Placing Friendship in Context

Personal relationships have long been of central interest to social scientists, but the subject of friendship has been relatively neglected. Moreover, most studies of friendship have been social psychological in focus. *Placing Friendship in Context* is a unique collection bridging social psychological and social structural research to advance understanding of this important subject. In it, some of the world's leading researchers explore the social and historical contexts in which friendships and similar informal ties develop and how it is that these contexts shape the form and substance the relationships assume. Together, they demonstrate that friendship cannot be understood from individualist or dyadic perspectives alone, but is a relationship significantly influenced by the environment in which it is generated. By analysing the ways in which friendships articulate with the social structures in which they are embedded, *Placing Friendship in Context* redescribes such personal relationships at both the macro and the micro level.

REBECCA G. ADAMS is Associate Professor in the Department of Sociology at the University of North Carolina at Greensboro. She has published widely on friendship, including two books with Rosemary Blieszner, *Older Adult Friendship: Structure and Process* (Sage, 1989) and *Adult Friendship* (Sage, 1992).

GRAHAM ALLAN is Reader in Sociology at the University of Southampton. His book publications include *Kinship and Friendship in Modern Britain* (1996) and, with Graham Crow, *Community Life* (1994).

D0096663

Structural Analysis in the Social Sciences

Mark Granovetter, editor

The series *Structural Analysis in the Social Sciences* presents approaches that explain social behaviour and institutions by reference to *relations* among such concrete social entities as persons and organisations. This contrasts with at least four other popular strategies: (1) reductionist attempts to explain by a focus on individuals alone; (2) explanations stressing the causal primacy of such abstract concepts as ideas, values, mental harmonies, and cognitive maps (thus, 'structuralism' on the Continent should be distinguished from structural analysis in the present sense); (3) technological and material determinism; (4) explanations using 'variables' as the main analytic concepts (as in the 'structural equation' models that dominated much of the sociology of the 1970s), where 'structure' is that connecting variables rather than actual social entities.

The 'social network' approach is an important example of the strategy of structural analysis; the series also draws on social science theory and research that is not framed explicitly in network terms, but stresses the importance of relations rather than the atomisation of reductionism or the determinism of ideas, technology, or material conditions. Though the structural perspective has become extremely popular and influential in all the social sciences, it does not have a coherent identity, and no series yet pulls together such work under a single rubric. By bringing the achievements of structurally oriented scholars to a wider public, the *Structural Analysis* series hopes to encourage the use of this very fruitful approach.

For a list of titles in this series, please see the end of the book.

PLACING FRIENDSHIP IN CONTEXT

Edited by

REBECCA G. ADAMS AND GRAHAM ALLAN

CAMBRIDGE
UNIVERSITY PRESS

PUBLISHED BY THE PRESS SYNDICATE OF THE UNIVERSITY OF CAMBRIDGE
The Pitt Building, Trumpington Street, Cambridge CB2 1RP, United Kingdom

CAMBRIDGE UNIVERSITY PRESS
The Edinburgh Building, Cambridge CB2 2RU, United Kingdom
http://www.cup.cam.ac.uk
40 West 20th Street, New York, NY 10011-4211, USA   http://www.cup.org
10 Stamford Road, Oakleigh, Melbourne 3166, Australia

First published 1998

Printed in the United Kingdom at the University Press, Cambridge

Typeset in Times NR 10/13 pt   [SE]

A catalogue record for this book is available from the British Library

Library of Congress Cataloguing in Publication data
Placing friendship in context / edited by Rebecca G. Adams and Graham
    Allan.
        p.   cm. – (Structural analysis in the social sciences)
    ISBN 0 521 58456 6 (hardcover) – ISBN 0 521 58589 9 (pbk.)
    1. Friendship. 2. Friendship – Sociological aspects. I. Adams,
    Rebecca G. II. Allan, Graham A. III. Series.
    BF575.F66P53   1998
    302.3'4 – dc21   98-15200 CIP

ISBN 0 521 58456 6 hardback
ISBN 0 521 58589 9 paperback

For Beth Hess and Eugene Litwak,
who were among the first to place friendship in context

Contents

Contributors

Rebecca G. Adams is Associate Professor in the Department of Sociology at the University of North Carolina at Greensboro. She received her Ph.D from the University of Chicago in 1983. Her major research interest is friendship patterns, especially as they are affected by geographic separation and by cultural and structural context. She has authored many articles on this topic and, with Rosemary Blieszner, co-edited *Older Adult Friendship: Structure and Process* (Sage, 1989) and co-authored *Adult Friendship* (Sage, 1992). Currently she is examining the cultural conventions and structural conditions affecting the development of friendships among the members of a non-territorial music subculture.

Graham Allan is Reader in Sociology at the University of Southampton, England. His research interests include many aspects of informal relations and domestic life. He has an MSc. degree from McMaster University, Canada, and a Ph.D from the University of Essex, England. As well as numerous papers on friendship, he is author of *Family Life* (Blackwell, 1985); *Friendship: Developing a Sociological Perspective* (Harvester-Wheatsheaf, 1989); and, with Graham Crow, *Community Life: An Introduction to Local Social Relationships* (Harvester-Wheatsheaf, 1994). *Family, Household and Society* (Macmillan), co-authored with Graham Crow, will be published in 1999.

William C. Carter is a Ph.D student in sociology at Louisiana State University. His other work with Scott Feld has examined tie strength in the contexts of foci of activity, including analyses of the effects of desegregation in schools on the development of interracial weak ties (published in *American Journal of Sociology*, 1998). He is currently working towards an understanding of how individual identities are affected by the surrounding network of social relationships.

Scott Feld is Professor of Sociology at Louisiana State University. He recently edited a special issue of *Sociological Forum* (March, 1997) devoted to making mathematical thinking more useful in sociology. He is most intrigued with paradoxes of social life, including 'Why your friends have more friends than you do' (*American Journal of Sociology*, 1991), and 'When desegregation reduces interracial contact' (with William C. Carter in *American Journal of Sociology*, 1998). His ongoing work focuses upon social networks, collective decision-making processes, and applying sociology. He is currently writing a book entitled *Closely Knit: Principles of Social Networks*, and working with Katherine Rossier to study Louisiana's recent social experiment with covenant marriage.

Kaeren Harrison is a Teaching Fellow in the Department of Social Work Studies at the University of Southampton. Her main research interests are concerned with intimacy, marriage, and women's friendships, a topic on which she is completing her doctoral studies. She is also conducting research on marital affairs.

Stephen R. Marks is Professor of Sociology at the University of Maine, where he has taught since 1972. His published work and his ongoing interests centre on the sociology of close relationships, perspectives on multiple roles, and feminist approaches to analyses of social settings. His current research draws on a theory of 'role balance' to understand how married people can balance multiple roles while avoiding problems of overload. His chapter on the Hawthorne women in this volume deals with a similar matter: how did these women, who became such fast friends at work, integrate these friendships into the rest of their personal networks?

Pat O'Connor is Professor of Sociology and Social Policy at the University of Limerick, Ireland. Her publications in the early 1990s reflected a concern with mother–daughter relationships and with the emotional reality and supportive potential of friendships and kin ties. With the publication of *Friendships Between Women* (Harvester-Wheatsheaf, 1992), she became increasingly concerned with issues related to women and power within relationships and organisations. These have been reflected in studies of organisational culture, 'male' and 'female' agendas, and consensual control. Her forthcoming book, *Changing Places – Women in Contemporary Irish Society* (Institute of Public Administration, Dublin, 1998), marks a further move to a macro level – locating women within the context of a changing but still patriarchal society. She is fascinated by the possibilities implicit in exploring the ways in which friendship can maintain or challenge established power structures, but has not figured out how to do this.

Stacey J. Oliker is Associate Professor of Sociology and Urban Studies at the University of Wisconsin–Milwaukee. Her book, *Best Friends and Marriage: Exchange Among Women* (University of California Press, 1989), received Honorable Mention for the American Sociological Association Jessie Bernard Award. Her recent work on welfare politics and on the family lives of women on welfare has appeared in *Social Problems, Sociological Quarterly*, and *Journal of Contemporary Ethnography. Caring and Gender* (Pine Forge Press), a sociology of caregiving, co-authored with Francesca Cancian, will be published in 1998.

Acknowledgements

The idea for this book developed over more than a decade. We originally met at the 1986 Conference on Interpersonal Relationships in Tel Aviv, Israel, organised by Steve Duck and Robin Gilmour. Without this venue, it is unlikely that our paths would ever have crossed or that the idea for this collection would ever have occurred to either of us. Although we both firmly believe that the most exciting social scientific research is often inter-disciplinary, we have retained strong identities as sociologists. Over the years, attending subsequent meetings of the International Society for the Study of Personal Relationships and of its sister organisation, the International Network on Personal Relationships, we recognised the need to articulate a sociology of friendship distinct from the perspectives offered by our colleagues in communications and psychology. At the 1994 International Conference on Personal Relationships in Groningen, Holland, with the encouragement of Program Co-Chairs Rosemary Blieszner and Bram Buunk, we began to organise this effort. Along with Robert Milardo, David Morgan, Pepper Schwartz, and Barry Wellman, we began an interest group on Contextual and Structural Perspectives on Relationships. Under the leadership of Michael Johnson, this group has continued to meet. At this same meeting, we organised a panel on Contextual Approaches to the Study of Friendship. Many of the contributors to this volume participated. It was during the discussion at this session that the idea for this volume emerged.

We would like to thank the colleagues mentioned above for contributing to the intellectual atmosphere that inspired us to organise this collection. In addition, we would like to acknowledge our department heads, David Pratto, University of North Carolina at Greensboro, and Roger Lawson, University of Southampton, for supporting our collaboration. We would also like to thank Jackie Rives for making Graham welcome at UNCG when he visited and Julie Capone for secretarial assistance. Finally our thanks to Sue, Chris, Kahla, and Peter Allan for not minding too much about Graham's absences from England, and Steven and Hadley Iliff, Rebecca's family, for tolerating, and even enjoying, his visits to the United States.

1

Contextualising friendship

Rebecca G. Adams and Graham Allan

It is clear that friendships play a significant part in many people's lives. Yet sociologists in general have paid these and other similar relationships relatively little attention in their efforts to understand the nature of social organisation. Even when their concern is explicitly with aspects of social integration, little heed is normally given to the specific realm of friendship. There are of course exceptions to this, as the work referenced in this volume attests, but generally sociologists have been content to leave the study of friendship to social psychologists. Most sociologists appear to take the view that, with modernity, and late modernity in particular, friendship and other linked informal ties are of small consequence socially and economically. The dominance of formal organisations is taken as synonymous with a decline in the importance of informal ties, though, as Silver (1990) has shown, the evidence for such a view is anything but convincing. Yet, with informal solidarities defined as being of only personal significance, analysis of them has largely been ceded to psychologists.

This is a challenge which social and other psychologists have taken on very actively. Over the past fifteen years, there have been major changes in the ways in which researchers analyse and understand friendships and other personal ties (Duck, 1990; Duck, Dindia, *et al.*, 1997). The starting point of this approach was a rejection of the dominant 'attributes' perspective within psychology, particularly for its disciplinary insularity and its focus on the properties of individuals within relationships rather than on the relationships themselves. Those involved made quite deliberate efforts to bring together specialists from a range of allied fields to inform one another of the different theoretical perspectives that could be applied to the study of relationships and to create a fuller and more sophisticated understanding of the internal dynamics of different personal relationships.

By the 1990s, this new paradigm of relationships was receiving considerable attention from scholars in different disciplines. Extensive research networks had been developed and new journals specialising in the analysis of personal relationships had been successfully established. Exciting new lines of research opened up, focusing on different aspects of relationship processes (i.e., affective, behavioural, and cognitive) and on different phases of relationships. (See Blieszner and Adams, 1992, for a summary of findings on these topics regarding friendship.) These researchers recognised the importance of treating relationships, be they ties of friendship, love, parenting, or whatever, as emergent ties with their own properties rather than as the consequence of the individual attributes each actor brings to the interaction. Put simply, this perspective recognised that it was *inter*action which mattered, and not just action. As part of their concern with relational properties, these researchers have highlighted *process* – the dynamic aspects of relationships and how they develop and change over time – far more than earlier attributional approaches did. They have also paid somewhat more heed to aspects of social structure lying outside specific relationships, particularly the effects of gender.

Yet, while the new paradigm has been interdisciplinary from its point of origin, this has been true more in principle than in practice. The new field of personal relationships is to be welcomed for generating fresh lines of enquiry and providing far better understandings of pertinent relationship processes than existed previously, but from a sociological perspective the portrayal they provide remains somewhat partial. To a degree, this is a criticism of sociology for its relative indifference to analysing informal ties like friendship at all, but especially in a fashion which fosters interdisciplinary discourse. The focus, however, in much of the research on relationships which has developed from a broadly psychological perspective over the past fifteen years remains very much at the dyadic level. While relationship research is no longer as individualised as it once was, the dominant framework is still relatively narrow and concerned mainly with the particular individuals who are the direct actors in the relationship in question (though see Duck, 1993; Duck, West, and Acitelli, 1997).

Of course, the individuals involved in a particular relationship are of crucial importance; no one would claim otherwise. The point, though, is that those individuals do not generate their relationships in a social or economic vacuum, any more than they do in a personal vacuum. Relationships have a broader basis than the dyad alone; they develop and endure within a wider complex of interacting influences which help to give each relationship its shape and structure. If we are to understand fully the nature of friendships, or for that matter of other personal ties, these relationships need to be interpreted from a perspective which recognises the impact of this wider complex, rather than from one which treats the dyad in relative isolation. Yet most empirical research on friendship has focused only on the internal form and dynamics of friendship without much regard for variation in setting and without much thought given to contextual explanations of findings.

In other words, what is largely missing from the new field of personal relationships is a consideration of the broader *contexts* in which such relationships are embedded (Duck, 1993). In essence, it lacks a sociological framework which locates the relationships within their broader environment. This is the concern of the present volume. Its aim is to show that a sociological perspective can not only make a contribution to our knowledge of personal relationships, but furthermore that studying these apparently personal ties can also increase our understanding of social change and thus inform more general sociological discourse. To achieve this, the volume brings together some of the foremost researchers now investigating aspects of the sociology of friendship. By looking at the different ways in which friendships have been constructed in different social milieux and in different historical periods, the chapters in the book demonstrate both the importance of context in the development and organisation of these ties and the advantages which accrue from bringing a sociological viewpoint into play in analysing them.

In demonstrating how a sociological perspective can add to our understanding of friendship, the chapters in the book draw on a wide set of contextualising factors to examine the structuring of these relationships and to account for the different forms they take. By doing this they all illustrate a simple yet key theme in this volume, and in the sociology of friendship more widely: that friendships do not operate in some abstract, decontextualised world. Like all other types of personal relationship, they are constructed – developed, modified, sustained, and ended – by individuals acting in contextualised settings. As the chapters which follow demonstrate, these contexts impinge directly on the emergent construction of the relationships, shaping the behaviour and understandings of the friends in myriad ways, some obvious and some more subtle. Some scholars view contexts deterministically, as shaping the relationships embedded within them but not as being shaped by the behaviours of the actors participating in the relationships. Others see contexts as social constructions. A good example of this pertinent to friendship is provided by Hochschild (1973) in her description of the 'unexpected community' that emerged in an age-segregated apartment building. Both types of scholars, however, think relationships need situating within a contextual framework if they are to be understood.

What do we mean by context? This is not as simple a question to answer as it seems, for, by its nature, the concept of 'context' is broad. Boundaries cannot easily be put around what is to be included within the term. Essentially, though, by 'context' we mean the conditions external to the development, maintenance, and dissolution of specific friendships. In other words, we are referring to those elements which *surround* friendships, but are not directly inherent in them, the extrinsic rather than the intrinsic. The difficulty is that the range of extrinsic elements which do 'surround' friendships are, in a literal sense, boundless. What counts as context, where boundaries are drawn around the extrinsic yet pertinent, is a question of interpretation and judgement rather than of fact. Researchers can contextualise a given phenomenon in quite different ways, each carrying its own assumptions, strengths, and limitations. In this sense there is no right or wrong; rather there are more or less informative ways of creating knowledge and understanding. What should be included as context is an open-ended question, the answer to which depends, at least in part, on the intention, perspective, and vision of the analyst.

It should be apparent that we would like to see a comparative sociology of friendship developing. As yet, we are some way from reaching this level of accomplishment. Even those studies which are germane to understanding the connection between context and friendship tend not to be comparative. Very few friendship researchers, for example, have used a longitudinal design that would allow for change in context to be studied. Instead, they have offered snapshots of contextual effects. So, too, few researchers have compared the friendships that form and flourish in different settings at the same point in time. Nor, in the main, are the papers in this volume explicitly comparative. None the less, we believe they do offer a starting point for such a comparative effort by identifying some of the key aspects of context which need to be considered in understanding friendship. We would hope that future studies will be able to build on the analyses they contain.

Characteristics of context

Contexts are not unidimensional. Many of their various aspects are of sociological importance. Certainly the structural and cultural qualities of context, as well as its spatial and temporal organisation, are relevant to understanding relationships embedded within them. It is important to remember, though, that these broad characteristics of context do not act independently of each other. It is in their interaction that the complexity of context emerges. For example, distinguishing between what counts as cultural and what as social structural is often problematic, as the boundaries inevitably merge. Jerrome (1984), for example, has shown how middle-class lifestyles shape the friendship behaviour of older middle-aged women in Britain. Stack (1974) demonstrated a quite different pattern of ties in her analysis of friendships in a poor black community in the Midwestern United States. There the exchange of material resources was a key element to compensate for the economic uncertainties they faced. And, in a quite different setting, Oxley (1974) demonstrated how the culture of egalitarianism in small-town Australia influenced the patterns of 'mateship' which developed. Similarly, the distinction between the effects of temporal and spatial aspects of context is often blurred. Duneier's (1992) description of interaction among customers of a restaurant in an integrated neighbourhood in Chicago illustrates this point. The establishment's regular schedule made it possible for patrons to see one another without planning to do so and thus provided opportunities for them to forge ties with one another. The regularity of the temporal structure and of having a convenient place to meet was so important to these people that, when the restaurant closed temporarily for repairs, they replaced their routine visits to the restaurant with visits to other settings nearby.

It is also important to remember that dimensions of context are not static; they are constantly changing. The characteristics of a context during one period of time may vary considerably from its characteristics during another. One needs only to consider for a moment how neighbourhoods, schools, and the work-place have changed over the past several decades to realise the importance of this observation. On a broader scale, think how different relationships can be during times of war and times of peace, during affluent periods and in the midst of massive depressions, or in eras when men and women are not allowed to be alone with one another as against eras in which they are free to interact whenever they like. Over time, the social structural, cultural, spatial, and temporal situations surrounding individuals can all change, and so the constellation of the characteristics we are subsuming under 'context' changes as well.

Continuum of contextual analyses

Friendship researchers have approached the study of contextual effects in different ways. In turn the methods they have used to study context are related to the level of context they have studied. By 'level of context', we mean how near to the individual the boundaries of the context in question are. In the discussion that follows, we describe the traditions that examine the personal environment of individuals, the social network, communities or subcultures, and societies. (See Adams and Blieszner, 1993, for a discussion of contextual levels, and Praeger, 1995, for an elaboration of their treatment.) The discussion thus proceeds from the individual level of analysis to levels of analysis more remote from the individual. As we have already noted, these boundaries between levels of context are heuristic. By their nature, they are not delineated from each other in a discrete way.

The personal environment level

The first level represents the 'personal environment' of those who are friends. By this we mean the immediate features of a person's life which affect the character and pattern of the friendships which they develop and sustain. This will include, *inter alia*, their economic circumstances, their domestic responsibilities, their work commitments, their leisure preferences, and the like. It encompasses all those features of an individual's personal environment which either limit or create the opportunities they have for engaging sociably with others and servicing friendships. Researchers do not normally incorporate all these features into any given analysis of friendship patterns, but usually they do concern themselves with one or more in explaining why friendships take the forms they do.

Most studies which draw on context at the level of personal environment do so by specifying how social structural or cultural variables influence an individual's friendship behaviour. In this regard, aspects of this level of context are amenable to being treated as independent variables with a framework that examines the impact different variables have on friendship patterns. As a result, this perspective on context is highly compatible with survey methodology in which both friendships and the factors influencing them can be treated as attributes or properties of the individual. Thus, many studies have looked at how gender, for example, interacts with friendship development or with the interactional styles occurring in friendships (e.g., Fischer and Oliker, 1983; Wright, 1989; Rawlins, 1992; Kaplan and Keys, 1997). Other studies have examined the impact of characteristics such as age, ethnicity, ill-health, care giving, or economic circumstances on the organisation of friendship (e.g., Nahemow and Lawton, 1975; Weiss and Lowenthal, 1975; Fischer and Oliker, 1983; Jerrome, 1990; Lamme, *et al.*, 1996).

Not all research which incorporates context at the level of personal environment depends upon survey data. Other methodologies are quite capable of producing data which provide information about the ways in which people's commitments and obligations structure their friendships. On the other hand, most survey-oriented studies of friendship are restricted to this level of contextualisation. Because of its individualistic character, it is harder for survey research to contribute to our understanding of other levels of context. This is not to say that context in the sense of personal environment is unimportant. It is difficult to see how an understanding of friendship patterns could emerge without this level of context being part of the analysis. Nevertheless, this is only one level. The range of contextual considerations which play a part in structuring friendship behaviour runs deeper than this type of feature alone. In some ways, the ease of doing survey research quickly and relatively inexpensively has seduced friendship researchers and so, by default, they have ignored the more labour-intensive and expensive methodologies required to reach an understanding of broader contextual effects.

The network level

The second level of context is linked closely to the personal environment level. It concerns the network of personal relationships which each person maintains. There are two basic elements to the network perspective. The first is the more obvious: different people become involved in social networks with different properties through their distinct patterns of social participation. Some have larger networks than others; some have denser networks in the sense that those in it are likely also to know others involved. Similarly, some people's networks involve multiplex relationships, whereas others have less complicated ties. In explaining how networks with different constellations of relationships emerge, researchers typically draw on the type of factor discussed under personal environment. However, networks can also have an independent influence on people's behaviour. Here, the key question is not so much why different patterns of network develop, but rather what the results of these different patterns are for the opportunities open to people and the constraints they face. A feature of this second perspective is that it can be concerned with the network configurations of larger social collectivities, such as work groups or communities, in which no particular individual is seen as central. (For a review of the development of network studies, see Scott, 1991, or Wellman, 1988.)

Both these perspectives indicate that friendship behaviour can be influenced by the overall patterning of networks as well as by the specific obligations embodied in particular personal relationships. The structural characteristics of the networks in which people are embedded become part of the context of their interactions. A simple way of recognising this with respect to friendship is to consider how patterns of kinship ties can influence a person's friendship behaviour. There is, for example, some evidence from Britain, admittedly now rather dated, that extensive involvement with kin living outside their household limits participation in (non-kin) friendship ties (Allan, 1979; Willmott, 1987). Similarly, people involved in relatively dense friendship networks are likely to develop fewer new friendships at any time than those whose friendship networks are more dispersed (Allan, 1989).

There have been relatively few studies which have tried to specify at all fully how the structure of people's networks influences friendship behaviour. There have been even fewer which focus on this from a perspective which considers networks wider than ego-centred ones (Milardo and Allan, 1997). In part this is because of the difficulties of researching such networks, especially using a social survey methodology. This is not the only approach used for generating data on networks, but it is undoubtedly the most common and the least time-consuming. Often such studies also ask only about a particular portion of an individual's network – those they see most frequently or those to whom they feel closest. (See Adams, 1989, for a discussion of the ways in which researchers have limited their operational definitions of friendship.) Given that different data collection instruments generate different depictions of network structure (Milardo, 1992), how useful more partial studies of personal networks are for providing contextual information relevant for understanding friendship patterns remains a moot question.

Community level

From the development of the Chicago School onwards, field researchers have provided many in-depth descriptions of the social lives of the inhabitants of specific places. The places and settings they have studied have varied widely, fostering a rich tradition in Europe in addition to the United States. (The classic American studies include Whyte, 1943; Gans, 1962; Liebow, 1967; and Stack, 1974. For a review of British studies, see Crow and Allan, 1994.) This body of research provides much insight into the friendships of those studied, though none of them focuses exclusively on these ties. What these studies illustrate exceptionally well is how the contexts in which sociability and friendship are embedded influence their internal organisation and dynamic. Woven into tapestries comprising threads about family, love, work, survival, and daily activities are narratives about the social lives and personal relationships of the participants. In this body of work the limitations of treating relationships solely as dyadic formations becomes most apparent.

A standard criticism of community studies is that only rarely are they cumulative. Each stands alone, difficult to generalise about or build upon. Researchers designed very few of them in a way that allows others to compare findings about friendship across them. Furthermore, few of the researchers used the results of previous community studies to inform their own research. In the main, they describe the complexities of friendship in one context, but do not evaluate how the different characteristics of contexts combine to affect friendship. None the less, one can begin to develop contextual hypotheses from some of these studies taken in combination.

For example, both Stack (1974) and Liebow (1967) described friendships among poor American blacks and emphasised the importance of friends for providing basic survival resources. This suggests that, in economies of scarcity, friendships become important as instrumental relationships. As the subjects in both Stack's and Liebow's work were American blacks, one might be tempted to offer a purely cultural explanation. The economic hypothesis gains strength when studies of unemployment elsewhere are considered (Binns and Mars, 1984; Wallace, 1987; Morris, 1990), or in the light of research like Hochschild's (1973) which examined the social lives of poor elderly white women living in an age-segregated housing complex. In these studies, too, respondents depended on material exchanges with one another, if not for survival, at least to improve their quality of life.

Societal level

The final level of context we want to discuss is the societal level. This is the level most removed from the individual, but it still frames patterns of friendship in a number of very important ways. In particular, the economic and social structures which dominate at any time have an impact on the forms which different personal relationships take (Silver, 1990). The best-known illustration of this concerns the ways in which industrialisation affected familial and domestic ties. Commonly, this is seen as entailing a move from a more collective past to a more individualised present, often expressed as a shift from an extended family system to a nuclear family one. The causes and time periods involved are frequently specified differently, but the consequences are usually seen as similar. In effect, industrialisation, the spread of wage labour, increased geographical mobility, and the decline in importance of familial property resulted in marital selection being increasingly based around ideas of love and personal compatibility rather than parental influence, with a concomitant reduction in solidarity and authority between kin outside the immediate household.

Of course, the impact of social and economic change on personal relationships did not stop with the grand nineteenth- and early twentieth-century transformations we commonly subsume under the term 'industrialisation'. Indeed, as modernity developed further, so our understandings of how personal relationships should be organised also altered. Giddens (1992), for example, has developed an account of the ways in which romantic and sexual ties have been modified under what he terms 'late modernity'. While this account can be criticised, it does have the benefit of recognising just how much relationships of intimacy are tied to the economic and social formations within which they occur.

Just as the wider changes occurring in the society affect the patterning of sexual and familial relationships, so too they influence the character of friendship. Perhaps the most dominant theoretical perspective here is that of 'privatisation', though this term actually embraces quite a range of distinct arguments. Essentially the idea behind it is that, with industrialisation and the development of modernity, the more communal solidarities of the past have been replaced by a dominant concern for the private world of home and family. Whereas once the social and economic conditions of people's lives encouraged a wide co-operation and dependency between those living near to and working with one another, contemporary social organisation no longer generates the same needs. In particular, affluence in general and the development of mass communication and personal transport systems more specifically have reduced the salience of the local in people's lives and freed them from any great need to co-operate with others living nearby. There has, as a result, been a major change in the organisation of sociability, though again there are quite different versions of what precisely these changes have been.

Some have argued that this has resulted in nuclear families, or perhaps more accurately nuclear households, becoming increasingly isolated, with individuals leading lives which are firmly centred on their home and immediate family. Others disagree with this isolationist perspective, suggesting instead that what has altered is the salience of structured public settings in people's social lives. Whereas once social relationships tended to be based around ties of locality and employment and enacted communally, this is no longer so. Instead, people are now more able to sustain friendships created in a variety of settings, but these ties tend to be 'privatised' in the sense that interaction is framed by domestic contexts rather than communal ones (Allan and Crow, 1991; Devine, 1992; Marks, 1994; Wellman, *et al.*, 1988). Such changes in friendship can be linked to other aspects of social change: for example, altered patterns of leisure, the greater 'compartmentalisation' of different aspects of people's lives, including the increased separation of domestic life and leisure from employment, and the development of greater conjugality within marriage.

Other scholars have adopted rather different perspectives, whilst still emphasising the ways in which historical change in socio-economic relationships pattern friendship ties. While Lopata (1991), for example, suggested that the development of commercial society led to a decline in the social significance and heterogeneity of friendship, Silver (1990) argued that commercial society actually encouraged friendship by ridding ties of the 'contamination' of instrumentality. 'Only with impersonal markets in products and services does a parallel system of personal relations emerge whose ethic excludes exchange and utility' (Silver, 1990, p. 1494). Litwak (1985, 1989) has also suggested that friendships become more significant with modernity because of the increased need for the flexibility which informal ties provide in societies dominated by bureaucratic organisations. Oliker (1989), too, was concerned with how friendships were patterned with the emergence of modernity, though she argued that the consequences were gender-specific. She particularly emphasised the historical importance of intimacy in women's friendships, whilst recognising that its mode of expression altered over time.

And, of course, change continues. Indeed, the arguments that have been made about the 'compartmentalisation' of sociable relationships can be seen as broadly compatible with arguments about the transformation of modernist society into post-modernity. Here the apparently secure base of knowledge and organisation which modernity represents is becoming more fragmented. One element in this is the greater freedom that people have to construct their own personal and intimate worlds. The rise of cohabitation, the developing recognition that marriage is not necessarily a lifelong commitment, the increased acceptance of gay identities and relationships, the growth of gender and ethnic politics, and so forth all point to the greater legitimacy of diversity in the construction of personal life. The friendships people form, the ties of solidarity which they generate, and the support (or otherwise) which they receive are likely to be important in these constructions.

But the issue here is not whether friendships are indeed becoming of greater consequence in social life, nor whether society can accurately be defined as post-modern. The point is simply that patterns of friendship are framed within a societal context. Thus, for example, the form they take, their salience in people's lives, the extent to which they are permitted to be influential, and the legitimacy and support they provide are all shaped by the constraints and opportunities people experience as a consequence of their specific location within the social and economic formation, framed by the general character of that formation. The impact of these broader social and economic influences needs recognising. They, as much as anything, provide a contextual frame for understanding friendship now or in any time and place.

Plan of the book

The chapters which follow all illustrate how the contexts within which friendships develop influence the forms which friendships take. The actual topics with which they are concerned vary quite considerably – from nine-teenth-century women's friendships to the implications for friendship of recent developments in electronic communication. Some of the chapters contain detailed empirical examinations of the friendships maintained by specific individuals; others are more theoretical, drawing on a range of sources to develop arguments about the transformations that are occurring in sociability. All, however, focus on the ways in which the organisation of friendship and people's understandings of the boundaries and exchanges that the ties entail are influenced by factors which lie outside the relation-ships themselves. As such, they illustrate very clearly why context matters and why it is important in analysing friendship to locate the ties within their wider framework.

The first chapter by Stacey Oliker is concerned specifically with the ways in which the development of modernity within the nineteenth-century United States influenced the patterning of middle-class women's close friendships. As noted earlier, while much has been written about the impact of changing economic and industrial conditions on family relationships, far less research has been published on the impact of these changes for ties of friendship. Oliker's argument is that the growth of individualism as a dominant ideology had quite distinct consequences for men and women because of their discrete structural locations. For men, individualism was associated with autonomy, self-interest, and competition; intimacy was typically contained within the familial sphere. In contrast, among middle-class women the expression of intimacy was positively fostered, both inside and outside the family. The institutional framework within which their lives were embedded encouraged an affectionate individualism to flourish and allowed for the development of intimate friendships in a fashion that would have been quite inappropriate for men.

Stephen Marks's essay is also concerned with understanding how the changing structural position of women – in his case working-class women from the industrial Midwestern United States – influenced the forms of solidarity generated between co-workers. In a fascinating analysis of the experiences of the women involved in the famous Relay Assembly Test Room experiments at the Hawthorne plant in Chicago in the 1920s and 1930s, Marks draws on archival material, as well as retrospective interviews with some of those involved, to reconstruct the pattern of solidaristic relationships which developed. He shows how the character of their friendships was patterned by the immediate circumstances of their domestic economies – and in particular the dominance of men's location within the household – as well as by the gendered realities of marriage and the local labour market. Interestingly, though, these friendships, starting circumstantially in their youth and lasting the women's lifetimes, did not involve particularly high levels of intimate self-disclosure. Rather, Marks characterises their solidarity as involving an 'inclusive' form of intimacy, which he contrasts with the 'exclusive intimacy' now so frequently taken as the hallmark of close friendship.

The next two chapters, by Graham Allan and Kaeren Harrison, follow the temporal theme by focusing on friendship patterns in the middle and later parts of this century. Allan is concerned with changes in dominant forms of male working-class friendship and sociability since the middle of the century in Britain. Building on the analyses contained in community and occupational studies in the immediate post-war period, he assesses the structural factors that influenced the ways in which sociable ties were then organised, and investigates how major changes in domestic, economic, and social relationships since then have modified how they are managed. The central theme of the chapter is that the boundaries constructed around sociable ties and the exchanges they involve are structured by the social and economic contexts within which they arise.

Like Oliker, Kaeren Harrison is concerned with middle-class women's friendship, though her focus is on married women in late twentieth-century Britain. Basing her analysis on a combination of interview and archival data, Harrison examines the integration of friendships within the broader contours of her respondents' lives. In particular, together with both Oliker and Marks, she is concerned with the expression of intimacy within friendships and, in turn, how these ties relate to the women's experiences of marriage and motherhood. Her argument is that the patterning and content of these close friendships can be understood only within the context of the women's domestic lives and, specifically, the failure of their marriages to meet their expectations for conjugal expressivity. She emphasises how the close friendships the women maintained provided an alternative forum for intimate disclosure, offered a means of situating their experiences, and validated their sense of self.

Pat O'Connor also focuses on women's friendships and the ways in which they are patterned by the wider structures in which they are embedded. However, her concerns are more broadly based, examining how elements of patriarchy and capitalism shape female friendships in a post-modern context. Within societies where both men and heterosexuality remain privileged, she argues that dominant discourses often portray women's friendships as fragile and of limited social consequence. She explores how, even when their significance in the construction of identity is recognised, such cultural portrayals still disguise the part women's friendships play in sustaining the prevailing social order. In addressing these processes, she assesses the transformative potential such ties have in a post-modern era where old stabilities are increasingly questioned.

Scott Feld and William Carter take a quite different tack in examining how context influences friendship ties. Building on Feld's earlier work (Feld, 1981), they examine how friendships are patterned by the foci of activity in which they are embedded. Their argument is that most friendships arise from one or more foci of activity, and that usually foci of activity involve individuals in quite dense networks of others. These networks of relationships form the context within which particular dyadic forms of tie, including friendships, develop. Feld and Carter use the example of divorce to illustrate the importance of considering the extent to which friendships are embedded in foci of activity, and in particular how changes in this embeddedness impact on the organisation of the friendships in question. By doing so, they show how apparently personal ties of friendship are typically rooted in broader sets of connected relationships which influence their development and form.

In the final substantive chapter, Rebecca Adams explores how technological changes shape the character of friendship. She begins by illustrating how the emergence of mass forms of transport and communications over the past 200 years altered the parameters of social participation. Her main concern, though, is contemporary, and lies in distilling the impact that the growth of electronic communication – principally e-mail and the Internet – have had on the social construction of informal relationships. Drawing on a conceptual framework developed in her earlier research (Adams and Blieszner, 1994), she examines how the special context of electronic communication raises important questions for our understanding and knowledge of friendship structure and processes. In probing these issues, she shows how a focus on electronic friendships helps explicate the limitations of some conventional approaches to analysing informal relationships, as well as highlighting the diversity of elements constituting 'context' in friendship analyses.

References

Adams, Rebecca G. (1989), 'Conceptual and methodological issues in studying friendships of older adults', in Adams and Blieszner (eds.).

Adams, Rebecca G., and Blieszner, Rosemary (eds.) (1989), *Older Adult Friendship: Structure and Process*, Newbury Park: Sage.

(1993), 'Resources for friendship intervention', *Journal of Sociology and Social Welfare*, 20: 159–75.

(1994), 'An integrative conceptual framework for friendship research', *Journal of Social and Personal Relationships*, 11: 163–84.

Allan, Graham (1979), *A Sociology of Friendship and Kinship*, London: Allen & Unwin.

(1989), *Friendship: Developing a Sociological Perspective*, Hemel Hempstead: Harvester-Wheatsheaf.

Allan, Graham, and Crow, Graham (1991), 'Privatization, home-centredness and leisure', *Leisure Studies*, 10: 19–32.

Binns, David, and Mars, Gerald (1984), 'Family, community and unemployment: a study in change', *Sociological Review*, 32: 662–95.

Blieszner, Rosemary, and Adams, Rebecca G. (1992), *Adult Friendship*, Newbury Park: Sage.

Crow, Graham, and Allan, Graham (1994), *Community Life: An Introduction to Local Social Relationships*, Hemel Hempstead: Harvester-Wheatsheaf.

Devine, Fiona (1992), *Affluent Workers Revisited: Privatism and the Working Class*, Edinburgh University Press.

Duck, Steve (1990), 'Relationships as unfinished business: out of the frying pan and into the 1990s', *Journal of Social and Personal Relationships*, 7: 5–29.

(ed.) (1993), *Social Context and Relationships*, Newbury Park: Sage.

Duck, Steve, Dindia, Kathryn, Ickes, William, Milardo, Robert M., Mills, Rosemary, and Sarason, Barbara (eds.) (1997), *Handbook of Personal Relationships*, London: Wiley.

Duck, Steve, West, Lee, and Acitelli, Linda (1997), 'Sewing the field: the tapestry of relationships in life and research', in Duck, Dindia, *et al.* (eds.).

Duneier, Mark (1992), *Slim's Table*, University of Chicago Press.

Feld, Scott L. (1981), 'The focused organization of social ties', *American Journal of Sociology*, 86: 1015–35.

Fischer, Claude S., and Oliker, Stacey (1983), 'A research note on friendship, gender and the life-cycle', *Social Forces*, 62: 124–33.

Gans, Herbert J. (1962), *The Urban Villagers*, New York: Free Press.

Giddens, Anthony (1992), *The Transformation of Intimacy: Sexuality, Love, and Eroticism in Modern Societies*, Cambridge: Polity.

Hochschild, Arlie R. (1973), *The Unexpected Community*, Englewood Cliffs, N.J.: Prentice Hall.

Jerrome, Dorothy (1984), 'Good company: the sociological implications of friendship', *Sociological Review*, 32: 696–718.

(1990), 'Frailty and friendship', *Journal of Cross-Cultural Gerontology*, 5: 51–64.

Kaplan, Daniel, and Keys, Christopher (1997), 'Sex and relationship variables as predictors of sexual attraction in cross-sex platonic friendships between young heterosexual adults', *Journal of Social and Personal Relationships*, 14: 191–206.

Lamme, Simone, Dykstra, Pearl, and Broese Van Groenou, Marjolein (1996), 'Rebuilding the network: new relationships in widowhood', *Personal Relationships*, 3: 337–49.

Liebow, Elliott (1967), *Tally's Corner*, Boston: Little, Brown.

Litwak, Eugene (1985), *Helping the Elderly: The Complementary Roles of Informal Networks and Formal Systems*, New York: Guilford.

(1989), 'Forms of friendships among older people in industrial society', in Adams and Blieszner (eds.).

Lopata, Helen (1991), 'Friendship: historical and theoretical introduction', in Helen Lopata and David Maines (eds.), *Friendship in Context*, Greenwich, CT: Jai Press.

Marks, Stephen R. (1994), 'Intimacy in the public realm: the case of coworkers', *Social Forces*, 72: 843–58.

Milardo, Robert M. (1992), 'Comparative methods for delineating social networks', *Journal of Social and Personal Relationships*, 9: 447–61.

Milardo, Robert M., and Allan, Graham (1997), 'Social networks and marital relationships', in Duck, Dindia, *et al.* (eds.).

Morris, Lydia (1990), *The Workings of the Household*, Cambridge: Polity.

Nahemow, L., and Lawton, M. P. (1975), 'Similarity and propinquity in friendship formation', *Journal of Personality and Social Psychology*, 32: 205–13.

Oliker, Stacey J. (1989), *Best Friends and Marriage: Exchange Among Women*, Berkeley: University of California Press.

Oxley, H. G. (1974), *Mateship and Local Organization*, Brisbane: University of Queensland Press.

Praeger, Karen J. (1995), *The Psychology of Intimacy*, New York: Guilford.

Rawlins, William (1992), *Friendship Matters: Communication, Dialectics and the Life Course*, New York: Aldine de Gruyter.

Scott, John (1991), *Social Network Analysis*, London: Sage.

Silver, Alan (1990), 'Friendship in commercial society: eighteenth-century social theory and modern sociology', *American Journal of Sociology*, 95: 1474–1504.

Stack, Carol (1974), *All Our Kin*, New York: Harper and Row.

Wallace, Claire (1987), *For Richer, For Poorer: Growing up in and out of Work*, London: Tavistock.

Weiss, L., and Lowenthal, M. F. (1975), 'Life-course perspectives on friendship', in M. E. Lowenthal, M. Thurnher, D. Chiriboga, and associates (eds.), *Four Stages of Life*, San Francisco: Jossey-Bass.

Wellman, Barry (1988), 'Structural analysis: from method and metaphor to theory and substance', in Wellman and Berkowitz (eds.).

Wellman, Barry, and Berkowitz, S. D. (eds.) (1988), *Social Structures: A Network Approach*, Cambridge University Press.

Wellman, Barry, Carrington, Peter J., and Hall, Alan (1988), 'Networks as personal communities', in Wellman and Berkowitz (eds.).

Whyte, William F. (1943), *Street Corner Society: The Social Structure of an Italian Slum*, University of Chicago Press.

Willmott, Peter (1987), *Friendship Networks and Social Support*, London: Policy Studies Institute.

Wright, Paul (1989), 'Gender differences in adults' same- and cross-gender friendships', in Adams and Blieszner (eds.).

2

The modernisation of friendship: individualism, intimacy, and gender in the nineteenth century

Stacey J. Oliker

Intimate friendship is a modern relationship. If we think of intimacy as the sharing of one's inner life or mutual self-exploration – not simply familiarity and interdependence – we can observe the flowering of intimate friendship in the past few centuries. The assertion that intimate friendship is modern contradicts the prevailing view that modernity drained intimacy and trust from the vibrant community of past times (Nisbet, 1953; criticised by Fischer, *et al.*, 1977). The conventional wisdom holds that, as marriage modernised and husbands and wives became romantic lovers and best friends, friendship faded in social importance. To the contrary, I will argue, intimate friendship and intimate marriage developed as intertwined cultural ideals and patterns amidst a widening culture of individualism.

In recent decades, social historians have unearthed and interpreted the history of sentiment (Cott, 1977; Stone, 1977; Smith-Rosenberg, 1979; Lystra, 1989). I use their work here to assemble an account of the modernisation of friendship, focusing on the exchange of intimacy. My account of modern friendship will centre on the articulation of a burgeoning culture of individualism with changes in social institutions.

The articulation of cultural change and social institutions

Wuthnow (1989) uses the term 'articulation' to refer to specific linkages in the 'fit' between cultural patterns and their social structural contexts. Cultural innovations that spread, Wuthnow maintains, are able to draw resources from their institutional contexts and then transcend them. Resources – like money, role flexibility, or events that provide useful symbols – enable a culture to spread and become routinised. Wuthnow shows how the creation, selection, and institutionalisation of cultural changes draw on resources in the social environment of cultural actors. Rather than simply 'identifying general affinities between ideological patterns and broad features of the social environment', Wuthnow advises that we closely link context to cultural change (1989, p. 541). His book, *Communities of Discourse* (1989), explores the articulation between world-changing cultural movements and the social structures in which they grew and which they altered. In his cases, social experience was both incorporated into cultural change and reworked in the context of cultural innovation.

Wuthnow's framework, adapted generally, rather than in conceptual detail, allows me to move from a social historical account to sociological analysis of change in patterns of friendship: I examine how intimate desires and practices emerged, spread, and became embedded in social institutions in ways that recreate a culture of intimate friendship in the absence of its generating historical context.

The complicating issue in my account will be gender: men's and women's intimate patterns, in marriage and friendship, seem to have differed. Nineteenth-century middle-class women were ardent innovators of an intimate 'world of love and ritual', to use Smith-Rosenberg's (1979) term for the culture, in which men participated more marginally and during particular life stages. I propose that contemporary differences in men's and women's friendships have roots in the emerging social structures and cultural patterns of nineteenth-century liberal, industrialising society.[1]

I originally proposed this argument in a 1985 study, published in 1989 as *Best Friends and Marriage: Exchange Among Women*.[2] The book is a qualitative study of contemporary married women's best friendships, and a chapter on the modernisation of friendship and marriage provided a historical backdrop for the contemporary patterns I analysed.[3] Scholars of American women's history had published a decade of remarkable work on middle-class women's friendships by the mid-1980s; but, since then, scholarship on private life and men's friendships has provided new evidence to draw on here. Thus, with new data on nineteenth-century friendships and new sociological work on cultural change, I refine earlier arguments about changes in friendship.

Although European historians have contributed a great deal to the study of intimate life, I have chosen American sources because I am better schooled in American history. I focus on the middle classes both because they were the pioneers of individualism and intimate culture, and because, compared to the working classes, they more often reflected on their experience in writing and thus preserved these records for posterity.

Data on the private behaviour and states of mind of unillustrious historical actors are always scarce, however. Much of the evidence still lies in the letters of the highly educated and in religious and philosophical tracts on private life. For this reason, I consider my analysis of the historic dynamics of intimacy to be a speculative project. None the less, imaginative social history has given me more confidence than ever to speculate.

Individualism and modernity

One might define 'intimacy' as extensive familiarity with another and the emotions, affects, interactions, and moral possibilities that accompany this knowledge. Using such a definition, I could identify the historical spread of a particular form of intimacy which centres on mutual self-disclosure and expression of emotional attachment. Instead, I will use the term 'intimacy' in this narrower sense: I define intimacy as the sharing of inner experience, mutual self-exploration, and the expression of emotional attachment. The narrower, more psychologically and communication-focused definition of intimacy corresponds best to the way we now use the term. Moreover, it allows me to use it here without appending adjectives specifying self-exploration and disclosure.

Intimacy, defined as mutual self-exploration, requires a culture of individualism. In societies with a more collective cultural ethos, attention to the self is dangerous and considered unworthy. It subverts the authority of tradition and the discipline of identifying with social roles. Those who became intimate in the eras before individualism was a primary ethos were sanctioned for behaving madly or badly (Romeo and Juliet, for example), unless they possessed the impunity accompanying great wealth and power.

The socially approved practice of intimacy required a valuation and sanctioned interest in each person's inner life, feelings, and self-regard. The cultural ethos of individualism encouraged people to view themselves as distinct, complex, and interesting – to develop identities that could not be specified by their social roles (Berger, 1977). Individualism's encouragement of self-interest and introspection cultivated individual selves and inner lives. Privileged access to another's individuality and self-exploration produced new makings of feeling, trust, and commitment. This is the dynamic of intimate friendship that I will describe in the nineteenth-century United States.

Thorough-going cultural change depends on concurrent institutional change. In examining the rise of intimate friendship in the modernising United States, we see a culture of individualism diffusing and becoming institutionalised through changes in a variety of social institutions. The changes we typically associate with individualism are the development of a market economy and a democratic polity. Participation as a free agent in a competitive market-place and as a citizen in a liberal polity are the best-known sources of spreading individualism. In most accounts, these individuated social roles then influence the expectations of family life, by eroding the functional importance of kin and the authority of household heads. Individual interests gain expression in the family. As a result, men and women are freer to choose spouses and stay married for love; free choice and love then make marriage more egalitarian. Individualism becomes the cultural ethos of economy, polity, and family.

The preceding account of the institutional underpinnings of individualism, which underlies most sociologies of the family, portrays a single current of individualism that is born in the public world of economy and polity and sweeps through private life. Yet, when we imagine individuals carrying a culture (their actions, as believers or doers, are the current that sweeps across institutions), we can see how small a role women appear to play as carriers of the culture in this model of change. In the modernising United States, women were not citizens; they were not supposed to be employed and most middle-class women were not. Did men's individualism simply infect them at home?

Prevailing notions treat individualism as a complex but single ideology, rather than a complex and diversified one. To the contrary, this paper argues, meanings and practices of individualism vary with the contexts of people's social participation. American women were not properly part of the market in the nineteenth century; their proper sphere was the home. The kinds of individualism they were positioned to embrace differed, I propose, from the kinds available to men. Modernity radically diversified the spheres of participation of men and women, and different sets of institutional resources became the makings of gendered forms of individualism. By looking more closely at the different lives of nineteenth-century men and women, and of people of different classes, I will show how varieties of individualism and intimacy articulated with social and institutional structures. In my account, women become the innovators and leaders in the spread of intimacy.

Nineteenth-century changes in social institutions

The nineteenth century witnessed massive changes in social, economic, and familial institutions. The unit of pre-industrial work was the family. There, the production of goods, food preparation, child care, sick care, trade, sociability, and rest alternated throughout the day. Work roles were allocated by age and sex, but everyone, including children, contributed productively to the family and worked, if not alongside each other, then within view (Demos, 1970; Ulrich, 1982).

The daily intermixture of work, trade, and sociability opened the household to the purview of neighbours and friends; families and family members neither found much privacy nor valued it. Neither friends, nor courting lovers, nor spouses did much apart from others. Families dined with servants and whomever was passing through the households and the same assemblage often shared a room to sleep. Adults and youth socialised in same-sex groups; often several groupings dispersed in a single church, tavern, or hall. In these formations, interdependence, familiarity, and the absence of privacy were the components of what might be labelled pre-industrial intimacy.

In the industrialising United States, work and family moved worlds apart and so did men's and women's lives. A confluence of religious, Enlightenment, and romantic ideas distilled in an 'ideology of separate spheres' that allocated distinct roles, identities, and forms of authority and influence to the institutions of work and family. The 'public sphere' was a realm of competitive individuals, pursuing self-interest in the market and the polity. Men, long authorised to represent and protect households and to subordinate emotion to duty or calculation, claimed ownership of the public domain. The 'private sphere' became a complementary world of sentiment, moral goodness, and communal commitment. Women, already viewed as the sex most tied to the household, presided over a much altered domain of private life. Their labours at home, previously represented as productive, were pastorally reconceived as the spiritual accomplishment of motherhood (Bloch, 1978; Ryan, 1979; Boydston, 1990).

Whereas in the past each sex was bound to its proper endeavour by tradition and religious duty, the ideology of separate spheres allocated duties according to newly conceived natural virtues of each gender: men were naturally calculating, competitive, and self-controlled; women were naturally emotional, tender, and virtuous. Natural inclinations gave each sex authority in its proper domain (Welter, 1978; Ryan, 1979).

Families turned inward in privacy and intensified emotionally as they became havens from a heartless world where economies were less tied to communal authority and exchange. Privacy and emotional intensity were aided by the spreading ideal of love-based companionate marriage, which replaced traditional ideals of distance and patriarchal deference (Stone, 1977; Degler, 1980). Perhaps more importantly, the idea of innocent and precious childhood replaced the pre-industrial view of a useful but naturally evil child. New doctrines of domesticity prescribed attentive and tender nurturance rather than harsh discipline, and endowed mothers with new authority to discharge this delicate mission. Affluent middle-class mothers delegated mundane domestic tasks and elaborated intense new mother–child relations of care and tutelage (Cott, 1977; Ryan, 1979; Zelizer, 1985).

Individualism in the public sphere

The ideology of separate spheres pronounced the public sphere to be the world of men. Yet the public sphere was not just men's *proper* place. Its *institutions* developed to incorporate men as central actors and its ideology of individualism simultaneously presumed and constituted modern male identity (Acker, 1990; Boydston, 1990; Rotundo, 1993). The institutions of work and the meanings of being a worker incorporated a person who was fully freed to compete and contract in a labour market, to sell long hours of labour for a wage, and to suppress non-pecuniary motives, needs, and emotions in service of his contract. In the American polity, the citizen's self-interest was defined by his responsibility for economic dependants.

In sum, the institutions of a capitalist and democratic society presumed both competitive individualism and institutional role occupants whose non-pecuniary needs were served by economically dependent domestic partners. Although men were not, in fact, the only participants in the arenas of public life, public institutions were fashioned in the image of individualised male actors (Acker, 1990). Simultaneously, men formed individuated identities that were significantly patterned by their roles in public life. Manhood in industrial society was defined by employment, competitiveness, hardness, and unemotionality (Mangan and Walvin, 1987; Rotundo, 1993).

Individualism in the private sphere

Once a public sphere developed, family, friendship, and secular and religious community became a segregated sphere of 'private life'. In private life, people exited the competitive, contractual, and segmented roles of public life and entered the holistic, morally ordered relations of communal compact.

English historian Stone captured the ethic of individualism that flowered in private life with the notion of 'affective individualism'. In his study, *The Family, Sex, and Marriage in England, 1500–1800* (1977), Stone coins the phrase to describe the characteristic *mentalité* of modern culture. With sources in the economic, political, and psychodynamic changes of modernity, affective individualism changed relations of authority, thinking, and feeling among people. Protestantism, Enlightenment and libertarian ideas and capitalist markets all spread the awareness and sanctioned expression of individuality, and rights of autonomy. These valued practices advanced personal intimacy, which replaced 'distance, deference, and patriarchy' as the ethos of human relations that were newly considered 'personal life' (Stone, 1977, p. 18). People developed self-conscious, self-expressive forms of intimacy, and with introspection they found and expressed sentiment towards intimates. The generalised ethos radiated from the eighteenth-century family, which featured an 'intensive affective bonding at the nuclear core' and the valuation of individual happiness, sexual pleasure, and privacy. Even public life became more concerned with tolerance, sentiment, and the avoidance of cruelty (ibid., p. 8).

In private life, Stone argues, both men and women imbibed the culture of affective individualism, becoming mutually introspective, self-disclosive, affectionate, and emotionally expressive. None the less, Stone, like others who write about individualism, does not note how differently men and women adapted its ideas. Their adaptations of affective individualism differed because the resources available in their different institutional positions differed. Women's affective individualism, much more so than men's, developed within the communal constraints of family responsibility and emerging formations of collective gender identification (Oliker, 1989). In divergent adaptations of individualism, masculine and feminine ideals, identities, and patterns of intimacy diverged.

In the nineteenth-century United States, industrial men fulfilled their primary family roles when they were 'breadwinners' or 'good providers' (Boydston, 1990). Pre-industrial men had been the rearers of sons past infancy, the managers of the work of all dependants, and moral and religious leaders of the household, as well as producers. Once men followed work out of the home, however, women became responsible for running households, rearing children, and conducting daily religious life and moral tutelage in the family.

A money economy marginalised the unpaid productive role of women in the household and made women more economically dependent on husbands. Yet, an ideology of 'moral motherhood' celebrated women's role as 'angel of the hearth', responsible for the newly conceived necessity of tender care and moral tending of children and husbands. New ideas about women's natural purity, piety, submissiveness, and sentimentality held them ideally suited for a role of growing importance in private life that made them morally equal with husbands even as they became more economically subordinate (Cott, 1977; Welter, 1978; Bloch, 1978; Ryan, 1979).

To discharge their role as homemaker, nurturer, and moral exemplar, women had to develop self-consciousness, empathy, and emotional intelligence, and harness them to relations of private life. This was a form of individualism: women became more autonomous (within their proper realm), self-aware (to morally inspire and serve others well), and intensely emotional (because of increased attentiveness to those needing care). Yet this individualism developed within communal bonds and obligations that demanded the subordination of self-interest and independence. Women's affective individualism was delimited by social exclusion and domestic duty.

Religious ideals and romantic expectations of marriage elicited affective individualism in men as well as women (Lystra, 1989; Yacovone, 1990). Romantic love had succeeded family calculation and negotiation as the proper basis of marriage, and courtship became an intensely romantic enterprise. Companionate ideals, holding that husbands and wives should be intimate best friends, replaced older marriage ideals that emphasised patriarchal authority and wifely deference (Rothman, 1984; Lystra, 1989).

Evangelical emphasis on feeling, as well as secular courtship expectations of romantic love and emotional communion, cultivated affective individualism in both sexes. In private life, men were supposed to be sentimental and disclosive too, even if these were virtues not considered natural to men (Lystra, 1989). Public and private role expectations were contradictory only in the same time and space. None the less, being breadwinners allowed middle-class men little time to practise private virtues. One advocate of male domestic involvement, who was read widely in the middle of the nineteenth century, considered the dinner hour an adequate investment in time with family (Marsh, 1990). Moreover, the space for practising domestic affection was increasingly under the authority and *de facto* control of women. Affective individualism was, thus, an awkward and perilous culture for men. To embrace it too heartily risked the charge of 'effeminate indulgence' and 'unmanliness' (Rotundo, 1993).

In observing the rise of romantic companionate marriage, sociologists and historians document changes in ideas more decisively than changes in practice. Romantic companionate ideals spread farther and deeper than the practices. Moreover, failures in practice were more often attributed to husbands by wives than the reverse. In the first decades of the nineteenth century, women who married after romantic courtships experienced 'marriage trauma' (Cott, 1977, p. 80; Smith-Rosenberg, 1979). Later in the century, young women still anticipated marriage with 'images of confinement, struggle, and loss', fearing that 'The thing is not its vision' (Rothman, 1984, p. 63; Stowe, 1983). While some courting men expressed the same fears, others welcomed the end of courtship, because 'I do not feel I will do one bit of good at any kind of business until we are married' (Rothman, 1984, p. 164).

It appears that men were neither as motivated by nor as practised at affective individualism as women were. Autonomy, competitiveness, and emotional self-control were the salient elements of masculine individualism. These elements constituted the individualism of the public sphere and they enabled men to fulfil their primary family role of provider. In the late nineteenth century, women's effective grounds for divorce were failures of economic provision and, increasingly, mental cruelty, but not failures of emotional communion (May, 1980; Griswold, 1990).

Affective individualism, in the form of romantic and companionate marital expectations, presumed a psychological structure of motives that conflicted with the motives reinforced in market roles and the primary family roles of men. As social psychological theorists like Chodorow, Benjamin, and Gilligan have shown us, the most exaggerated forms of autonomy entail the psychological denial of relationship and dependence, while the latter are necessary for self-conscious attachment to others and empathy (Chodorow, 1978; Benjamin, 1981; Gilligan, 1982).

Affective individualism emerged in private life. It was not an application of the competitive individualism of the market or the polity, but a cultural complex that developed in the reformed institutions that were newly labelled private life. In important ways, it was a culture that favoured women's interests and desires. As women became more economically dependent on marriage and men, they had much to gain by men's emotional dependence. Both men and women became affective individualists, but they adapted the culture differently because they were positioned so differently in the institutions of modernity.

Separate spheres?

Male and female complexes of individualism were different and contradictory but mutually constitutive, like the institutional spheres in which they developed. There could be no world of men of the market without a world of women at home. Men were autonomous in the market-place, able to sell a long day's uninterrupted labour and free to pursue self-interest and concentrate energy in work and competition because the labour they needed to dress, eat, rest, raise children, be consoled, and conduct their religion was performed by domestic spouses. Similarly, women could devote themselves to care, nurture, empathy, and preservation of values that withered in the public realm only if they were economically supported and politically protected by public men. And just as gender-diversified individualism articulated with gendered institutions, so did gendered patterns of intimacy.

The rise of intimate friendship

Historians disagree about exactly where and when widespread patterns of intimate friendship arose. Yet, regarding the United States, few disagree that, by the middle of the nineteenth century, the middle classes were engaged in a fervent and valorised culture of intimacy. In courtship, marriage, family life, and friendship, people mutually explored their inner lives and emotions and feelingly expressed their attachment to one another (Degler, 1980; Lystra, 1989). Practices of intimacy appear to have been widespread in the nineteenth-century United States, but they were most elaborate where the actors were inspired to and could easily draw ideas, resources, and strategies of intimate exchange from their primary institutional settings. Consequently, the upper and middle classes found intimacy most appealing and practicable. And women became the culture's most ardent practitioners.

The romantic friendships of middle-class women

The lives of middle-class women were especially favourable to the cultivation of emotionally intense and intimate friendships with other women. First of all, pre-industrial patterns of sociability, interdependence, and affection had carried into modern domesticity, even though industrial work undermined them for men. Domesticity allowed continued practices of collective work (like quilting or canning) and regular exchanges of help (like child or bedside care). Upon this solid ground of traditional friendship, modern intimacy developed. Middle-class domesticity provided both constraints on competitive individualism and the opportunities to establish intense, emotional relationships with family members and networks of similar (more knowable) others and, with them, to partake of the symbols and substance of affective individualism.

Evangelical 'Awakenings' in the eighteenth and nineteenth centuries drew the United States' female majority of active parishioners – whom ministers now charged with the cultivation of husbands' and children's moral goodness and psychological comfort – into friendly communions of spiritual self-consciousness and feeling (Welter, 1974). 'I do not believe that men can ever feel so pure an enthusiasm for women as we can feel for one another', Catherine Sedgwick recorded in her diary in 1834 after meeting Fanny Kemble, 'ours is nearer to the love of angels' (Cott, 1977, p. 173).

As industrial commodity production and a growing middle class (with servants) increasingly freed middle-class women of responsibility for domestic tasks, religious sorority was augmented by the sisterhood of maternal, charitable, and moral reform organisations. Here, secular canons pronounced 'the culture of the heart' a virtue of republican womanhood, and secular as well as religious duty directed 'self-conscious mothers and wives' to shine the light of the home in a wider sphere. In these new forms of association, passionate friendships developed along with the sensibilities that shaped this 'caring' female sphere of public life (Cott, 1977; Ryan, 1979). European romantic culture, yet another source of inspiration, also augmented secular and sentimental friendships. With burgeoning audiences of avid readers, novels (and growing numbers of female novelists), maga-zines, and a fast-growing domestic advice literature, helped to spread the culture of romantic friendship (Cott, 1977; Douglas, 1977; Degler, 1980).

First girls, then women, recorded their ardent feelings for one another in passionate letters, diaries, and novels. Smith-Rosenberg, Cott, and Faderman cite an abundant literature of letters exchanged between edu-cated young women throughout the nineteenth century, who addressed 'My Beloved', requested that they should 'lay our hearts open to each other', and closed, 'Imagine yourself kissed a dozen times my darling' (Smith-Rosenberg, 1979, pp. 315, 328; Cott, 1977; Faderman, 1981). Mature women soon adapted the romantic conventions of friendship, evident in a diary entry in which a woman describes her friend: 'Time cannot destroy the fascination of her manner . . . her voice is music to the ear' (Smith-Rosenberg, 1979, p. 320).

The letters of women separated from friends are especially passionate: 'Dearest Darling – How incessantly I have thought of you these eight days – all today – the entire uncertainty, the distance, the long silence – are all new features in my separation from you, grievous to be born' (ibid., p. 314). A bride writes to her friend from her honeymoon trip in 1857: 'Darling, do you think every day that in my heart, I am close, close by your side?'(Degler, 1980, p. 146). Carroll Smith-Rosenberg documents the ways overlapping networks of family and friends enacted rituals of emotional attachment and sustained lifelong relations of intimacy (1979).

Romantic styles of intimate friendship thrived in an era in which modern ideas of pandemic sexuality had not yet arrived. The era's doctrines of 'true womanhood' had replaced pre-industrial conceptions of women's carnality and moral weakness with new images of women's superior moral virtues, including natural 'passionlessness' (Cott, 1979). Thus, romantic friends' passionate yearnings, their language of love, and sensual liberties appeared sexually innocent and were unreproached by parents, teachers, husbands, or suitors (Smith-Rosenberg, 1979; Faderman, 1981). (Faderman even argues that women's nineteenth-century progress in education and aspiration, along with post-Civil War sex ratios that assured that many women would not marry, encouraged some male commentators to herald passionate friendship as an alternative to marriage.)

Although some historians question the extent of romantic friendship among the middle classes, none disputes the rise of intimate modes of friendship among middle-class women, as American culture hallowed self-awareness and individuality, and as middle-class women found more opportunities to devote time and attention to their husbands, children, friends, and themselves (Degler, 1980; Rothman, 1984).

Nineteenth-century men's friendships

Affective individualism became a generalised cultural current that influenced men's friendships as well. Yet the daily lives of American men provided fewer opportunities for the cultivation of intimate friendship. Commerce and industrial work drew men of all classes away from forms of association that prevailed in the pre-industrial economy. Their days were clocked by industrial timetables rather than the task-paced flow of work and sociability of pre-industrial work and modern domesticity. The role of worker, in whatever stratum of work, demanded the subordination of emotions, rather than their cultivation, and the bracketing of concerns about self and private life (Boydston, 1990; Rotundo, 1993).

Traditions of male sociability proceeded in the tavern and the club when the workday was over. But the social traffic of public sociability at these sites was better suited to maintaining older patterns of intercourse than the new forms of introspection and disclosure that flourished in the paired interactions of private life. Men probably became familiar, affectionate, even committed, in long association with friends in public places, but they were not likely to have become as intimate as women friends who met privately and who carried on friendships at home amidst the tasks and rituals of private life.

Modern ideals defined masculinity in terms opposed with feminine impulse and sentiment in a way that polarised the personalities, capacities, and desires of men and women more than before. The 'man of feeling' was a fleeting masculine icon who was quickly displaced by the hard, competitive, and unemotional man of the market (Stone, 1977, p. 266). Not only were the primary tasks of men unwelcoming of intimate attachment, but new standards of masculine identity and personality were also. Christian brotherhood and romantic love circumscribed the play of intimacy (Yacovone, 1990; Rotundo, 1993).

Historians have tapped evidence of romantic friendships among men, none the less (Rotundo, 1989; Yacovone, 1990). In 1800, Daniel Webster, for example, described his best friend as 'the partner of my joys, griefs, and affections, the only participator of my most secret thoughts' (Rotundo, 1989, p. 1). Rotundo maintains that Webster's statement was characteristic of the ardent sensibilities of young male friends in the nineteenth century. Letters and diaries of men in their late teens and twenties reveal intimate attachments to friends that seem similar to those of young women of that time. One diarist prays, for example, that God 'ever keep us as we are now in oneness, one life, one interest, one heart, one love' (ibid., p. 5).

Evoking the unselfconscious physicality of women friends of this time, men left accounts of sharing kisses and beds 'and in each others arms did friendship sink peacefully to sleep' (ibid., p. 5). Romantic friendships among middle-class young men that included ardent emotions and sensual embraces were accepted among parents and peers and considered compatible with heterosexual courtship. An era with no label of 'homosexual' or specific sexual identities allowed more latitude for physical expression than later eras would (D'Emilio and Freedman, 1988; Rotundo, 1989, 1993).

Rotundo notes a pattern that significantly distinguished the romantic friendships of men and women, none the less. He found the male pattern in only one stage of life, the decade or so between childhood and adulthood. Still preparing to stage a career, close in time to the sentiment and shelter of domestic childhood, and living in worlds of school, boarding house, and club that were segregated by sex, class, and age, young men turned to each other without the constraints of competitive career and 'manly independence' (Rotundo, 1989, p. 13). Rotundo considers brief romantic friendship among youth as a staging ground for both career and the intimacy of marriage. These friendships were different from the aggressive play of boys and from the instrumental friendships of male adults. And young men anticipated their certain end with marriage and career (ibid.). Romantic friendships of young women, by contrast, were continuous with the attachments of girlhood and domestic female adulthood (Smith-Rosenberg, 1979).

A note on working-class intimate friendship

There is still very little historical evidence that we can use to portray intimacy among the nineteenth-century working classes. Some historians have disagreed with suggestions that intimacy blossomed first in the middle classes, maintaining that the working classes pioneered it (Shorter, 1977). Individualism in marriage choice, for example, was easier to forge where little property was at stake in marriage. And working-class youths who left the countryside for work in the cities were freer of parental control of friendly association as well. Some essential ingredients of intimacy may have been more concentrated and wider spread among the nineteenth-century working classes than the middle classes (Shorter, 1977; Stone, 1977). None the less, it seems likely that lack of leisure, domestic space, secular education, and reading constrained the spread of affective individualism and intimacy. There is, however, a literature on working-class intimate friendship.

Examining letters and diaries of literate day labourers, teachers, and farmers – both white and black – in the antebellum Northeastern United States, Hansen (1994) found evidence of intimate and romantic friendships, as well as intense sociability. Addie Brown, a seamstress and domestic servant, wrote often to her 'only dear and loving friend', Rebecca Primus, sharing news and feelings. 'I cannot be happy if I was to stay a way from you. Rebecca, my *Dearest Love*, could any one love a person as I love you?' (ibid., pp. 55–6).

Hansen found fewer letters between men, but cites a correspondence between two men who probably met while working together in a box factory. J. Foster Beal wrote to Brigham Nims that he 'Can not forget those happy hours [th]at we spent . . . But we are deprived of that privilege now, we are separated for a time we cannot tel [*sic*] how long perhaps before our eyes behold each other in this world' (ibid., p. 69).

The letters Hansen cites suggest friendships as intimate and romantic as those found among middle-class women and among young middle-class men. These are all letters between *young* women and men, however, and their friendships generally ended with marriage. While middle-class women's friendships seem to have survived courtship and marriage, Hansen suggests that 'in the agrarian and working classes, scarce resources made demands on marriage that occasionally placed female friends in direct competition with husbands' (ibid., p. 61). Moreover, working-class friends seemed to have had fewer resources to bridge geographical distances when marriage moved friends apart. One woman wrote to a faraway friend: 'I had given up all hope of ever hearing from you again and concluded that you was either dead or married' (ibid., p. 66).

While Hansen found far more intimate letters between women than men, other evidence makes it plausible to suggest that, in contrast to the middle classes, working-class men may have had more resources for establishing and sustaining intimate friendships. Working-class men were more autonomous of family and more frequent actors in the public arenas that cultivated individualism and choices in friendship. Young working-class women, employed primarily as paid domestics, were more isolated from peers than men were and less exposed to the individualism of the market-place. Those who lived at home were more likely than their brothers to have heavy responsibilities for housework and child care after work, to turn over paychecks to parents, and to have family supervise their movement outside the home (Peiss, 1986). Working-class girls also lacked the individuating context of schooling, which was so important to middle-class female friendships. Moreover, late nineteenth-century immigration lowered their literacy rates.

In sum, until the turn of the twentieth century, working-class young women entered few structures of peer aggregation that paralleled those of working-class men; and they had less time, space, and cultural inspiration than middle-class women for cultivating affective individualism. When young women entered non-domestic urban employment, their low wages made them exceptionally dependent on male companionship if they wished to participate in urban sociability. As a result, reports Kathy Peiss (1986), young working-class women's friendships at the turn of the century were oriented instrumentally to linking up with male companions.

Once married and mothers, nineteenth-century working-class women had less leisure and were more enmeshed in and dependent on kin exchanges than their men were. The need to venture into the streets to borrow, trade, and scavenge made working-class women more publicly active than middle-class women may have been. But their time with co-operating kin and neighbours, both inside and outside the home, was consumed by relentless work and mutual aid, as in pre-industrial society. Working-class women friends had little of the leisure that might open a space for self-reflection and intimacy (Stansell, 1986). Working-class men, on the other hand, tended to use their somewhat greater leisure time to be with friends at the tavern or club (Peiss, 1986).

These comments on working-class intimacy are speculative. That said, it is plausible that self-exploration, free choice of friends, and time to invest in intimate exchange were more accessible to working-class men than women, although many conditions that favoured affective individualist intimacy were constrained for both. If so, intimacy may have been engendered differently across the social classes.

Twentieth-century changes

By the turn of the twentieth century, changes in the lives of women and men of the middle classes began to undermine the intense romanticism of intimate friendships. Changes in marriage, education, work, and influential ideas about sex contributed to its decline. One set of changes affected friendship by way of affecting male–female relations. Education for women, especially coeducation, assimilated the experience and views of young men and women and brought them into daily contact. The expansion of women's labour force participation and urban recreations did the same. As the worlds of men's and women's experience increasingly overlapped, men and women became more companionable and intimate heterosexual bonds more central (Oliker, 1989). By the 1920s, dating became a widespread institution that isolated couples more thoroughly than courtship in the past and drew time and energy from same-sex friendship (Modell, 1983). In marriage, companionate ideals became more practicable, eclipsing the singular success of romantic friendship.

Popular sexology and psychoanalytic ideas labelled formerly unclassified behaviours and feelings as erotic and lifted the mantle of innocence that protected passionate feelings and sensuality between romantic friends (Faderman, 1981; D'Emilio and Freedman, 1988). Masculine fears of 'effeminacy' were magnified by the association of the feminine with newly labelled 'homosexual' persons. The labelling of homosexuality as a sturdy psychosexual identity moved same-sex eroticism into the makings of sexual identities. Passionate love for a friend posed the danger of establishing a deviant sexual identity and threatening heterosexual courtship. This was more the case for men than women, who continued to be viewed as naturally unsexual (Faderman, 1981; D'Emilio and Freeman, 1988). None the less, regarding girls, teachers and school administrators who once encouraged romantic friendship began to condemn it. The 'lesbian threat' shadowed the 'crushes' and passionate friendships of young women and forced them into a deviant underground (Simmons, 1979).

Responding to a divorce rate that rose along with expectations of companionate marriage, the new professionals of marriage-helping more heartily prescribed companionship in marriage, emphasising mutual disclosure, couple socialising, and joint endeavour. Temperance and moral movements targeted the masculine immoralities and dissipations of the tavern and the club (Oliker, 1989). Employers scrutinised and colonised the leisure activities of good company men. And in a different prescriptive mode, and targeting women, advertising promoted consumption as the royal road to individuality, romanticising the household as the centre of leisure and consumption and galvanising the invidious pursuit of beauty. One's best friend became a competitor (ibid.).

All of these forces undermined the culture of romantic friendship and cultural recognition of intimate friendship as an institution of private life and individual identity. Companionate marriage occupied – entirely – the lighted space of culturally recognised intimacy; indistinct, friendship became viewed as part of the benign world of sociability. This is not to say, however, that intimacy between friends declined, at least not for women. Rather, intimate friendship persisted as an important but unheralded institution of middle-class women's private lives. Indeed, it became more widespread, as new groups of women adapted individualism and leisure through expanding access to social privilege (see in this volume: Marks; Harrison; O'Connor).

The increasing practicability of companionate marriage helped to deflate the culture of romantic friendship, but women's centrality in private life, as nurturers and consumers, allowed them to enlarge ideals of marital companionship successively. Over the course of the twentieth century, literature, cinema, television, and religious and therapeutic advice publicised marital ideals of mutuality, attentiveness, disclosure, empathy, emotional communion, and sexual pleasure, in images of intimacy that often best served women's desires and interests. Marital ideals continued to outpace realities, leaving women dissatisfied with the gender gap in intimacy. Seven decades of empirical research on marriage document women's greater dissatisfaction with companionship and a consensus between men and women on the predominance of women's self-sacrificing marital 'adjustment' (Oliker, 1989).

Although intimacy between close women friends was displaced by marriage in cultural centrality, intimate friendship persisted as a social pattern responsive to the gender asymmetries in marriage. Like romantic women friends, but without their exaltation, twentieth-century friends continued to practise intimacy that compensated for the intimate shortcomings of spouses. Sociologists were always more captivated by marriage than friendship, yet throughout the century they noted, if only tangentially, both the intimacy of women's friendships and the contrast with the greater distance of men's. The sociologists who restudied Middletown in the 1970s found 'overwhelming' evidence that marital communication had improved, and offered, without comment, a 'typical example from one housewife': 'I feel there is nothing I couldn't go to him and ask . . . I mostly talk to my best friends, but I feel that you should look to your own husband for basic communication' (Caplow, *et al.*, 1982, p. 125). By the 1970s, Bernard (1976) had distinguished 'his marriage' and 'her marriage', and by the 1980s titles like Rubin's *Intimate Strangers* (1983) appeared in scholarly and popular writings. My 1980s work on married women's best friendships shows how women's intimate friendships shore up their commitments to and satisfaction with marriages, compensating for husbands' shortcomings in realising the widely shared ideal of intimacy (Oliker, 1989).

In the past two decades, numerous studies of friendship have documented a pattern in which women's same-sex friendships are more self-disclosive and emotionally expressive than those of men (Oliker, 1989; Umberson, *et al.*, 1996). Yet the social structures that once favoured intimacy between women and constrained it between men are no longer so unequally dispersed as they were a century ago. Men and women, especially those without children, are likely to be employed, educated, and included in an array of activities in public life. It is true that the majority of employed women are in occupations with short mobility ladders that minimise the gains to competition. None the less, the social structures and ideologies of public individualism and competition reach both sexes. Similarly, popular culture more pervasively enshrines emotional expression and self-disclosive intimacy for both heterosexual relationships and male friendships. Why would patterns of relationship that grew in the context of separate spheres persist after both ideas and realities of separation have eroded?

The answers most frequently offered to explain contemporary gender differences in intimate styles have been dispositional arguments rooted in gender socialisation. Once the structural constraints on intimacy weaken, one cannot so easily bracket such explanations. Perhaps I have neglected sources of intimate friendship in the psychodynamics of the Victorian family. To acknowledge how my argument might accommodate hypotheses about gender dispositional causes, however, I must first turn once more to issues of structural change.

While women now participate in 'men's worlds' of paid work and politics, the structures of domesticity have changed much less dramatically. Women remain the primary co-ordinators and executors of housework, child-rearing, kin-keeping, and elder care (Abel and Nelson, 1990; Finch and Groves, 1983). Persistent structures of private life continue to elicit women's practices of intimacy and create investments in intimate relationships, in the nineteenth-century mode. The most persuasive arguments about gender dispositional differences in intimacy place disposition in this institutional context.

Chodorow (1978), for example, explains gender differences in intimacy with a Parsonsian (in psychology, 'object relations') adaptation of psychoanalytic explanation. She argues that, when mothers are the primary nurturers of children, both boys' and girls' individual identities emerge out of primary attachment and identification with the mother. Boys develop masculine identification by renouncing both identification and attachment to their mothers, in favour of identification with fathers. They accomplish that difficult renunciation by distancing themselves from all that is feminine, adopting a defensive masculinity centred on exaggerated autonomy. Girls must renounce their primary attachment to mothers and transfer attachment to fathers and then men. Yet, elements of maternal attachment persist in girls' unchallenged identification with their mothers. Less propelled by psychic conflict towards autonomy, their identities remain embedded in relationships.[4]

Through this dynamic, argues Chodorow (1978), male and female adult identities are differentially oriented to relationship and intimacy. Chodorow argues that these 'gender asymmetries' produce 'heterosexual knots', out of which married women, disappointed with husbands' capacities for intimacy, turn to intimacy with women kin, friends, and children. This desire to nurture children, and men's lack of it, begins the cycle anew.

A variety of other theorists have also posited internalised dispositions towards intimacy, suggesting that the persistent structures of child nurture may pattern identity, personality, cognitive development, and moral orientation in boys and girls, and may have done so in the past, as well. Bem (1993), for example, focuses on how, in child socialisation, institutional patterns become internalised in cognitive schema, such that individual cognition, not just psychological inclination, shapes gendered patterns like intimacy. Gilligan (1982) posits that persistent modes of child nurture produce distinctive patterns of moral development. The predominantly masculine pattern is oriented to ethics of justice and the feminine to ethics of caring. Each gendered moral 'voice' is missing crucial moral commitments developed in the other. Ruddick (1983), focusing on dispositions that develop in adulthood, suggests that both knowledge and moral voice develop in institutionally gendered practices. Nurturing children generates cognitive and moral frameworks that favour intimate knowledge and commitment.

Thus, a range of theories – of cognition, moral development, and psychological disposition – would take the persistent institutional arrangements of child nurture as the starting point for explaining gendered intimacy. Twentieth-century changes that undermined the brief reign of the breadwinner–caregiver family and accelerated gender equality in public and private life left the structure of child nurture in place, and, with it, perhaps, gendered dispositions towards intimacy.

Conclusion

Intimate friendships developed alongside intimate courtship in an affective individualistic culture of private life. The makings of disclosive, emotionally expressive intimacy were changes in both ideas and institutions as they influenced middle-class lives. Varieties of individualism, along with the ideology of separate spheres, articulated with emerging modern institutions in ways that unevenly encouraged intimate styles. Nineteenth-century middle-class men's and women's distinctive social locations and experiences offered them different opportunities and constraints as they adapted cultural currents of individualism and intimacy.

For men, the industrial economy and democratic polity in which they participated elicited an individualism which emphasised autonomy, competitive self-interest, and emotional control. These harsh practices pushed them towards the family for relief and consolation. There, men were offered the pleasures of intimacy, care, and connection, in exchange for economic provision.

Yet, if the pleasures of intimacy were heightened by its exclusion from public life, intimate practices were temporally and psychologically contradictory with competitive individualism in ways that made intimacy a more arduous pleasure for men than it was for women. Once past the intense and distracting intimacy of courtship, men found that their daily lives positioned them awkwardly and ambivalently for the practice of marital intimacy. The public and group structures of male sociability and men's increasing worries about effeminacy and erotically charged friendship made intimate friendship less accessible, particularly once men entered career and marriage. In the nineteenth century, intimacy was less practicable, less facile, and more ambivalent for men than women.

Middle-class women's practices of intimacy were more consistently elicited and better supported by their institutional participation; and female intimacy was less constrained by cultural stigma and the psychodynamics of the private sphere. Intimacy articulated seamlessly with the daily structures of middle-class girlhood, young womanhood, and adulthood. Relations in the small, private worlds of family, parish, school, and sociability made women's networks homogeneous and normatively affective. Even courtship, where young women were positioned to compete, elicited shared intimacies and excitements between intimate peers. Intimate inclinations blossomed in relations of attentive and nurturant motherhood and wifehood. Women gained power resources in emotional interdependence as they lost them in their economic dependence on marriage, whereas men lost traditional resources of authority amidst the riches of intimacy.

Affective individualism spread desires and practices of intimacy through heterosexual relations and same-sex friendship, but the culture was incorporated most thoroughly in women's desires for marriage and in their friendships. In the eras of the nineteenth century in which women's and men's experiences were most distinct and most difficult to reconcile in intimate knowledge, romantic same-sex friendships filled the gap between romantic ideals of marriage and marriage realities. Young men and women of all ages elaborated an intense and sensual culture of intimate same-sex friendship.

As the century turned, and companionship and intimacy between men and women became more practicable, and as modern sexology spread, the culture of romantic friendship faded for both men and women. When it faded, intimate friendship persisted, among women, though not, perhaps, among young heterosexual men. The continuing marginality of women in public life and, more importantly, the continuing marginality of fathers in housework and child nurture recreate the gender asymmetries of marital intimacy. Even as the ideology of separate spheres receded, social institutions continued both to differentiate experience and to polarise psychodynamic dispositions by gender. Women in my study of contemporary best friendship reported a 'gulf of experience' that emerged in marital understanding once couples had children (Oliker, 1989). These women and those in larger-scale studies tend to believe their mates need and want less intimate disclosure and emotional expressiveness than they do themselves (Rubin, 1983).

For the entire twentieth century, the ideology of separate spheres has been contended by enlarging egalitarian ideals and changes in women's public participation. Yet, egalitarian ideals of parenthood notwithstanding, participation in the private sphere remains distinctly gendered in ways that recreate gender differences in desires and behaviours of intimacy. And formal rights of access notwithstanding, economic and political institutions have retained their gendered character in gender-neutral guise: man or woman – anyone who is cared for and whose children are cared for by someone else – can achieve in work or politics. Both men and women may want children, but men have the social resources and, perhaps, the psychological reluctance that enable them to decline to rear them (Polatnick, 1983). Twentieth-century egalitarian-minded families thus often recreate the gendered institutional and psychological structures of intimacy: even without rigidly separate spheres, men primarily invest time and identity in work, women in family. Gendered institutions recreate gendered patterns of intimacy.

Acknowledgements

A fellowship at the Center for Twentieth-Century Studies at the University of Wisconsin–Milwaukee supported this research.

Notes

1. A historian would more intricately periodise changes in nineteenth-century intimacy, and chart the pre-nineteenth-century origins of many of them. I treat the nineteenth century more as a sociological ideal-type, that is, as the period in which the effects of modernity on gender and personal relations appear in concentration and the dynamics are readily observable.
2. Allan's *Friendship: Developing a Sociological Perspective*, published the same year (1989), also proposes a close look at the links between social structure and cultures and patterns of friendship.
3. Sources for the arguments in this chapter are more abundantly provided in the book (Oliker, 1989).
4. Jessica Benjamin (1981), also using object-relations psychoanalytic theory of identity, emphasises the internal makings of domination and obstacles to individuality in gender identities that rigorously divide masculine autonomy and feminine relationality. Authentic autonomy depends on recognition and authentic relationality depends on autonomy. When only women nurture, the dynamic of gender identity uncouples these essential relations and infuses male autonomy with authoritarian impulse and female intimacy with dependency.

References

Abel, Emily K., and Nelson, Margaret K. (1990), *Circles of Care: Work and Identity in Women's Lives*, Albany: State University of New York Press.

Acker, Joan (1990), 'Hierarchies, jobs, bodies: a theory of gendered organizations', *Gender and Society*, 4: 139–58.

Allan, Graham (1989), *Friendship: Developing a Sociological Perspective*, Hemel Hempstead: Harvester-Wheatsheaf.

Bem, Sandra L. (1993), *The Lenses of Gender*, New Haven: Yale University Press.

Benjamin, Jessica (1981), 'The oedipal riddle: authority, autonomy, and the new narcissism', in John P. Diggins and Mark E. Kann (eds.), *The Problem of Authority in America*, Philadelphia: Temple University Press.

Berger, Peter L. (1977), *Facing up to Modernity*, New York: Basic Books.

Bernard, Jessie (1976), *The Future of Marriage*, New York: Bantam Books.

Bloch, Ruth H. (1978), 'American feminine ideals in transition: the rise of the moral mother, 1785–1815', *Feminist Studies*, 4: 103–13.

Boydston, Jeanne (1990), *Home and Work: Housework, Wages, and the Ideology of Labor in the Early Republic*, New York: Oxford University Press.

Caplow, Theodore, Bahr, Howard, Chadwick, Bruce, Hill, Reuben, and Williamson, Margaret (1982), *Middletown Families: Fifty Years of Change and Continuity*, Minneapolis: University of Minnesota Press.

Carnes, Mark C., and Griffen, Clyde (eds.) (1990), *Meanings for Manhood: Constructions of Masculinity in Victorian America*, University of Chicago Press.

Chodorow, Nancy (1978), *The Reproduction of Mothering*, Berkeley: University of California Press.

Cott, Nancy F. (1977), *The Bonds of Womanhood*, New Haven: Yale University Press.

　(1979), 'Passionlessness: an interpretation of Victorian sexual ideology', in Cott and Pleck (eds.).

Cott, Nancy F., and Pleck, Elizabeth H. (eds.) (1979), *A Heritage of Her Own: Toward a New Social History of American Women*, New York: Simon and Schuster, Touchstone.

Degler, Carl N. (1980), *At Odds*, Oxford University Press.

D'Emilio, John, and Freedman, Estelle (1988), *Intimate Matters: A History of Sexuality in America*, New York: Harper and Row.

Demos, John (1970), *A Little Commonwealth*, London: Oxford University Press.

Douglas, Ann (1977), *The Feminization of American Culture*, New York: Avon Books.

Faderman, Lillian (1981), *Surpassing the Love of Men*, New York: William Morrow.

Finch, Janet, and Groves, Dulcie (eds.) (1983), *A Labour of Love: Women, Work, and Caring*, London: Routledge and Kegan Paul.

Fischer, Claude S., Jackson, Robert M., Steuve, C. Ann, Gerson, Kathleen, and McCallister Jones, Lynne, with Baldassare, Mark (1977), *Networks and Places*, New York: Free Press.

Gilligan, Carol (1982), *In a Different Voice*, Cambridge, Mass.: Harvard University Press.

Griswold, Robert L. (1990), 'Divorce and the legal redefinition of Victorian manhood', in Carnes and Griffen (eds.).

Hansen, Karen V. (1994), *A Very Social Time: Crafting Community in Antebellum New England*, Berkeley: University of California Press.

Lystra, Karen (1989), *Searching the Heart: Women, Men, and Romantic Love in Nineteenth-Century America*, New York: Oxford University Press.

Mangan, J. A., and Walvin, James (eds.) (1987), *Manliness and Morality: Middle-Class Masculinity in Britain and America, 1800–1940*, Manchester University Press.

Marsh, Margaret (1990), 'Suburban men and masculine domesticity, 1870–1915', in Carnes and Griffen (eds.).

May, Elaine Tyler (1980), *Great Expectations*, University of Chicago Press.

Modell, John (1983), 'Dating becomes the way of American youth', in D. Levine (ed.), *Essays on the Family and Historical Change*, Arlington: University of Texas Press.

Nisbet, Robert A. (1953), *The Quest for Community*, New York: Oxford University Press.

Oliker, Stacey J. (1989), *Best Friends and Marriage: Exchange Among Women*, Berkeley: University of California Press.

Peiss, Kathy (1986), *Cheap Amusement: Working Women and Leisure in Turn-of-the-Century New York*, Philadelphia: Temple University Press.

Polatnick, M. Rivka (1983), 'Why men don't rear children? A power analysis', in Trebilcot (ed.).

Rothman, Ellen (1984), *Hands and Hearts: A History of Courtship in America*, New York: Basic Books.

Rotundo, E. Anthony (1989), 'Romantic friendships: male intimacy and middle-class youth in the northern United States, 1800–1900', *Journal of Social History*, 23: 1–25.

  (1993), *American Manhood: Transformations in Masculinity from the Revolution to the Modern Era*, New York: Basic Books.

Rubin, Lillian B. (1983), *Intimate Strangers*, New York: Harper and Row.

Ruddick, Sara (1983), 'Maternal thinking', in Trebilcot (ed.).

Ryan, Mary P. (1979), *Womanhood in America from Colonial Times to the Present*, New York: Franklin Watts, New Viewpoints.

Shorter, Edward (1977), *The Making of the Modern Family*, New York: Basic Books.

Simmons, Christina (1979), 'Companionate marriage and the lesbian threat', *Frontiers*, 4: 54–9.

Smith-Rosenberg, Carroll (1979), 'The female world of love and ritual: relations between women in nineteenth-century America', in Cott and Pleck (eds.).

Stansell, Christine (1986), *City of Women: Sex and Class in New York, 1789–1860*, New York: Alfred Knopf.

Stone, Lawrence (1977), *The Family, Sex, and Marriage in England, 1500–1800*, New York: Harper and Row.

Stowe, Steven M. (1983), 'The thing is not its vision: a woman's courtship and her sphere in the southern planter class', *Feminist Studies*, 9: 113–30.

Trebilcot, Joyce (ed.) (1983), *Mothering: Essays in Feminist Theory*, Totowa, N.J.: Rowman and Allanheld.

Ulrich, Laurel T. (1982), *Good Wives*, New York: Alfred Knopf.

Umberson, Debra, Chen, Meichu D., House, James S., Hopkins, Kristine, and Slaten, Ellen (1996), 'The effect of social relationships on psychological well-being: are men and women really so different', *American Sociological Review*, 61: 837–57.

Welter, Barbara (1974), 'The feminization of American religion: 1800–1860', in Mary Hartman and Lois W. Banner (eds.), *Clio's Consciousness Raised*, New York: Harper and Row, Torch Books.

  (1978), 'The cult of true womanhood: 1820–1860', in M. Gordon (ed.), *The*

American Family in Social-Historical Perspective, New York: St Martin's Press.

Wuthnow, Robert (1989), *Communities of Discourse: Ideology and Social Structure in the Reformation, the Enlightenment, and European Socialism*, Cambridge, Mass.: Harvard University Press.

Yacovone, Donald (1990), 'Abolitionists and the "language of fraternal love"', in Carnes and Griffen (eds.).

Zelizer, Viviana (1985), *Pricing the Priceless Child*, New York: Basic Books.

3

The gendered contexts of inclusive intimacy: the Hawthorne women at work and home

Stephen R. Marks

In 1927, a group of men from the Western Electric Company's Industrial Relations branch initiated a new series of studies at the Hawthorne plant in Chicago. They began by removing five female operators from their regular department, and they relocated them in a separate room where they could be studied doing their familiar jobs. Thus began the famous Relay Assembly Test Room (RATR) – the longest and most hotly debated of the various Hawthorne studies.

Since the ending of the RATR over six decades ago, new waves of analysis have revisited every detail bearing on the women's work productivity, and this singular focus has dominated more than one discipline. In psychology, Bramel and Friend (1981) provoked a flurry of controversy with a Marxist approach, recasting the drama inside the RATR as a class struggle between bosses and workers, and attacking other analysts for giving short shrift to the strategies of 'resistance' the women employed. Sociologists have sought the comfort of multivariate statistical models, asking, for example, if there really *was* a 'Hawthorne Effect' on the women's productivity (Jones, 1992). In business administration, the women became minor celebrities. Rediscovered in the 1980s, they were invited as a panel to a 1986 conference, where they reminded their interlocutors that their productivity rose in the RATR because they were happier there, they liked each other, and they earned more money.

The obsession with the circumstances surrounding the women's production is both curious and unfortunate, because there are other aspects of the women's lives that are no less worthy of interest. Along with factory output, the women produced what I shall call *inclusive intimacy* – a friendship pattern marked by regular group gatherings, by a readiness to expand group boundaries to include anyone important to any of the members, and by a tacit notion that the fulfilment of friendship is in the gatherings themselves.

Exclusive intimacy, or what Giddens (1991, 1992) terms the 'pure relation-ship', is typically dyadic rather than group-oriented, and it is given to the elaboration of private thoughts, feelings, and experiences through acts of self-disclosure. (See also Oliker, this volume, for a similar definition.)

Attention to co-worker closeness – whether inclusive or exclusive inti-macy – was a road not taken in the sociology of workers. Nearly twenty years after the RATR closed down, Homans (1950) did get close to this focus when he borrowed data about the men working in the Bank Wiring Observation Room, not far from the RATR women. Homans linked the men's sentiments of mutual liking to their joint activity, but his proposi-tions were so decontextualised that his readers could easily forget that these were *workers* who were generating this fellow feeling, and that a *work-place* was the institutional setting that was harbouring this feeling. As for the RATR women, no one ever forgot that they were workers, but there was never any interest in anything they produced besides factory output. Even Whitehead (1938, p. 167) – the analyst who seemed most interested in their overall lives – could write: '[Their] ordinary chitchat [in the RATR] . . . was devoid of any general interest; in fact it is so boring as to be almost unread-able.'

The theoretical context of this chapter

The lopsided focus on the instrumental significance of co-worker bonds prevailed until the 1980s, when feminist researchers led a general explora-tion of women's 'work culture', often focusing on expressive and non-util-itarian aspects of these ties (see Westwood, 1985; Cooper, 1987; Lamphere, 1987; Zavella, 1987; Hessing, 1991). In my own work (Marks, 1994), I have sought to understand co-worker bonds from within a general theory of inti-macy and societal context. If the different institutional spheres of society (such as work, family, education, health care, much of leisure) become seg-regated 'foci of activity' (Feld and Carter, this volume), individuals must then move back and forth among these different foci to carry out their func-tionally specific purposes. As they do so, and as they regularly encounter other people pursuing these same purposes, selective intimacy may arise, especially if they share specific activities, as co-workers often do (Homans, 1950; Feld, 1981; see also Feld and Carter, this volume). Modern intimates, however, are often outside one another's purview, except within the foci of activity that bring them together. If I have a close co-working friend, and we do not see or talk to each other at night or during the weekend, our respective lives outside our work-place will remain more or less mysterious to each other. Some form of self-disclosure work may then be required if we want to bridge these *en*closed and separate worlds. I suggest that people will be most eager to bridge their separate worlds when their cultural context encourages them to see themselves as unique and private individuals, in possession of important, separate identities (see also Oliker, this volume). In this case, exclusive intimacy will be the preferred pattern, and disclosure work may become quite complex and elaborate, at times including emotional aspects of one's inner experience. However, if people see and experience themselves not as unique individuals but as members of categories or groups (in large part because this is how they are treated by others), then inclusive intimacy will be their preferred pattern. In this latter case, disclosure accounts may be limited to reports of one's 'outside' activities and to storytelling about others. Comfort will be drawn more from being surrounded by members of one's group or category than by seeking exclusive ties in which one can fully disclose the finely elaborated inner world of thoughts and feelings.

There remains the problem of how, if at all, people integrate segregated foci of activity, such as home and work. Modern theories of work-to-family 'spillover' (Small and Riley, 1990) are clearly premised on the notion that the unique exigencies of the work world may erode or enhance the exclusive intimacies of the home world, and they imply that the 'business' of each of these domains is at the very least different from, if not disruptive of, that of the other.

Analyses of this sort have little relevance to the Hawthorne women. They did their best to make each focus the same rather than different, by pulling one another back and forth between them – from work, to home, to leisure in some third place – so that the same little circle of like-minded women would be close at hand wherever they went. As a point of contrast, consider Wellman's findings about contemporary Toronto, where 'people are not wrapped up in traditional, densely-knit, tightly-bounded communities but are floating in sparsely-knit, loosely-bounded, frequently-changing networks' (1994, p. 32). Wellman notes that 'these are fragmented networks', and he adds that 'people must actively maintain each supportive relationship rather than relying on solidary communities to do their maintenance work' (pp. 32–3). Again, these networks contrast sharply with the tightly bounded, group-oriented networks of the Hawthorne women, even though these women *did* 'float' together among myriad social settings. Are we dealing, then, with differences that are a function of different historical periods, and, if so, what aspects of the contexts of friendship have changed? And what is the nature of these changes?

Perhaps the Hawthorne women's intimacy was specific to the edge of history on which they were standing – the *Gemeinschaft* platform that had not yet been fully displaced by the emerging individualistic, privatised *Gesellschaft* order. If this is the case, we will need non-modern eyes to see the distinctness of the patterns these women evolved. Or perhaps their style of friendship was not historically unique, but may still be found within certain contemporary settings, in which case we will need to uncover the contexts that are most likely to foster the appearance of this pattern. I shall return to this issue at the end of the chapter.

My principal task here concerns two interrelated questions – a substantive one and a contextual one: first, how did these women do friendship on a day-to-day basis? How did inclusive intimacy unfold among them? Secondly, we need to understand the changing contexts of these friendships – cultural, social structural, and historical. The substantive and the contextual features of friendship stand in a dialectical relationship. Put abstractly, the various contexts always provide a framework, or point of departure, for the *doing* of friendship work. Yet, in these doings, friends may transform the very contexts that gave rise to them as friends.

For the Hawthorne women, the social structure and the culture of gendered womanhood were among the most important contextual elements. That is, they took their places as friends within a gender system framed by men, but they then used these friendships, in part, to *continue* to construct themselves as women. One might say that they were involved in a gender-*making* process as well as a gender-taking one; and, while they inherited a patriarchal legacy and to some extent maintained it, they also erected a woman-centred alternative alongside it. In brief, my argument is that the structure and culture of gender were such pervasive contextual elements in these women's friendships that it is reasonable to claim that their doing of friendship was at the same time a doing of gender.

In the remainder of this chapter, I draw on a variety of materials to reconstruct some of the cultural and social structural contexts bearing on four of the RATR women throughout their life-course – Mary, Geraldine, Theresa, and Wanda (their names have now become a matter of public record). In the long data section, I maintain an inductive strategy. My purpose is to elucidate the phenomenon of inclusive intimacy as it wends its way through five or six decades of slowly shifting forms. There is a cumulative impact, I believe, of staying close to the wealth of concrete details about these forms and the women who evolved them, and of course the proof of this strategy is whether the reader emerges with a rich understanding of this type of intimacy.

Sources of data

The succession of observers in the RATR kept a 'Daily History Record' (DHR). In it, they recorded project developments, noted outside events in the women's lives, and wrote down conversation about a broadening array of topics as the experiment wore on. This DHR and other project reports, available from the Baker Library at Harvard, constitute one of the three sources of data for the present analysis. A second data source comes from interviews with all four women conducted between 1981 and 1986 (see Greenwood, *et al.*, 1983; Bolton, 1994). Most of these interviews were either audio- or videotaped, and the tapes were kindly made available to me by Al Bolton. My final source of data comes from my own interviews early in 1993, not long after I learned that two of the women – Mary Volango and Wanda Beilfus – were alive and well and still living in Chicago, some sixty years after the end of the experiment. Mary was then eighty-four and Wanda was eighty-six, and both agreed to interviews. Geraldine Sirchio had died just a year earlier, but I was able to interview two of her brothers – Jim Sirchio and Joe Sirchio – and also Joe's wife Nancy. Joe and Nancy were especially good sources, as Geraldine lived with them for thirty-six years, and their home became a frequent gathering place for all the women. Finally, an unexpected bonus of interviewing Wanda at her home was the presence of her daughter-in-law Arlene, who had been living with Wanda for the past twenty-two years, ever since Arlene's husband – Wanda's son – died at age thirty-one. Arlene joined Wanda and me for part of the interview, and she had vivid insider knowledge of the other women and their connections with each other. For the convenience of the reader, table 1 charts the names and domestic statuses of the people who appear repeatedly in this study.

Some limitations of the data

In the recent interviews, the retrospective data sometimes reach back more than sixty years. Details were often murky, especially concerning the approximate year that something happened, such as the women's return to the Hawthorne plant in the years following their layoffs. As for the DHR, it was hardly a complete record of what the women said to each other in the Test Room. There were too many different record-keepers, and not enough consistency in what was held to be important enough to record. Moreover, the various observers must have missed much of the conversation. While some of the talk was loud and intended for everyone to hear it,

Table 1. *The relay assemblers*

MARY VOLANGO* – lived all her life with her sister JEANNE VOLANGO. Neither ever married.

GERALDINE SIRCHIO – lived with her brother JOE SIRCHIO* and her sister-in-law NANCY SIRCHIO* for thirty-six years. Geraldine never married; she was like another mother to Joe and Nancy's three children. JIM SIRCHIO* was another of her brothers.

THERESA LAYMAN – married John and had four daughters.

WANDA BEILFUS* – married Art, had two sons, and was widowed after nine years. One son married ARLENE*. After that son died, Wanda and Arlene lived together (twenty-two years at the time of the interview).

ANNA HAUG – married prior to the RATR. She was never drawn in to the intimacy of the other four.

Note:
* Interviewed by the author in 1993.

much of it was 'hardly audible' (see DHR, 1-27-1932; note that dates are given month-day-year), either because of the considerable machinery noise or because of the efforts of the women to protect their privacy.

Limitations notwithstanding, these data offer a unique research opportunity. Despite the many unrecorded conversations, we shall see that the DHR in its five-year totality is a virtual catalogue of the interests of young women at work, spotlighting many aspects of their current lives, as well as their hopes for the future. The later interviews add a longitudinal dimension, revealing the fit between their early aspirations and the ensuing realities.

The composition of the Test Room

The supporting personnel in the RATR included a layout operator, a succession of men who had supervisor/experimenter/observer duties, and a clerical assistant. For most of the study, the assemblers were the four women already named plus Anna Haug (for detail about the two assemblers who were soon replaced by Mary and Geraldine, and about temporary replacements later on, see Gillespie, 1991; Roethlisberger and Dickson, 1939). Of these five 'subjects', only Anna was married when the study began, and, at twenty-eight, she was eight years older than her next oldest co-worker. The others' continuing single status throughout the five-year study, as well as their closeness in age, must have figured prominently in their fast friendships. As with homogamy in mate selection, so with friendship: like is attracted to like, and age, sex, and marital status were surely important contextual factors that helped fuel the attraction (see Allan, 1989). In any case, since Anna contributed little to the recorded conversation in the RATR, the present analysis will focus on Mary, Geraldine, Theresa, Wanda, and those who were most central to their lives.

Life before the Test Room: the family backdrop

In many respects, life in the RATR must have seemed an extension of home life, and to see this is to appreciate the historical context that shaped these women's style of intimacy with one another through their life-course. All four women grew up in working-class families. They were daughters of immigrants – Geraldine's parents from Italy, the others from Poland. Three of the four had many siblings; Mary had just two, but Geraldine and Theresa each had six, and Wanda had eight. Privacy was not often found in this crowded family setting. Mary's situation – only five people living in an eight-room house – must have been unusual. More typical was Geraldine's family. Her brother Jim told me that their older sister married at sixteen, moved in with them, and had three or four children by the time the rest of the family moved elsewhere to separate housing. 'At one time', Jim recalls, 'there were twelve or thirteen of us living in six rooms.' At Wanda's and Theresa's houses, the situation must have been similar.

Horizons were limited largely to one's own neighbourhood, and to romantic fantasies stimulated by Hollywood. Television was still decades away. Few people had cars; Wanda said that her father was the first in their neighbourhood to have one, and this was not until he was in his fifties: 'All the kids would jump in the car in front of the house just to get a ride to the garage', and she laughed at the memory of her mother telling her father that he wasn't choking the car right to start it up. Neither Wanda herself nor her husband ever drove, and her daughter-in-law Arlene, whose own mother must have been in the same age cohort as Wanda, elaborated the quality of this neighbourhood rootedness: 'My mother had eight sisters, and they all lived two blocks from one another. And the kids we grew up with . . . just the gangways separated us, and we'd all go outside and we'd play together. You grew up differently. It wasn't so separated; you didn't have cars to jump in and run around and find different friends. You stayed right in your little area.' (For more on the impact of technological developments on friendship, see Adams, this volume.)

Like many working-class girls and boys in this era, as fourteen- or fifteen-year-olds these women were expected to go to work full-time and turn over their earnings to their large families, while their mothers stayed home and did reproductive work and care (see Tentler, 1979, p. 74; Cooper, 1987, p.

194; Lamphere, 1987). All of these women went to work – willingly, even eagerly, sacrificing their completion of high school, often seeking jobs with their friends. When Wanda was fifteen, three of her friends recently had exchanged school for work and, wanting to be with them, Wanda did likewise. They all got jobs making car cushions, but then 'one quit, so we all quit', she recalls.

Patriarchal standards delineated the division of responsibilities among siblings. A young, unmarried woman framed her interests in terms of the males in the family; she was not expected to have economic needs of her own, as she would soon be attached to a male and his more primary earnings. If anyone got to go straight through high school, it would typically be a son, not a daughter. Mary, who had dropped out of school, was working over forty hours per week when her brother was a high-school senior (the small size of this family was perhaps a factor in his staying in school). Theresa, who had four younger siblings, began full-time work at fourteen, and Geraldine also dropped out of school at age fourteen to help gear up for her three younger brothers' education. When Geraldine joined the Test Room, she already had worked full-time for over five years. When her mother died soon after that, Geraldine not only remained a major breadwinner for her family but also became principal household manager; and, when her father and brother were laid off just a few weeks later, she was now her family's *only* breadwinner – all this before she was twenty-one.

To summarise: life in these families taught girls to blend with, to fit themselves to the needs of those close to them, not to escape from them on behalf of separate needs. When your family needs your wages from the time you are fourteen, the chances for individual distinction become circumscribed accordingly. Moreover, these women never experienced the walls of privacy – both physical and psychological – that would have fostered their individuation (see Marks, 1994). Their self boundaries thus were fluid (Chodorow, 1978), their close relationships marked by a readiness to integrate themselves with others. We shall see that their woman-centred intimacy was oriented to celebrating group life far more than the separate existence of private individuals.

The Test Room period

The cultural context: science and industry as patriarchy

From the women's point of view, the little RATR must have seemed like instant relief from the impersonal discipline of the larger department –

closer, again, to family life at home. To them, the men whose interests created the RATR were anything but villains. Their comfort seemed to be a genuine concern, and they were treated as honoured employees. The women knew that they were enjoying a kind of industrial largesse that was most unusual. That said, the fact remains that this largesse was squarely within the male-defined context that framed most wage-earning women's experience around the time of the Great Depression. In the Hawthorne plant, it is always men who give women their jobs or take them away, cut back their hours, or lay them off altogether. Men arrange for these women to work in a separate, special little room where they are even consulted in advance about some experimental changes to which they are subjected. It is men who then reprimand them for too much talking, and decide later to permit them to talk. Put simply, men presume to give these women their voices, and to take their voices away.

It is men who decide, to quote Roethlisberger and Dickson (1939, p. 82), 'that in the general interest of the experiment the operators should submit to periodic physical examinations' – this at the hands of a male company doctor whose first examination was so daunting to at least one of the operators that she was dreading the next one. Men penetrate into all the details of the women's lives, probing for accounts of their eating habits, their bedtimes, their wake-up times, and their activities outside work. A man always serves as observer in the RATR, listens to as much of their conversation as he can, and records them for other men to scrutinise and interpret. And men manipulate the conditions under which the women work – give them rest periods, take them away, and give them back again; change their hours; and temporarily change their seating in the room, despite the fact that it disrupts the patterns of interaction to which the women had grown attached.

Some three years into the study, the researchers shift their focus from the RATR to their study of the men in the Bank Wiring Observation Room. They herald this new research venture as a pure observational study that will obviate the problem of the observed behaviour being an artefact of the process of experimentation. But note the sequence: when the research was seen as a classic field experiment that entailed a lot of manipulation of the experimental subjects, women rather than men are selected to be these subjects. And when the research strategy shifts to a more ethnographic mode in which every effort is made to *avoid* manipulative intrusions caused by the research process, men rather than women are selected. To be sure, no one advances the idea that it might feel easier to manipulate women rather than men, but this is the way it works out.

Life in the Test Room

The women do not go quietly into this more honoured control over their voices, their bodies, and their livelihoods. Through a combination of humour, secrecy, ironic commentary, protest, and conversation in Polish among those who speak it, they alternate between loudly celebrating their new privileges and protecting themselves from these newer forms of invasion. Several times on any given day, Theresa will loudly trill up and down the musical scale, as if to trumpet the gift of their voices, much to the uproarious delight of her co-workers. 'I must have my vocal lesson', she jokes; 'maybe I will sing in a concert some day' (DHR, 2-1-1932). The women frequently sing to each other. Typically, the choice of whom to ask for a song entails skipping across adjacent women, thus maintaining the flow and feeling of group connection between those prevented by the noise from conversing. (For other functions of singing, see DHR, 9-7-1928, and 8-1-1930; see also Tentler (1979).)

Aside from singing, the women talk and joke while they work. Seeing that no one will punish them, their lively exchanges often become clamorous. One day when the Department Chief comes into this room, filled, in the words of the observer, with 'hilarious and noisy conversation', he asks the observer, 'Doesn't that chatter get on your nerves sometimes? It does me. Sometimes it is so meaningless, and they say nothing' (DHR, 4-14-1932).

The Department Chief is mistaken. The 'chatter' is not meaningless, and the women are saying everything, not nothing, to each other. Their talk reflects an eagerness to stay in the process of relationship. If a vacation separates them, they are sure to talk about where they went, who they saw, and what they did as soon as they return. If one of them is involved with a man, they whisper and joke about it. They share their upcoming plans for dates over the weekend. They discuss religion, and politics, though the DHR notes very little detail. They talk at length about current movies, recalling scenes and retelling them. *Tarzan of the Apes*, starring Johnny Weissmuller, becomes the subject of some humorous, ongoing banter. Theresa initiates talk about dreams, when she remembers them. They talk about everything in their sensuous surround – about sitting in the sun and getting tanned, and about the moon from the night before, Theresa often taking the lead on this topic. 'You and your stars', Wanda jokes one day to Theresa, 'I hope you fall in a bucket of mud some day while you are looking up in the sky' (DHR, 1-26-1932). And one day they have a detailed chat about sleep: what time they go to bed, how long it takes each one to fall asleep, how many hours they sleep, what time they get up in the morning, whether they roll around in bed a lot – Geraldine says that her brothers roll around so much that they wake up with their covers tied up in knots.

Central topics of conversation

Much of the women's recorded conversation centres around the three social spheres that are most important to them: work, family of origin, and men and marriage. I shall explore their recurrent concerns about each one, looking especially for the groundwork they laid to keep themselves available to each other, in the face of the centrifugal forces that could easily have pulled them apart when the Test Room ended.

Shop talk

Talk about work and about the experiment covers a broad spectrum – their hours, the adequacy of their materials and parts, the burden of repairing already completed relays, the volume of their production and the amount of 'percentage' they are making on a given day, and, late in the experiment, the omnipresent threat of cutbacks and layoffs. I shall not elaborate here on these conversations, as this is the focus of most of the literature. (Interested readers should see Whitehead (1938) and Roethlisberger and Dickson (1939), and then use Gillespie's (1991) superb work to trace the ensuing literature.) Suffice it to add, here, that the women's habit (learned at home) of fitting themselves to the needs of those close to them was abetted by the group wage rate, which made each woman's pay dependent on the others' productivity as well as their own.

Family talk

The women's talk ranges far beyond work. They often talk about family members and their own responsibilities to them. When quitting time is changed from 5:00 to 4:30, Geraldine reacts in terms of her mother, who was then still living: 'It's too good to be true. When I get home now, I can help my mother with supper, and as long as we make as much money, it's fine' (DHR, 1-31-1928). And when the half-day of work on Saturdays is eliminated, her reaction is again familial, this time in terms of helping her married sister in the evening (DHR, 7-3-1928).

Towards her brothers, Geraldine maintains an adoring, protective, and sometimes boasting stance. She eagerly reports on everything from their love affairs, to their baseball allegiances (DHR, 5-24-1932), to their education and how she might fund college for them (DHR, 4-8-1930). When a brother tries his hand at boxing, she frets to her co-workers that 'his face is all battered up' (DHR, 7-3-1930). When a war erupts in Shanghai and the United States has sent warships to the area, she worries that her brothers could be drafted (DHR, 1-29-1932). And when her brothers were about to get laid off from the jobs they had at Western Electric, she implores her supervisors to intercede with management on her behalf, as her family needed their income. (Wanda does likewise for *her* brother (DHR, 5-15-1930). Both appeals were unsuccessful.)

The women constantly support each other's kin-keeping talk. Even their banter aligns them with family concerns. When Theresa jokes that she will ease Geraldine's boredom by buying her a trip to Europe, Mary quips that Geraldine would then ask for a trip for her brothers and father as well. The women seem to stay abreast of all important family matters. When Theresa's sister has an operation, the others ask about her repeatedly (e.g., DHR, 4-4-1930). Everyone keeps up with each other's family members' job status. Geraldine's brother had been out of work, and, when Mary asks if he had been 'getting up' to go job-hunting, Geraldine replies with the stark humour that had become the women's rhetorical stock-in-trade in the teeth of the Depression: 'Oh yeah, my brother is still a man of leisure. He works for the government; he walks the streets for them' (DHR, 7-28-1930). Nearly two years later, cutbacks and layoffs had become endemic, and the women's hours had been cut by more than half. Wanda offers a quick family status-check, again using sardonic humour: 'The whole family was home yesterday. We don't see enough of each other, so we stay home during the day' (DHR, 5-24-1932; Milkman (1979, p. 525) also notes that Depression family members saw more of each other 'whether they wished to or not').

The women's family interests eventually extended from work-place talk to visiting each others' homes. Mary told me of a monthly rotation: 'Our mothers would cook a meal, and we'd have a little party, like. My sister played the violin and I played the piano, and we'd sing the old songs. Sometimes there'd be bad weather, and we'd stay overnight. We even slept three in a bed; now you couldn't do that, because you'd be called something.'

As the women became familiar with each other's families, some of the siblings got pulled into their social activities, especially Mary's sister Jeanne, who became fully integrated into their tight little circle. These connections apparently spilled over into co-worker gift-giving. For example, both Mary and her sister Jeanne contributed to a gift of pyjamas for Theresa's birthday (DHR, 9-10-1931).

Thus began a pattern of bridging the people at work with the people at home, forming a tightly knit network of co-workers and their families. Inclusive intimacy is inherently expansive, and these women maintained a readiness to share their group energy with the other people close to any one of them. Later, those who married tried their best to manoeuvre between their husbands and these pre-existing co-worker network ties (see Bott, 1971). While still single, however, the women used much of their talk to strategise about their presumed futures as married women.

Marriage talk: options and contradictions

In the RATR, the women often talk as if marriage is their primary mission in life. They have countless exchanges about matters of physical appearance. They talk about their weight – what it is and what it should be. They strategise about hair styles, and about clothing they want to buy, and discuss how long a pair of stockings should last before they tear. They talk about food – again, almost in the spirit of strategy. Geraldine gives Wanda technical instruction about arching her eyebrows; she should tweeze the bottom hairs, not the top (DHR, 6-15-1932). All of this is clearly gendered talk and gender-*making* talk. Not once in the conversational record for the men in the Bank Wiring Observation Room do we find exchanges reflecting a concern with matters of grooming. Their own gender-making draws on more 'masculine' materials.

Throughout the study, marriage talk continues, often held up as a great escape from economic dependence on work: 'I wouldn't mind marrying someone with money', Geraldine says; 'I'm bored at coming down to work every morning. I'd like to be able to spend and spend and spend, whenever I felt like it' (DHR, 9-8-1930). And when Theresa says that she will marry 'for love' – the man she marries 'won't have diamond rings or money' – Wanda challenges her: 'Get a guy with money; don't be dumb' (DHR, 2-27-1930).

At times marriage becomes almost a group threat to the Western Electric establishment: 'Wait till the test is over and watch how quick we get married', Geraldine admonishes, no doubt mindful that returning to the larger department would mean losing some of the RATR privileges (DHR, 11-8-1928; for another instance, see 4-29-1930). And threat or no threat, talk about marriage remains a group ritual that the women often celebrate: 'Starting this year in September to next year in September', Geraldine declares, 'we will all be married' (DHR, 5-10-1930).

In their orientation to marriage, the women both mirror and reproduce the patriarchal cultural context, which has instructed them that their good standing as adult females depends upon their marital connection to men. By that standard, they use friendship to constitute themselves as 'good women'; they talk to each other about weddings and marriage even when they are not attached to particular men. On the other hand, in their shrewd assessment of their options, they come close to unmasking the subordination that the patriarchal context implies. Geraldine declares, 'I don't intend to get married until I'm thirty-five, and if I get [a job] in the office, I won't get married as soon' (DHR, 2-19-1930). Wanda similarly surveys her options, drawing on a blend of fantasy and reality: 'They ought to free the slaves', she says, referring to herself and the other RATR operators; 'I'd give ten votes to the president who would free them so they wouldn't have to work anymore' (DHR, 10-9-1928). But Wanda knows that neither this mythical president nor a husband will be the shining knight who liberates her from work: 'Well if I get married', she says a year and a half later, 'I won't leave this place' (DHR, 4-15-1930).

In most of the talk about marriage – both serious and bantering – there lurks an unspoken question: what good would marriage do me if I couldn't even stay home and be a homemaker? The question remains implicit, so the women cannot directly question the patriarchal framework itself. They question only whether they as individuals can wrest the presumed advantages from that structure, and their answer is equivocal. In a world of free options, they would choose what they have been taught is their best bet – to get married and stay home, at least as soon as they have children. But their world is not free. Their families of origin need their earnings, and, even freed of that need, a husband's income may not be enough in the Depression economy to free them from work. Besides, despite the drudgery of relay work, they take pride in their collective effort, and they enjoy coming to work. 'At work is the only place I have fun', Geraldine says; 'there are too many worries when you get home' (DHR, 2-19-1930). And Theresa remarks, 'If I didn't come down to work I wouldn't know what to do' (DHR, 2-17-1930). Then too, the money is good; they have that breadwinner's pride that is more often conceded to the province of males. 'Boy, that was the biggest pay I ever got', Geraldine exclaims, a few months after joining the Test Room. 'When I showed my sister my paycheck, she said, "And you want to get *married*?"' (DHR, 10-18-1928).

The biggest potential contradiction of marriage was the likely gulf between their own rich relationships with each other as single women, and the more limited intimacy available from the men in their immediate social surround. As evidenced by the men's conversations and antics in the Bank

Wiring Observation Room, it is not likely that many men were attuned enough to female worlds to engage much with women. Consider how finely intertwined these women's lives were, both at work and outside the work-place: they went to events sponsored by the Western Electric Girls' Activity Organization – for example, the Girls' Masquerade Party, and the hike to the Great Lakes Naval Training Station, after which they talked all week at work about their sailor acquaintances. They went roller skating, and to the movies together, and to the Aragon Ballroom – a favourite dance hall fea-turing big bands. They went to the rodeo at the Chicago Stadium. Some of them planned a trip to a rustic cabin for a vacation together. They visited each other at their homes, and held several sleep-overs. They went on double or triple dates together. Back at work, they created a variety of rituals to celebrate their lives together: a day-before-Thanksgiving lun-cheon together; an exchange of presents at Christmas time; a little party after their six-week physical examinations; a birthday ritual – everyone brought gifts of lingerie to the birthday person, whose responsibility was to reciprocate with a half-pound box of Fanny May chocolates. And after several years of all this intertwining went by, they devoted some of their talk to reminiscing about pieces of their group history.

Small wonder that the women kept close watch on their own relation-ships – sometimes jealously. They had certain standards about staying in touch outside work, enforced through joking forms of moral suasion. Wanda chides Mary for being 'the only one who never calls up [on the phone]', and when Mary protests ('What would I talk about?'), the other women keep on ribbing her (DHR, 1-29-1932). When Theresa misses one of the women's hikes, she too is teased enough to spark a defensive retort: 'I can't help it if my aunt had a baby, can I? It wasn't *my* fault!' The other women laugh (DHR, 6-28-1932), thus honouring her excuse, but the point about group responsibilities has been made. One final example: when Geraldine joins a neighbourhood sorority, her Test Room friends react strongly, through teasing. Wanda and Mary threaten to show up uninvited at a sorority party, and learning that 'Epsilon' is part of the sorority's name, they begin to call it 'The Epsom Salts' (DHR, 4-19-1932; 4-29-1932). One is reminded here of the threat to cohesive groups of 'dyadic withdrawal' (Slater, 1963), only here the danger is withdrawal into a sorority instead of a dyad. One is also reminded of Rich's (1980) 'lesbian continuum', which includes forms of female bonding and intimacy that are not necessarily sexual. Perhaps none of these women would have entertained the thought of lesbian experience, though we cannot be certain. The fact remains, in any case, that what they got from (and gave to) one another by this point in their lives was enormous; what they might get from turning their attentions to men was, aside from the likelihood of children, untested and uncertain.

The middle years: life after the Test Room

Of course, at this point the women's solidarity as friends had never been tested either. There is no evidence that Geraldine's sorority ever offered much competition to her bonds with the Test Room women, nor had relationships with men interfered with the women's almost daily involvement with each other. The disbanding of the RATR was the first real test, as the work-place had been their most regular point of contact. Here I describe the final weeks and days, and piece together what information we have about the aftermath. Then I shall explore the impact of the second great test of the women's bonds – the marriages of two of the women.

The ending of the Test Room

By 1932, layoffs had become more pervasive, and even the RATR was vulnerable. In April, the women face a two-week layoff, and Geraldine becomes pensive. She leans her head on Wanda's shoulder. 'This is our last day together for a long time', she laments. Wanda chimes in, 'And we'll hold hands, Darling, all day', attempting, through her parody of two parting lovers, to lighten the gravity of Geraldine's mood. But Geraldine will not be swayed. 'You know', she says, 'I'm really going to miss you dames' (DHR, 4-29-1932).

Two months later, the RATR closes down for good, a casualty of the Depression's unyielding spirit of contraction. The women are not all laid off on the same day; those with more financial need are kept a few days longer than the others. The order of departure is Mary and Theresa first, then Wanda and Geraldine. The last few weeks are tense and fretful. The women expect the layoffs, because they are happening all over the plant, but the staff choose not to reveal the specific timing. Even without the information, the women discuss the inevitable – what they are going to do once they are laid off. They talk about 'relief' funds and the investigations they might have to undergo as a condition of getting any aid; they will hide their jewellery and whatever else might hinder their chances. They wax indignant about Mayor Cermak's $12,000 salary and the fact that he is 'worth six million bucks'. 'This is going to be like Russia', Geraldine declares. 'You can stand [it] just so long. Then you are going to have a revolution' (DHR, 6-20-1932).

In the final two weeks, every time the foreman comes into the room, the women stiffen with apprehension. The procedure is for the Section Chief to send the woman who will be laid off to the foreman, outside the room. He then tells her the news. On 29 June, Mary is sent out in this fashion. The observer notes that Theresa and Wanda appear frightened, and Geraldine is forcing a cynical smile. A few minutes pass, and Mary returns. In a strained voice she says, 'They got me, pal.' Moments later, it is Theresa's turn. By now, Geraldine is 'unable to restrain her emotions any longer', and she 'rushes out of the Test Room and returns a couple of minutes later', with puffed eyes and some fresh make-up. Mary resumes work, making a 'supreme effort' to keep from breaking down. When Theresa returns she sits down silently. Before long the rest period arrives, and the women can barely drag themselves out of their chairs. When they return, Mary and Theresa look dazed, and Geraldine has been crying again. Mary and Geraldine have an exchange about their financial situations, and soon Mary's feelings overrun her, and she rushes out of the room. Somehow, they all compose themselves, and Geraldine expresses the feelings she had had when Mary and Theresa were called out to be told of their layoffs: 'I felt like I lost my best pal when you went out', she says to Mary or Theresa or both of them.

After the layoffs

Memories were vague about how long the women remained unemployed. At different times, they all returned to Western Electric and once more became co-workers. Mary returned around 1937 and remained there for nearly forty years. Geraldine came back around the same time, but retired in 1955. In the meantime, by 1936 both Wanda and Theresa had married. At first Wanda worked very little, but when her husband died in 1945 and her sons were just three and five, she too returned to 'Western', depending on her mother and a sister-in-law for child care, and she worked there for another thirty years. Theresa did what she had yearned to do: she stayed home with her daughters, until in 1953 she returned to Western and worked there for another twenty-three years.

Following the Depression, assembling relays became more automated, and the four women became 'instructors'. 'You had five girls under you on the conveyor', Wanda told me; 'you'd fill their little baskets with parts. It was more interesting, and we made more money. You kind of inspected them on the end, and repaired bad parts.' The changes in work status radically altered the women's work-place contacts with one another. For a number of years, Mary was downstairs in a different department from the others. 'We'd still bump into her', Wanda said. 'And sometimes we'd go down to see one another, or she'd come up.' Though Mary later came up to work in the others' department, it is doubtful that the women ever again created at work the social intensity of the RATR. They were no longer enclosed together in a small room with only a few others, nor were they co-ordinating their work together, or depending upon one another to keep up a group wage rate, and their attention was focused on the women working under them. By now, however, these older friendships were so well estab-lished, and so well implemented away from work that they no longer required much fine-tuning while on the job.

Still, the women did see one another every day at work, and that was probably important to them, as evidenced by Mary's decision to stay in the factory instead of moving to the office job she had trained for by finishing high school and going to business college at night. When Western Electric finally called her for the office job, she turned it down. She told me, 'I was used to the girls already at work.'

Even before the women returned to Western Electric after the layoffs, the pattern of outside contact persisted. 'We had jobs in different places', Wanda recalls, 'but Geraldine and I used to go dancing every weekend at the Aragon Ballroom, and Mary would come with us sometimes. And even after work I'd go on the streetcar to visit Geraldine and spend a few hours there.' The rotating home visits also continued, Wanda added.

Changes in domestic status

Theresa and Wanda both married around 1936. Neither Geraldine nor Mary ever married. After the Test Room days, Mary continued living with her mother and father and with her sister Jeanne, who also never married. When their parents died, Mary and Jeanne remained together. Eventually, they bought their own home, where they still lived together in 1993. 'The two sisters were inseparable', Nancy Sirchio told me, a view corroborated by everyone else I talked to. Indeed, Mary and Jeanne were treated by every-one as a couple. When respondents recounted gatherings that the women had, Mary's name was rarely mentioned alone; it was always 'Mary-and-Jeanne'. This had been true even in the days of the Test Room; Jeanne was included in whatever the women did away from work.

Geraldine's situation was more complex. We know she was involved at different times with at least two different men. With one of them – Dominic – she had an on-again, off-again relationship for seven or eight years, starting from the Test Room days. Back then, she felt responsible for her younger brothers, while Dominic felt responsible for his mother. In Jim Sirchio's terse words, 'Dominic wasn't going to leave his mother, and [Geraldine] wasn't going to leave us. It was an impossible situation.' Still, after Geraldine's brothers married, she did *not* follow the path of marriage. She invited Nancy and Joe to live with her, and, when they eventually bought a new home, she and her father came along. There she remained for most of her adult life.

For the present exploration, this mix of domestic statuses is fortuitous. With two women who became wives and mothers, and two who never married, we have a strategic opportunity to trace the impact of these differences on the women's continuing bonds.

The impact of men and marriage

Seen from a short- to intermediate-term view, the marriages of Wanda and Theresa were disruptive of the group patterns, which, paradoxically, often had been oriented to finding eligible men. Mary told me that, after Wanda met her fiancé, it was only Geraldine and herself (Mary) who still went to the Aragon Ballroom; and, by then, Theresa too was involved with her husband-to-be; after both women married, Mary did not see either Theresa or Wanda as often, although they still all maintained their tradition of monthly dinners together. Similarly, Wanda said that, before her husband died after just nine years, she did not see the others as much as before. 'When you love the man, you just *want* him', she told me, 'you want to *be* with him always . . . It was harder [to get together with the women]; I guess you just hated to be away. It was different.'

As for Theresa, Nancy Sirchio thinks that she 'pulled away' from the group following her marriage. She noted that Theresa's husband John 'was very jealous of her', and both Nancy and Wanda independently recalled an episode in which all the women went to Nancy's for dinner, and John arrived and demanded that Theresa leave, which she did.

Seen from a longer-term perspective, however, the earlier pattern of work, leisure, and friendship among single women was simply no longer tenable once two of the women had their families, and it must have taken time to work out a new vehicle for the close group bonds. In the meantime, even if Theresa did pull away from the single women, she kept up a solid tie with Wanda, the other mother in the group. The two women bonded around their children, and Wanda recalls a period of reciprocal visits, children always in tow. Theresa's daughters welcomed the birthday cakes and holiday cookies that Wanda would bake for them, and they called her 'Aunt Wanda'. Though Wanda remembers no couple-to-couple occasions, these two families must have stayed closely connected through the women. When Theresa died in 1984, it was Wanda to whom Theresa's husband John went to see photographs and to reminisce about Theresa. And even recently, Theresa's four daughters – long since grown-up and married – came to pay Wanda a visit and share news about their current lives, shortly before the 1992 Christmas holidays.

Inclusive intimacy as family-centredness

Theresa's tie with Wanda, rooted as it was in their shared status as mothers, was not the 'inclusive' intimacy we are exploring here. It was a more bounded relationship, less group-oriented; it did not tend to expand to pull others in. And it did not seem to include Geraldine, who had always been the presumptive leader and the sparkplug for the other women. After 1936, the centre of gravity for inclusive intimacy seemed to follow Geraldine into Nancy and Joe's house, abetted by Nancy's celebrated Italian dinners and her welcoming personal style. For nearly twenty years following the Depression, Geraldine continued to work, while Nancy had three children and remained a homemaker. Geraldine paid rent to Nancy and Joe, and she also provided child care. She '*adored* the children', Nancy told me emphatically: 'To my kids, she was like a second mother', buying them clothes and such, and remaining involved in their schoolwork, even typing their college papers for them later on. Geraldine made full use of her 'other mother' status, often boasting about Nancy and Joe's children to the other women. Wanda's sons called Geraldine 'Aunt Gerry' and Nancy 'Aunt Nancy', just as Nancy and Joe's children called Wanda 'Aunt Wanda'. In turn, Geraldine was a regular visitor to Wanda's house. The two sets of children were all around the same ages. 'They knew each other from the time they were *born*', Nancy emphasised, and she told me of countless gatherings for picnics, 'little birthday parties', communions, confirmations, and, much later, weddings.

Unlike Geraldine, Mary and Jeanne did not have the opportunity to mother. Still, they remained part of the child-oriented facets of the other women's lives. At the constant stream of dinners and child-centred events, they were an ever-reliable presence. Wanda said that any time Mary returned from a vacation, she would come to Wanda's house bearing gifts for Wanda's sons. And Mary herself recalls arriving home after a trip to the Greek islands, and immediately rushing off to the festivities for the wedding of Geraldine's nephew (Nancy and Joe's son). Theresa, too, would appear at these more ceremonial occasions.

Bridging the differences

More than anything else, it was the dinners and ceremonial occasions together that ritualised the feeling of energy and group connection that had arisen back in the Test Room days, and bridged the marrieds with the singles, the mothers with those who remained childless, and the workers with the ones who were not working for pay. Some of the dinners were at Wanda's house, and Nancy recalls a number of occasions at Mary and Jeanne's, but most of them were hosted by Nancy. Sometimes the women would invite one or two other women who worked with them at Western, and, as Nancy began to describe the feeling of these gatherings, her words became more measured and her tone radiated a sense of almost reverential nostalgia: 'We had a lot of good times, a lot of good, happy times. A lot of laughs. We sometimes would be laughing the whole evening' – and she then broke into warm laughter, remembering these occasions.

The gatherings were woman-centred, fuelled by the energy of a core group of women, but they were expansive enough to include anyone close to them – husbands, children, and, later, children's spouses. Arlene, who married Wanda's son, recalls being brought over to 'pass inspection' at the hands of 'the ladies' and, after their marriage, Arlene remembers being routinely included in these female-centred gatherings.

Geraldine, Mary, and Jeanne: forging new womanhood

Apart from all this family-centred activity, Mary, Jeanne, and Geraldine took advantage of some leisure opportunities as single women. Nancy recalls that the three women often went out together. 'Every Saturday they would meet and go either to the theatre or see some play, and then go out and have dinner . . . And then every once in a while I would say to [Geraldine]: 'After you girls get out of the theatre or the movie, come on over and have something here.'

There were also annual vacations taken by Mary and Geraldine (Jeanne stayed home, not wanting to travel in the heat of July). Geraldine feared flying, so they went by bus or train – for example, a train trip to a dude ranch in Colorado, a bus trip to Mexico, and a bus trip to New England. On these group charters, organised by Western Electric, Mary and Geraldine were roommates and 'travel partners', in Mary's words. Other travel – plane trips to Germany, France, and England – Mary took without Geraldine.

In 1971, a stroke left Geraldine physically immobilised, and she lived her last twenty years in nursing homes. For some fifteen of those years, her mind remained alert and active, and the homes became a new gathering place for the women. In all these years, Mary was the most frequent visitor, aside from Nancy and Joe. 'I went several times a week to see her', Mary told me. 'I would take the bus from work. I just felt it would be good for her to see me. And Jeanne would come too; she'd take the "El" [Chicago's elevated railway] from work downtown . . . Toward the end [Geraldine] didn't talk at all . . . She was just lying there, not knowing time, [and then] I thought it would be okay to go only every other week' (Wanda also visited Geraldine prior to her final decline).

Implications: inclusive intimacy and woman-centredness

The women we have been following were woman-centred, beginning with the days in the RATR. At the same time, they were male-defined; they were constrained to make their way as best they could within the overall system of opportunities available to them in a man's world. The RATR could only be a microcosm of the larger social surround, within which a woman *might* gain an advantage, as these women did, if there were men around who had reason to bestow it on them. They encountered few women with the power to define jobs and environments; there was little to inspire them to reach beyond the kind of wage-labour they were doing. Hawthorne was not a unionised plant, so there was no political vehicle for mobilising their attention beyond their own immediate environment. And there was no strong women's movement to draw them to a radically alternate definition of womanhood, independent of the interests of men. Given these conditions, the women were none the less shrewd about assessing their options.

One of those options was marriage. Women were supposed to marry – i.e., it was not a real option. Neither Nancy nor Wanda saw Dominic as a good match for Geraldine, yet both had the couple over for dinner on numerous occasions. And following their final breakup, when Geraldine fell headlong in love with someone they perceived as even less desirable, again both Nancy and Wanda recall having the couple to dinner. Greatly relieved when this relationship soon ended, they had done what they could to integrate it into their lives together. If the road to full womanhood is paved with marriage, one's duty as a close friend is to help the vehicle along.

When Geraldine, Mary, and Jeanne did not marry, all the women had to revise their understanding of authentic womanhood. This was probably easy enough to do. Those who remained single needed only to expand their boundaries to include their married friends' husbands and children. Involvement in children's lives then helped to keep them women in good standing, even if they did not themselves marry. By expansion and inclusion, then, the Hawthorne women bridged differences that emerged among them. Through real or fictive kinship, single women became 'aunts' and had children to fuss over. Through domestic partnership, two sisters got included as a couple in ritual gatherings and festive celebrations among married women. Through welcoming children and husbands into many such gatherings, the women harmonised potentially competing interests, without compromising the unique energy they generated among each other. And, through working together, all the women elaborated a common work culture. Even Nancy, the only one who remained a homemaker, got to participate vicariously in that work culture. She told me of Western Electric retirement parties: 'A group of girls – maybe fifteen, twenty – would go out to dinner in a restaurant, and I was always included; my sister-in-law [Geraldine] would always want me to come along. So I . . . knew a lot of girls that worked with my sister-in-law. And we had a lot of good times.' Here is a reversal of the pattern of bringing close co-workers home, as Nancy, a close family member, is pulled in the opposite direction – from her home into some of the social spinoffs of the other women's work life.

To understand this inclusive intimacy is to resist projecting more exclusive styles on to these particular relationships. In my recent interviews, as I set about plumbing the depths of what these women shared, there were cues that ultimately served notice of a different kind of closeness. There was Wanda's reply to my query about topics the women did not talk about: 'Well, we never discussed sex or anything like that' – and on further probing she was clear that not even Geraldine (who was anything but reticent) would have broached that topic. There was also Wanda's response to my query about some 1932 DHR entries, in which Mary is being teased by the other women about her presumed crush on Davisson – the last of the Test Room observers: 'With Mary', Wanda noted, 'you would never know. She was so quiet, she wouldn't tell you.' What kind of intimacy was this, if a close friend would not even disclose her crush on someone?

And then there were all those vacation trips taken by Mary and Geraldine. Unlikely travel companions with their opposite personalities, they nevertheless spent long days together on buses and trains, and nights in motel rooms. Did their intimacy intensify through these trips? I told Mary, 'I've found that when you travel with a friend, you get closer to that person.' She replied, 'Oh yes, you reminisce about what you saw and things like that', and then she recounted the New England bus trip and an all-you-can-eat crab fest in Maine: 'I was eating them like mad, and Geraldine didn't care for too many.' The trip here seems to be only the external one, and further probing revealed no more than that.

There is little sense of any joint exploration of *internal* processes, as that was not these women's pattern of connection. Wanda could tell me, an inquiring stranger, that as a youngster she 'felt the [city kids] were smarter than we were [in Cicero]' and that she 'always felt kind of backward', but it is unlikely that this kind of reflective disclosure of feelings found much expression in her friendships. Closeness with dearest friends was best expressed through laughing and singing and exchanging stories in large, expansive, family-like gatherings, not through little, self-disclosing dyads. The Hawthorne women did support one another devotedly, much like the nineteenth-century women made familiar to us by Smith-Rosenberg (1975), but the latter women came from smaller, highly educated, middle-class families. They usually attended boarding schools, where they often formed lifelong dyadic bonds with other young women – bonds that were emotionally intense, sensual and physical, and self-disclosing, especially once their marriages created physical gaps that were bridgeable only through letters and occasional visits. In contrast, the Hawthorne women were more inclusive, more continuous with the expansive social patterns of the antebellum New England working women described by Hansen (1994).

The Hawthorne women had neither the physical nor the emotional space to carve out a private sense of self – an individual, *enclosed* self – which would then require not simply acts of self-*dis*closure but also acts of self-*ex*posure to feel known (see Marks, 1994; see also Erickson, 1976, for a similar analysis within a different context). They grew up sharing rooms with siblings and attending to the needs of the entire family group, and in the Test Room they again found themselves in a little environment, sharing their days with sibling-like co-workers and attending to the needs of *that* entire group. It was like a double exposure, the work-place side of the image faithfully replicating the home-place side, and so they did the natural thing: they simply pulled the images together into sharp focus, bringing one another to their families on such a regular basis that the very boundaries of these families had to stretch themselves to become more inclusive. It was only a matter of time, then, before the language of fictive kinship would put the finishing linguistic touches on what was already a *fait accompli*.

In the beginning, these women could resist any sharp differentiation of their factory world from their home world because life in the little RATR reduced the gap, unlike their experience in the larger department. Segregated though the two worlds were, they connected them through an elaborate system of bridges. And when they later became shop-floor 'instructors', each with five or so women working under them, and they no longer sat side by side, chatting and singing to each other all day long, nothing needed to change. They still knew that their long-time companions were working nearby, and they still saw them nearly every day. And by then they knew they had ample opportunity to see these family-like people away from the work-place, through all the occasions of inclusive intimacy they created to keep themselves together.

Whom do the Hawthorne women represent? Of which women were they typical? We stand here on shaky ground, and generalisations are risky. The woman-centredness we have explored was fragile. By her own testimony, Wanda's nine-year marriage disrupted some of her involvement with the other women. Had her husband lived longer, his own needs or simply the exclusive intimacy of marriage may have overridden her woman-centredness, just as there is evidence that Theresa's husband John may have interfered with Theresa's continuing involvement with the other women. If all the women had married, the potential barriers to sustaining these bonds would have multiplied, either through husband interference or through network alliances reorienting around some of the husbands' kin. In the latter case, woman-centred inclusive intimacy still may have thrived, but no longer with a group of unrelated co-workers at its nucleus.

Today, bonds among co-workers are most likely to take the form of dyadic, shorter-lived exclusive intimacy, rather than to replicate the Hawthorne women's lifelong group 'convoy' of social support (Kahn, 1979). Small families and households, frequent job mobility, and an ideology and practice of privacy are all conditions that promote exclusive intimacy among those who 'discover' each other in the specialised settings that compose their daily life. Of course, these same conditions may foster a tendency to remain self-contained, if not self-absorbed, and to avoid intimacy with the people one encounters within any of these settings. Exclusive intimacies and seemingly impenetrable self-boundaries are both products of the same social forces, so it should come as no surprise to find the same person alternating between these different modalities.

As for inclusive intimacy, it will probably survive as a social form, both in mainstream industrial urban life and in pockets of the rural United States. Wherever social networks remain dense and 'tightly-knit' (Bott, 1971), and the forces of privatisation are resisted through ideologically driven choice (see Zablocki, 1971), through a lack of opportunity for individual social mobility, or through the sharing of some important ethnic, religious, linguistic, and/or other minority status, inclusive intimacy may emerge. Even the Hawthorne women's variant of this form may survive, in so far as groups of co-workers remain for many years at the same work-place, provide each other with some of their most cherished social support, and integrate one another into their family and kin networks. Perhaps contemporary workers who choose to remain single, as Geraldine and Mary did, are among the most likely to forge friendships among other single co-workers and to integrate these friends with kin. In the 1986 General Social Survey (GSS), I found that 5.4 per cent of full-time workers had close friendships *only* with co-workers, and in the 1985 survey, 6.6 per cent of full-time workers have only co-workers as the people with whom they 'discuss important matters' (see Marks, 1994). Although we cannot know from the GSS what kind of intimacy these co-worker-centred workers are forging with their friends, my hunch, again, is that, if they see themselves as separate and private individuals, they will have 'exclusive' friendships, and, if they see themselves as continuous with some group or category, their friendships will tend to be more 'inclusive'.

Acknowledgements
For help and support at various stages of this project, I wish to thank Rebecca Adams, Graham Allan, Katherine Allen, Michael Johnson, Ralph LaRossa, Kyriacos Markides, Joan Marks, and Alexis Walker.

References
Allan, Graham (1989), *Friendship: Developing a Sociological Perspective*, Boulder: Westview Press.

Bolton, Alfred A. (1994), 'Relay assembly testroom participants remember: Hawthorne a half century later', *International Journal of Public Administration*, 17: 255–457.

Bott, Elizabeth (1971), *Family and Social Network* (2nd edn), New York: Free Press.

Bramel, Dana, and Friend, Ronald (1981), 'Hawthorne, the myth of the docile worker, and class bias in psychology', *American Psychologist*, 36: 867–78.

Chodorow, Nancy (1978), *The Reproduction of Mothering*, Berkeley: University of California Press.

Cooper, Patricia A. (1987), *Once a Cigar Maker: Men, Women, and Work Culture in American Cigar Factories, 1900–1919*, Urbana: University of Illinois Press.

'Daily History Record' (1927–32), *Hawthorne Studies Collection* – Microfiche Set, Baker Library, Harvard University, Graduate School of Business Administration, Boston.

Erikson, Kai T. (1976), *Everything in Its Path*, New York: Simon and Schuster.

Feld, Scott (1981), 'The focused organization of social ties', *American Journal of Sociology*, 86: 1015–35.

Giddens, Anthony (1991), *Modernity and Self-Identity: Self and Society in the Late Modern Age*, Stanford University Press.

  (1992), *The Transformation of Intimacy: Sexuality, Love, and Eroticism in Modern Societies*, Stanford University Press.

Gillespie, Richard (1991), *Manufacturing Knowledge: A History of the Hawthorne Experiments*, Cambridge University Press.

Greenwood, Ronald G., Bolton, Alfred A., and Greenwood, Regina A. (1983), 'Hawthorne a half century later: relay assembly participants remember', *Journal of Management*, 9: 21–229.

Hansen, Karen (1994), *A Very Social Time: Crafting Community in Antebellum New England*, Berkeley: University of California Press.

Hessing, Melody (1991), 'Talking shop(ping): office conversations and women's dual labour', *Canadian Journal of Sociology*, 16: 23–50.

Homans, George (1950), *The Human Group*, New York: Harcourt, Brace, and World.

Jones, Stephen R. G. (1992), 'Was there a Hawthorne Effect?', *American Journal of Sociology*, 98: 451–68.

Kahn, Robert L. (1979), 'Aging and social support', in Martha White Riley (ed.), *Aging from Birth to Death: Interdisciplinary Perspectives*, Boulder: Westview Press.

Lamphere, Louise (1987), *From Working Daughters to Working Mothers: Immigrant Women in a New England Industrial Community*, Ithaca: Cornell University Press.

Marks, Stephen R. (1994), 'Intimacy in the public realm: the case of coworkers', *Social Forces*, 72: 843–58.

Milkman, Ruth (1979), 'Women's work and the economic crisis', in Nancy F. Cott and Elizabeth H. Pleck (eds.), *A Heritage of Her Own: Toward a New Social History of American Women*, New York: Simon and Schuster, Touchstone.

Rich, Adrienne (1980), 'Compulsory heterosexuality and lesbian existence', *Signs*, 5: 631–60.

Roethlisberger, Fritz, and Dickson, William J. (1939). *Management and the Worker*, Cambridge, Mass.: Harvard University Press.

Slater, Phillip (1963), 'On social regression', *American Sociological Review*, 28: 339–64.

Small, Stephen A., and Riley, Dave (1990), 'Toward a multi-dimensional assessment of work spillover into family life', *Journal of Marriage and the Family*, 52: 51–61.

Smith-Rosenberg, Carroll (1975), 'The female world of love and ritual: relations between women in nineteenth-century America', *Signs*, 1: 1–29.

Tentler, Leslie W. (1979), *Wage-Earning Women: Industrial Work and Family Life in the United States, 1900–1930*, New York: Oxford University Press.

Wellman, Barry (1994), 'I was a teenage network analyst: the route from the Bronx to the information highway', *Connections*, 17: 28–45.

Westwood, Sallie (1985), *All Day, Every Day: Factory and Family in the Making of Women's Lives*, Urbana: University of Illinois Press.

Whitehead, Theodore N. (1938), *The Industrial Worker*, Cambridge, Mass.: Harvard University Press.

Zablocki, Benjamin (1971), *The Joyful Community*, Baltimore: Penguin Books.

Zavella, Patricia (1987), *Women's Work and Chicano Families: Cannery Workers of the Santa Clara Valley*, Ithaca: Cornell University Press.

4

Friendship and the private sphere

Graham Allan

Introduction

One of the central arguments of this book is that friendship is a social relationship, and not just a personal one. Of course, it *is* a personal one, and
one over which people can exercise a good deal of agency. However, it is
also a relationship which is socially patterned – shaped and constrained by
factors over which the individuals involved have only limited control
(Duck, 1993). In particular, the forms which friendships take vary historically with changes in the dominant characteristics of the social and economic formation in which they occur. Expressed differently, the nature of
the obligations and solidarities which arise between friends – and indeed
who is recognised as a friend and what this represents – is influenced by the
web of other commitments and obligations which an individual has. And
these other commitments and obligations are themselves rooted in the economic and social 'realities' which confront the individual. Exactly how
these impact on each individual will depend on their specific location
within the social and economic structure. Class, ethnicity, gender, kinship,
caste, age, and whatever other social divisions are most pertinent to that
society at that period will impact on the 'freedoms' there are to develop
forms of informal relationship and shape the consequent solidarities that
emerge.

As discussed in the introductory chapter, this type of argument has long
been accepted in the field of family studies. Just as sociology itself was
founded on a desire to understand the causes and consequences of the
fundamental transformations which industrialisation and urbanisation sig-
nalled in the nineteenth and early twentieth centuries in Europe and the
United States, so too much family sociology has focused on the ways in
which these and other structural transformations impinge on the character
of domestic life. From quite different theoretical perspectives, numerous

studies have shown how the demographic, economic, and social organisation of households has altered in response to external events (Parsons,
1949; Goode, 1963; Laslett with Wall, 1972; Young and Willmott, 1973;
Harris, 1983). The central tenet of these different approaches has been that
the family – whatever that comprises – does not remain unchanged while
the social and economic environment in which it is embedded evolves into
new forms. As employment, housing, leisure, health, and education practices alter, so relationships within the household respond, generating modified patterns of solidarity and commitment.

The same kinds of arguments apply to friendship (and other types of
informal relationship). The character of the solidarities they entail and the
form of exchanges they involve are influenced by wider social and economic considerations. As these change, so the routine organisation of
friendship also alters. Oliker's and Marks's chapters in this volume attest to
this, as does Silver's (1990) examination of changes in friendship with the
development of commercial society. Silver showed how, far from having
historical precedence, friendships based on principles of non-instrumental
solidarity arose as a direct result of the transformation in social relations
which a market economy fostered. But, as with 'family', variation in the
organisation of friendship does not arise only as a result of such major
social and economic transformations as these. Changes in friendship patterns develop across the life-course as people's responsibilities, commitments, and opportunities alter (Feld and Carter, this volume). But more
importantly here, friendship patterns also change as the social and economic conditions of life are gradually modified. Sometimes in later eras
these modifications are recognised as elements within major transformations – industrialisation, commercialisation, or urbanisation, for example
– but at other times they are not.

Importantly, these processes whereby patterns of friendship are matched
to the wider context of people's experience – their economic and social
environments – operate continuously. In this sense, patterns of friendship
are emergent. They depend upon the normative conventions which attach
to friendship, but they are also influenced by the personal circumstances in
which individuals construct their friendship relations. (These constructions
in turn act collectively upon normative convention, thereby generating historical shifts in the dominant modes of friendship.) As the social and economic environments under which people live out their lives alter, so their
friendship patterns will reflect the new circumstances. Thus, for instance,
shifts in the organisation of domestic life, in work and employment, in
gender relations, or in community involvement are all likely to impact at

some level on the character of the friendship ties and networks which individuals sustain. Here agency and structure are conjoined with personal and historical transformation. Individuals make decisions about their friendships in the context of their structural location, while the characteristics of this structural location alter over time as they age and as material conditions evolve, usually gradually, though on occasion more radically.

This chapter will be concerned with exploring how one particular aspect of material and social change has influenced the organisation of men's friendship. Drawing on British experience, it will examine how the development of different conditions of domestic life has modified the ways in which friendship solidarity is expressed. In particular, taking class as a key determinant of experience, it will assess how working-class male friendship patterns are influenced by the character of the home, and how shifts in this, together with concomitant changes in domestic and community relationships, can shape the boundaries which are constructed around these ties. In this, the chapter will focus on aspects of 'privatisation' as a dominant trend in domestic and community relationships in the second half of the twentieth century. While this concept has received much critical evaluation, not least in Britain (e.g., see Pahl and Wallace, 1988; Proctor, 1990; Allan and Crow, 1991), it none the less provides a useful framework for exploring the impact that changes in housing, social mobility, marriage, and locality have upon dominant forms of male sociability. To do this, the chapter will start by examining in general terms how friendship has been shaped by class position in the recent past.

Friendship and class: the traditional picture

Class has long been seen as a crucial variable in understanding patterns of sociability. In particular, the traditional argument, in Britain and elsewhere, has been that kin played a more significant role in working-class life than they did amongst the middle class, for whom friendship with non-kin appeared more important. Typically, working-class families relied more at a day-to-day level on the support of primary kin living nearby, and were often able to name relatively few others as friends. In contrast, middle-class individuals and families led lives which, at least in terms of face-to-face interaction and routine support, relied little on kinship (Allan, 1996). Friendship seemed to play the larger role in their lives. It was their friends in whom they confided more, and their friends to whom they turned for assistance in resolving the everyday contingencies they faced. By the late 1970s numerous studies of kinship, community, and work-place had provided support for this orthodoxy. (See Allan, 1979, for a summary of many of the more important British studies.)

Of course, such claims as were made were generally more qualified than this bald summary allows. Moreover, later research built on earlier, less subtle work. Thus, for example, Bell (1968, 1990) and Firth, *et al.* (1970), argued that kinship was more significant for middle-class families than had been previously indicated. Contact may not have been as frequent as it was in 'traditional' working-class areas, but the advantages of a middle-class lifestyle were protected through the transfer of wealth across the generations in middle-class families. Thus, socially, primary kin remained of consequence even if the pattern of solidarity was distinct from that found among working-class families. In addition, though, the typicality of some of the working-class locations which had been studied began to be questioned (see Crow and Allan, 1994). In particular, their declining local economies, the material inadequacy of their housing stock, and the lack of significant inward migration (at least at the time of the studies), combined with the outward migration of young families to new public housing estates, led to patterns of social incorporation of the remaining residents which were not fully mirrored in other working-class locations.

Rather less was written in these studies about friendship than family, neighbouring and kin ties. The picture that prevailed, however, suggested that in some measure working-class individuals lacked the necessary social skills to develop friendships in the manner in which the middle class did. Whereas friendship offered an important route for social integration amongst the middle class who were apparently used to forming new ties of solidarity with those others they met, as a form of relationship it appeared quite 'foreign' to working-class practice. Yet such a finding sat uneasily with other images of working-class solidarity. In particular, occupational studies frequently celebrated the solidarity which those engaged in manual labour exhibited in seeking to protect their material interests. Similarly, community solidarity was generally perceived to be a more compelling phenomenon in working-class localities than in middle-class ones. Why, then, did the working class lack the necessary cultural experience, ability, or commitment to form ties of friendship and informal solidarity with non-kin in the way the middle class did?

In examining these issues, I have argued elsewhere (Allan, 1977, 1979) that in reality it was not an absence of social skills as such which discriminated between middle-class and working-class sociability. I maintained, instead, that different patterns existed in the ways in which non-kin sociable ties were organised. The dominant middle-class pattern of developing sociable relationships involved an extension or broadening of the contexts in which interaction occurred. That is, when individuals met others with whom they felt a sufficient degree of compatibility, they tended to foster the relationship by involving themselves with that person in settings other than that in which they first met. Thus, for example, people met in the work-place would be invited to the home or to some sporting or cultural event, often with their partners. In this way, the rules of relevancy (see Paine, 1969) governing the relationship were altered. Rather than the relationship being confined, and thereby defined, in terms of a particular context or setting, they were broadened out in a way which helped emphasise the primacy of the relationship above that of specific contexts. This mode of organising informal sociable relationships was entirely congruent with cultural understandings of what friendship entailed.

In contrast, a close reading of the research literature suggested that both male and female working-class sociability with non-kin was organised differently. In particular, the rules of relevancy constructed around these ties gave greater emphasis to context and setting and, as a consequence, underplayed the significance of the tie in its own right. That is, when people met with non-kin, rather less attention was given to developing the relationship through interaction in a variety of settings; instead, relationships tended to stay bounded within the initial context – or focus of activity in Feld's term (see Feld and Carter, this volume) – whatever that was. In particular, it was quite rare for men to socialise in the home, which remained the province of 'family'. As a result, there was less emphasis placed symbolically on the individuality of relationships. Whereas much middle-class sociability was planned and organised for its own sake, working-class sociability often appeared to be more fortuitous, being dependent on joint participation in activities, with participation being defined in terms of the activity rather than the relationships involved. The distinction here could be quite subtle. While activities were routinely undertaken in the knowledge that particular others would be there, even these more significant relationships usually remained bound to the setting without a conscious attempt to broaden their basis.

And because these working-class constructions of sociable relationships downplayed the significance of the abstracted relationship in favour of context, the terminology of 'friendship' often seemed to be inappropriate. Culturally, friendship involves an emphasis on the particularity of relationships over specific contexts of action. As this ran counter to much working-class practice, there was a hesitancy about describing these relationships as 'friendships'. Instead, the term 'mate' tended to be used, especially by working-class men, as this signified a different form of solidarity, one more in line with established working-class patterns. For this reason, and not because of an inability to develop sociable ties appropriately, working-class respondents in many surveys reported having fewer friends than middle-class respondents. And, interestingly, it was not just in Britain that such arguments appeared to apply. Research in other Western countries, including the United States, France, and Australia, seems to offer a degree of support for the general notion that working-class and middle-class sociability with non-kin were ordered differentially around context and relationship (Oxley, 1974; Ferrand, 1985; Rosecrance, 1986).

Contexts of difference

In terms of the focus of this volume – how different contexts mould patterns of friendship – the key question is why this class-based division in sociable relationships arose. What was it about the circumstances of middle- and working-class individuals – but men in particular – which led to different forms of non-kin sociability emerging? And to what degree was this differentiation rooted in a particular era – in the case of Britain, the broad period spanning the middle years of this century? In order to examine such questions, it is necessary to analyse more fully the characteristics of friendship – understood broadly – and then relate these to the material and social conditions under which these sociable ties were framed. As suggested above, the patterns of friendship and sociability which develop amongst any social strata in any era cannot be divorced from the broader social and economic structures which shape the opportunities and resources they have available. Even while friendship appears at times to lie outside these structures, they none the less contour the manner in which these ties are routinely organised.

One of the principal features of friendships and other such non-kin sociable relationships is that those involved regard and treat one another as social equals. Of course this does not mean that those who are friends – or whatever – *are* equal in every respect. Difference is certainly sanctioned. What it does mean, though, is that such difference should not interfere with the representation of equality within the relationship. Difference can be tolerated provided it does not undermine the sense that each party has of the other treating them as of equal social worth. Where such balance is missing, sustaining the relationship as friendship becomes problematic. In practice, most friendship ties are between people who share similar social and economic locations, thereby rendering the signification of equality easier. Similarly, friendships often lapse if one side's structural location alters sufficiently to make the routine portrayal of equality difficult (Allan, 1989a; Feld and Carter, this volume).

To express this in a different way, the principle of reciprocity is important in all forms of friendship. Such reciprocity impacts on a range of different aspects within these relationships, including whatever material exchanges occur within them; the favours and services each individual provides for the other; the commitment the parties show in the tie; and the status or sense of worth they bestow on each other. Such reciprocity is not necessarily short-term; the exchanges do not have to match immediately. Rather, what typically matters is the overall balance of the tie over the middle term. However, for how long the middle term extends, and how much 'credit' or 'debt' is permitted, will vary from one relationship to another, depending in part upon its history and on the current circumstances of those involved. The key issue, though, is that being able to reciprocate and sustain a balance of material and symbolic exchange is normally seen as central to the management of non-kin sociable ties of a friendship type.

Because of the importance of reciprocity, maintaining a level of control over the exchanges involved can become a prime concern, especially when available resources are unequal or limited. In such instances, strategies need to be developed for containing the level of commitment. In his community study of a small Australian town, Oxley (1974) provided an example of this which appears to have a much wider applicability. He examined how men from different class positions managed to sustain equality in their 'mateships' in the pubs and bars which served as the main locus of male sociability in the town. In essence, his argument was that tightly framing these relationships around the drinking setting, and deliberately excluding from them areas of activity which would make social and economic difference more apparent, fostered an ethic of equality in which reciprocities could be managed unproblematically. This theme can be applied more generally in the management of sociable relationships.

In particular, the dominance of mateship, as distinct from friendship, in the patterns of informal ties maintained by working-class men in the studies summarised above is certainly likely to be linked to their material position and the need to limit expenditure. That is, the relative poverty in many of the working-class areas studied, the insecurity of employment, and consequently of domestic economies resulted, it can be argued, in the need to ensure that control was maintained over sociable expenditure. A pattern by which ties were restricted to specific settings, rather than being framed more openly, meant that this could be achieved, both generally and in particular when resources became most scarce. Put simply, if interaction depends on being in a particular leisure setting, then episodes of interaction are relatively easy to control. At times people can stay away and thus avoid committing their resources in this way. In addition, to a degree, they can determine their participation in any episode by entering and leaving it when they will. Most importantly, because involvement is defined in terms of settings rather than individual relationships, the reciprocal commitments generated within relationships are more readily bounded and consequently contained.

But there is another element of people's material resources that is important in this: their housing. As many of the relevant studies indicated, the quality of housing was very poor. In Britain, many of the areas studied contained housing which was old, overcrowded, lacking amenities, and built to inadequate standards by contemporary definitions. Thus the 'traditional' working-class areas studied were typically inner-city slum areas which had suffered badly from war damage and lack of investment. As mentioned above, many of the younger families from the areas were being rehoused in new estates in more suburban locations. Those who remained generally had little domestic space and usually shared basic amenities – in some cases including cooking as well as (external) toilet facilities. In addition of course, due to poverty, the furnishings and other accoutrements within the home were often worn and otherwise inadequate.

The material poverty of these homes had a significant impact on the way they were used. Specifically, the home became very much the preserve of 'family', including close kin. Only rarely, and then, it would seem, on quite formal occasions, were non-kin ever entertained. Unlike the middle-class pattern, the home was not a place to invite others into; it was not a place to 'reveal' the symbolic familial order which had been constructed. Its standard did not encourage this. Moreover, the close-knit character of local social networks discouraged this further. In the absence of significant inward migration, most people knew, and were consequently known by, a large number of others. As a result, they were readily 'placed' within the local social structure and thus entwined in gossip networks. Keeping the 'family space' as private and not giving 'outsiders' access to what went on within the home was one mechanism for protecting privacy and maintaining respectability. In reality it was extremely difficult to keep family business private, as the housing infrastructure with its thin walls and shared amenities meant that much could be overheard as well as overseen. None the less a pattern developed, especially among those families who most valued respectability, of building strong boundaries around the home and keeping it as exclusively family space. Except in special circumstances, even well-liked 'outsiders' were not encouraged inside (Klein, 1965; Williams, 1983; Allan, 1989b).

In addition, the dominant pattern of marriage also appeared to have an influence on both the use of the home and the organisation of sociability. While it is easy to stereotype, the research reports indicate that many of the couples in the study areas led relatively segregated lives. In particular, aside from kin, their sociable ties were largely individual rather than 'joint'. They had few, if any, non-kin relationships in which they interacted as a couple. Two consequences follow from this. First, it fostered a pattern whereby non-kin were not entertained in the home. The more segregated the couple's social life, the less likely it is that men especially would define the domestic arena as an appropriate place for mixing with others, particularly when the space available was as limited as it typically was in these working-class households. Bringing people into the home is much more likely when the adults in the family share sociable relationships together. Secondly, where the couple's social activities and relationships are separate, then this of itself is liable to foster stronger contextual boundaries being placed around relationships. While not inevitably so, the non-involvement of spouses reduces the potential 'cross-over' between different foci of activity or spheres of social participation. Activities can, in this sense, be 'compartmentalised' and relationships bounded more readily.

Thus the working-class pattern of socialising, whereby non-kin relationships tended to be confined to specific settings rather than broadened or extended in the middle-class manner, can be recognised as rooted in the broader conditions of working-class life which then pertained. As a cultural construction of sociability, it did not arise haphazardly, nor did it represent a lack of social skills on the part of those involved. It was an adaptive pattern arising out of the specific conditions of working-class life in these localities at that time. In particular, it facilitated a degree of control over resource allocation for people with limited and often uncertain means, thereby allowing them to sustain respectability and manage reciprocity. Thus, the argument is that the structuring of men's lives – in particular, their economic circumstances, their housing conditions, and the organisation of their marriages – fostered a pattern of sociability distinct from that established by the middle class. Given their different structural location, the latter had concerns different from those of the working class and as a result generated distinct patterns of 'friendship'.

Changes

But if the social and economic conditions of the middle of the century and immediate post-war period fostered this form of sociability, what have the consequences been of the massive social changes that have occurred in domestic life over the past two generations, since, say, 1960? How have such changes altered patterns of non-kin sociability, particularly for working-class men? A full answer to such questions would require a much broader examination of contemporary social transformations than is possible in this chapter. For space reasons the impact of a changed employment structure – including rapid rises in married women's employment, a decline in the unskilled male manual labour force, and increasing levels of short- and long-term unemployment – and of changed demographic patterns – including lower levels of (and later) marriage, more divorce, major increases in cohabitation, and a higher proportion of births to single mothers (Allan and Crow, 1999) – will not be examined. The analysis will concentrate instead on changes in housing, in marital partnerships, and in conceptions of the home. As above, the focus here will be predominantly on the British context, though many of the changes in social and economic circumstance apply more widely, at least in broad terms.

There is no question that housing conditions have improved significantly for the majority of the population during the second half of the twentieth century. In the 1990s Britain still has major housing problems, with significant numbers of families in inadequate and/or temporary housing, and underinvestment in public housing. None the less, on all standard measures of housing adequacy and comfort, the average individual's housing circumstances are markedly better than they were two generations ago. For example, housing densities were 0.7 people per room in 1951 compared to less than 0.5 in 1991; in 1961 nearly a quarter of all households lacked a fixed bath/shower or inside toilet compared to only 1 per cent in 1991; as late as 1972 only 37 per cent of households had any form of central heating, while by 1995 the equivalent figure was 86 per cent (Halsey, 1988; General Household Survey, 1997; Social Trends, 1997). The level of household equipment and furnishings – carpeting, home entertainments, laundry, and food preparation appliances – has also increased significantly in the post-war period.

Other changes in housing have also been important. First, facilitated by new transport developments as well as cheaper production costs, there has been significant suburban 'drift', with most new housing, whether public or private, being built on the urban fringes. Secondly, tenure structure has altered dramatically since 1951 when 69 per cent of the population rented, either publicly or privately. In the last decade of the twentieth century, it is home ownership which stands at nearly 70 per cent, though arguments remain about the real significance of this in terms of people's 'ontological security' and their commitment to familial/domestic relationships (Saunders, 1990; Forrest, *et al.*, 1990). Thirdly, there have been less well-documented but none the less important changes in domestic architecture. In particular, the popularity of 'open-plan' lounge/dining/kitchen areas reflects changes in beliefs about the ordering of familial relationships and the appropriate use of domestic space. Here, in particular, it is noticeable how frequently in older, traditionally designed housing walls have been removed to make one large room rather than two small ones. Keeping a room for 'best' rather than allowing routine family use is now not seen as important in the way it was when the traditional working-class studies were conducted (see Hoggart, 1957; Roberts, 1973).

Overall these changes in housing have contributed to forms of domestic environment which are quite distinct from those which pertained in the era discussed above. A further element within this concerns the character of contemporary marital partnerships. As the growth of cohabitation and divorce implies, the ways in which marriages (including here longer-term cohabitations) are constructed have shifted noticeably over the past two generations (Cancian, 1987; Clark, 1991). While in Britain the division of domestic and employment responsibilities has altered less than is some-times imagined, it is evident that people's early expectations of the emotional and companionable satisfactions of marital relationships have changed. That is, there has been a growing emphasis on marriage as a personal commitment and as a relationship through which self-expression and self-realisation can be achieved (Giddens, 1992; Hawkes, 1996).

While this operates at an ideological level, providing a blue-print (Cancian, 1987) of what marriage is normatively, it does not mean that particular marriages are actually experienced in this way (Duncombe and Marsden, 1993, 1995). Indeed, it is arguable that the increased incidence of divorce is a direct consequence of many marriages not fulfilling the aspirations and dreams originally held. None the less, with this normative 'mapping' of marriage, couples are usually more involved in one another's social and leisure lives than was typically the case in the studies discussed earlier. Thus the segregated form of conjugal relationship famously described by Bott in the late 1950s is perceived in the 1990s as a sign of an unsatisfactory marriage rather than an alternative form of marital organisation (Bott, 1957). While not all activities will be shared, couples expect to lead more integrated social and leisure lives together, including some sharing of friends in common. There may still be a tendency for gender segregation within sociability, but it is far less marked – and apparently less desired – than was the case in previous eras. Contemporary marriage is constructed as a socially active and personally fulfilling tie and not simply as a domestic, familial, or economic relationship. As a result, couples – whether married or cohabiting – normally expect to share more of their significant informal relationships in common (Mansfield and Collard, 1988).

The final change to be discussed here concerns the meaning which the home holds for people. As with the other shifts examined, the impact of this has not been uniform. However, in general, the home has come to signify a different set of understandings and occupy a different place in people's lives than previously (Crow and Allan, 1990). Tied in with changes in housing facilities and marital expectations, the home, for couples especially, has come to be perceived as more fully a place of relaxation and self-expression, and not just as the site of domestic and family organisation. It is easy to be over-romantic here; the home is still the setting for much conflict and disharmony, and, in no small number of instances, abuse and violence. Overall though, the changes there have been – in housing standards and amenities, in comfort and ambience – have resulted in the home as personal and social space having an altered significance. Indeed, constructing the home, symbolically and materially, has become very much part of the 'couple project' – one of the key ways through which contemporary couples express their solidarity (Mansfield and Collard, 1988).

This represents a major shift for working-class men in particular. While the home has long been viewed by men as a refuge from the harsh realities of employment and other elements of the public sphere (Lasch, 1977; Oliker, this volume), what has happened over the past two generations is that men's lives have generally become more 'home-centred' (Allan and Crow, 1991). Rather than just being a refuge or retreat, constructed largely by women, it holds a more positive, more *active* place in their consciousness. Linked to other changes in the domestic sphere, men expect to take more pleasure from and in the home – to be more involved in its social construction and to spend more leisure time there than in the past. Of course the domestic division of labour remains highly gendered; women are much more fully involved in its day-to-day organisation than men. And of

course, the home is experienced as less satisfying at times of domestic conflict or economic impoverishment. None the less, by the end of the twentieth century, the idea of the home as an arena in which men can find
expression and fulfilment is, in general, much more firmly rooted in cultural
understandings of domestic and familial life than it was in earlier times.

Privatisation, home-centredness, and sociability

Changes like the ones discussed here cannot occur without having repercussions on other spheres of activity. Certainly they have influenced the
ways in which people construct their domestic and family life. Put simply,
the domestic options open to most individuals, couples, and families are
different to those available to their grandparents, as indeed are the constraints they face. But, equally, these changes have consequences for other
areas of activity too. They become part of the structural context within
which other relationships are framed. The central argument of this chapter
is that, as changes such as these occur, they have an impact on leisure activities, communal solidarities, patterns of sociability, and styles of friendship,
as well as on domestic and family organisation. It is also important to
recognise that the changes discussed have not affected everyone equally. In
particular, while for example material standards have improved overall, the
economic restructuring of the past twenty years has resulted in many individuals experiencing periods of long-term unemployment, severely inadequate housing, and chronic poverty. The patterns of sociability they
establish will be shaped by these experiences. Thus, in generalising about
change, the inevitable variations there are should not be forgotten, even if
it remains possible to talk about broader collective shifts.

The implications of these changes for sociability and friendship are not
as obvious as they are sometimes taken to be. As mentioned in chapter 1,
one of the commonest ideas is that, with affluence and changing housing
circumstances, community solidarities have been undermined and a process
of 'privatisation' has occurred. However, the concept of 'privatisation' is a
broad one that incorporates diverse ideas. Perhaps the main theme is the one
indicated above: whereas once the locality provided both the personnel and
the settings for much sociable interaction, this is no longer so. The development of rapid transport technologies, together with high levels of geographical mobility and other characteristics of urban growth, is thought to have
destroyed the communal bonds that once supposedly provided the fabric of
most people's lives. Instead of collective sociability – not altogether dis-
similar from the form described above as typical of sociability in traditional

working-class localities in mid-century Britain – increasingly people are taken to live far more privately, apparently content to focus predominantly if not exclusively on relationships 'internal' to the household. These are seen as the relationships which matter to people, not ties to neighbours, workmates, or others in the locality.

Thus, within privatisation theories, there is an opposition between public, communal participation and an isolated, private lifestyle. However these two patterns are not the only alternatives. There are others, and in particular others which are neither communal nor isolated. Indeed, one of the most interesting, though frequently ignored, issues here is the way in which 'noncommunal' participation develops through the 'privatisation' of sociability. For example, the traditional middle-class form of friendship is one which in most respects is non-communal, yet runs counter to at least some of the elements emphasised in most ideas about the privatisation of family and domestic life. It is a pattern which is 'privatised' in the sense of not solely (or even predominantly) involving 'communal' settings, but is not so in the sense of being concerned only with immediate issues of home and family.

Similarly Wellman and his colleagues (Wellman, *et al.*, 1988; Wellman and Wortley, 1990) have consistently argued that conditions of late modernity have indeed rendered the communal solidarities of the past redundant, but that people's personal networks are not barren as a result. Instead, they are able to maintain relationships with those people they define as significant through different technologies – cars, telephones, and more recently e-mail (see Adams, this volume) – irrespective of where they live. The result is the geographical dispersal of relationships within an individual's personal network in a manner that was far less common two generations ago. For many (though by no means all, particularly if they have no private transport available or are otherwise 'trapped' in the neighbourhood (see Wellman, 1985)), the locality is no longer a significant source of sociability, just as it is no longer the site of employment. It is just a place to live, often enough valued for the privacy, even anonymity, it allows. But the consequence is not social isolation. It is a greater selectivity of important sociable ties, and sometimes a more fragmented, as well as dispersed, network. That is, significant individuals in the personal network do not necessarily know each other well or meet particularly often. This of course allows for greater control and privacy, though not in the sense usually portrayed by theories of privatisation. By managing their networks so that particular others within them have little contact, somewhat different portrayals of self can be sustained because those 'in the know' are not in a position to reveal 'secrets' (Feld and Carter, this volume).

Evaluating these arguments is not straightforward. In Britain, there have been few empirical studies of friendship in recent years. Moreover, the sorts of community and occupational research that in the past revealed such rich information about the structuring of sociability, leisure, and domestic life became quite unfashionable in the late 1970s and 1980s (Murdoch and Day, 1993; Crow and Allan, 1994). Not surprisingly, given the economic circumstances of the period, many of the studies that were undertaken in this tradition were concerned predominantly with the impact of economic restructuring and historically high levels of unemployment in different localities. Moreover, they tended to focus mostly on routes back into employment, the re-negotiation of domestic tasks within the household, and the development of informal economies. (See, for example, Pahl, 1984; Harris, 1987; Westergaard, *et al.*, 1989; Morris, 1990; Anderson, *et al.*, 1994.)

Generally these studies report that the poverty and sense of stigma associated with unemployment resulted in reduced social participation. Existing non-kin relationships were serviced less extensively; fewer visits were made to sites of sociability; and access to the home was restricted so as not to reveal the material deprivations of domestic life. However, some of the research suggests different patterns to this. Binns and Mars (1984), for example, reported that the young unemployed men in their study who had not had jobs since leaving school sustained friendships which were not framed by specific contexts. They interacted across different settings, including their homes, unlike the older respondents with significant employment histories who tended to respond to unemployment by restricting all sociability (see also Wallace, 1987).

Few recent studies have examined changes in male working-class sociability in circumstances other than redundancy and unemployment. And those that have done so, including some concerned with privatisation, do not include a great deal of material on the organisation of friendship, focusing more on kin, colleague, and neighbour relationships. However, the material available does indicate that patterns of male working-class sociability are altering. While aspects of the 'traditional' model still apply, there none the less appear to have been changes in sociable practice which undermine the model. In particular, it seems that the 'boundaries' constructed around informal ties are becoming more permeable than they were in the past. Although emergent forms of working-class sociability do not simply mirror middle-class patterns, recent studies do indicate that changes in material and ideological context have had some impact on the routine ordering of domestic and leisure sociability.

Devine (1989, 1992) conducted research in Luton, the site of the influential *Affluent Worker* studies (Goldthorpe, *et al.*, 1969). Through interviews with both husbands and wives, she examined the changes which had occurred in automobile workers' lifestyles in the intervening period. In particular, she analyses patterns of informal solidarity with kin, neighbours, and workmates in some depth, as well as domestic organisation and family commitment. In general, her respondents' lives were focused far more around the domestic arena of home and family than seems to have been the case a generation earlier. Much of their free time was given to family projects and relationships, though much of this, especially for those whose wives were also employed, was spent doing mundane domestic tasks. Within this account, however, there is little evidence of the home being framed tightly, with non-kin excluded; nor is there the same sense of 'boundedness' of foci of activity evident in earlier accounts of manual workers' sociability. The terminology of friendship is used quite readily, with the personal qualities of those involved being emphasised over specific activities and contexts. However, it is worth noting that most of the friendships reported on appear to be individually rather than couple-oriented. That is, while the couples in the study frequently interacted with close kin together, they did not appear to do so to the same extent with friends.

Overall Devine's research demonstrates both that patterns of working-class social incorporation have been altering since Goldthorpe, *et al.*'s original study and moreover that an increased family- or home-centred orientation does not result in ties of informal sociability becoming inconsequential. This is a theme echoed by Proctor (1990) in his study of a working-class area of Coventry. Like Devine, Proctor examines the extent to which ideas of privatisation are reflected in his respondents' lives. The data he presents on friendship patterns are frustratingly limited, both because he is concerned primarily with ties in the locality rather than personal networks more widely, and because, surprisingly, no heed is paid to gender. However, like Devine, the picture he presents is one in which his respondents – people living with spouses and at least one dependent child – are more socially active than traditional privatisation theories imply. Here too it would seem that non-kin sociable relationships are typically bounded less tightly than earlier accounts suggest. For example, in this research over a fifth of the respondents socialised outside the home with a neighbour at least monthly; 30 per cent did so with a workmate; and a similar number did so with some other friend. While the data reported do not allow friendship issues to be addressed more fully, Proctor's analysis none the less suggests that patterns of sociability are being framed differently to the ways described in earlier research.

In their study of class structure and social mobility, Marshall and his colleagues (Marshall, *et al.*, 1988) were also concerned with the degree to which there had been an increasing privatisation of social life. The questions they asked about friendship were – once again – minimal but none the less suggestive. They report, for example, that a third of the non-work activities their respondents reported enjoying were undertaken alone, a third with family, and a third with friends. As well as finding that 'working-class associational activities' were more likely to be pursued in the home than were similar middle-class activities, they also record that nearly 40 per cent of their working-class respondents engaged in these activities with friends. While these data are limited, and leave unanswered questions about how the category of 'friend' was constructed, Marshall, *et al.*'s study portrays a greater similarity between the classes in patterns of non-kin sociability than earlier studies.

Conclusion

The theme of this chapter is that the demographic, material, and social changes working through society impact on the dominant forms which sociable ties take. Just as these changes influence family life, so too they will influence the patterning of non-kin sociability. In this sense, friendships and other such ties are a product of their time and place. More specifically, the ways in which working-class male sociability was organised in Britain in the middle period of this century can be understood in the context of working-class experience, in particular with regard to material resources, housing, and marital organisation. Limited finances, marriages typified by a high division of labour and leisure, and poor-quality housing contributed to patterns of socialising in which context was prioritised over the relationship in the construction of sociability. That is, in general, sociable relationships were not developed by extending the settings for interaction; rather they typically remained bounded within a given interactional site. As argued above, this allowed a degree of control over them which would otherwise have been more problematic.

But the social and economic conditions that fostered this form of sociability are no longer as pertinent as they were. The parameters of much working-class life have altered significantly in the second half of the twentieth century. As we have seen, a major element within this has been changes to domestic 'ambience', including shifts in housing standards, conjugal ideology, and perceptions of the home. These have clearly not been experienced by all equally – the rise in unemployment and divorce in particular have ensured marked divisions in individual experience. None the less, for the majority of men the conditions under which they live are noticeably different to those of, say, their grandfathers. These changes in the social and material parameters of male working-class life foster modes of sociability which are more consonant with these new circumstances, especially for the more secure and advantaged sections of the male working class. Rather than needing to control reciprocity through, in effect, keeping relationships tightly framed, modified patterns of sociability emerge which reflect the altered material, social, and domestic environment of those involved.

Given the analysis developed above, there are three conceptually distinct, though potentially contingent, elements of contemporary male working-class sociability that warrant particular consideration. The first concerns the degree to which the contextual 'boundaries' constructed around non-kin sociable relationships are more permeable, less firm, than they traditionally were. To what extent has the dominant mode of organising such sociability shifted from a (public/communal) context-defined one to one which is more relationally signified? Secondly, has the development of a conjugal ideology emphasising shared participation impacted on male non-kin sociability? Has there been a decrease in the extent to which male sociability is insulated from partner/family ties? And, thirdly, are friends brought into the home more often than in the past? Is the domestic environment now conceived of as an appropriate arena for working-class male sociability?

Note here that it is quite possible for individual relationships to be sustained for their own sake, i.e., without prioritising the activities involved, and still be enacted in interactional contexts which are 'public' rather than 'private'. Indeed, ultimately here the boundary between prioritising activity ahead of relationship may be difficult to define. None the less, when partners are at some level incorporated into the relationship, and when the home is used as an interactional setting, sociable ties become more clearly 'marked' as ties sustained for their own purpose. Forms of sociability which involve partners foster a fuller access to aspects of the other's life, thereby making context-defined constructions of the relationship less appropriate. Similarly, because the domestic world is private, controlled space, the incorporation of others into this arena symbolises the personal solidarity and commitment there is, particularly for men whose work is rarely framed domestically.

It is a pale ending to argue that current research does not allow these issues to be examined extensively. This is, however, the case. As discussed above, the available evidence does suggest that there has been a significant level of change occurring. In particular, it does appear that the boundaries being constructed around male non-kin relationships are less rigid than they were in the earlier community, occupational, and kinship studies. It is also evident that claims of privatisation in which working-class men are seen as becoming comparatively isolated, committed only to their home and family, are without much foundation. What is less certain is the degree to which working-class husbands and wives share many of their friends in common, and whether these men are now using their homes more for socialising with non-kin. There is likely to be wide variation in these matters as new practices replace older ones, but, if men have indeed come to be more home-focused with the domestic arena playing a larger part in their definitions of self, then permitting others access to this sphere becomes much more consonant with their personal and social identity. Such changing patterns can be interpreted as a form of embourgeoisement or, indeed, as part of the 'slow march of history' to which Young and Willmott (1973) refer. Both of these perspectives are open to criticism. However, in this chapter, the question has not been the relationship between middle-class and working-class cultural practices *per se*, but rather how modifications in the social and material circumstances of different sections of the population – in this case, working-class men – have repercussions for emergent forms of solidarity.

References

Allan, Graham (1977), 'Class variations in friendship patterns', *British Journal of Sociology*, 28: 389–93.

(1979), *A Sociology of Friendship and Kinship*, London: Allen & Unwin.

(1989a), *Friendship: Developing a Sociological Perspective*, Hemel Hempstead: Harvester-Wheatsheaf.

(1989b), 'Insiders and outsiders: boundaries around the home', in Allan and Crow (eds.).

(1996), *Friendship and Kinship in Modern Britain*, Oxford University Press.

Allan, Graham, and Crow, Graham (eds.) (1989), *Home and Family: Creating the Domestic Sphere*, Basingstoke: Macmillan.

(1991), 'Privatization, home-centredness and leisure', *Leisure Studies*, 10: 19–32.

(1999), *Families, Households and Society*, Basingstoke: Macmillan.

Anderson, Michael, Bechhofer, Frank, and Gershuny, Jonathan (eds.) (1994), *The Social and Political Economy of the Household*, Oxford University Press.

Bell, Colin (1968), *Middle-Class Families*, London: Routledge and Kegan Paul.

(1990), 'Middle-class families', in C. C. Harris (ed.), *Family, Economy and Community*, Cardiff: University of Wales Press.

Binns, David, and Mars, Gerald (1984) 'Family, community and unemployment: a study in change', *Sociological Review*, 32: 662–95.

Bott, Elizabeth (1957), *Family and Social Network*, London: Tavistock.

Cancian, Francesca (1987), *Love in America: Gender and Self-Development*, Cambridge University Press.

Clark, David (ed.) (1991), *Marriage, Domestic Life and Social Change*, London: Routledge.

Crow, Graham, and Allan, Graham (1990), 'Constructing the domestic sphere: the emergence of the modern home in post-war Britain', in Helen Corr and Lynn Jamieson (eds.), *Politics of Everyday Life*, Basingstoke: Macmillan.

 (1994), *Community Life: An Introduction to Local Social Relations*, Hemel Hempstead: Harvester-Wheatsheaf.

Devine, Fiona (1989), 'Privatised families and their homes', in Allan and Crow (eds.).

 (1992), *Affluent Workers Revisited: Privatism and the Working Class*, Edinburgh University Press.

Duck, Steve (ed.) (1993), *Social Context and Relationships*, Newbury Park: Sage.

Duncombe, Jean, and Marsden, Dennis (1993), 'Love and intimacy: the gender division of emotion and emotion work', *Sociology*, 27: 221–41.

 (1995), '"Workaholics" and "whingeing women". Theorizing intimacy and emotion work: the last frontier of gender inequality', *Sociological Review*, 43: 150–69.

Ferrand, Alexis (1985), *Amis and Associés*, Grenoble: Ministère de l'urbanisme du longement des transports.

Firth, Raymond, Forge, Anthony, and Hubert, Jane (1970), *Families and Their Relatives*, London: Routledge and Kegan Paul.

Forrest, Ray, Murie, Alan, and Williams, Peter (1990), *Home Ownership: Differentiation and Fragmentation*, London: Unwin Hyman.

General Household Survey (1997), *Living in Britain: General Household Survey 1995*, London: Stationery Office.

Giddens, Anthony (1992), *The Transformation of Intimacy: Sexuality, Love, and Eroticism in Modern Societies*, Cambridge: Polity.

Goldthorpe, John, Lockwood, David, Bechhofer, Frank, and Platt, Jennifer (1969), *The Affluent Worker in the Class Structure*, Cambridge University Press.

Goode, William (1963), *World Revolution and Family Patterns*, New York: Collier-Macmillan.

Halsey, A. H. (1988), *British Social Trends Since 1900*, Basingstoke: Macmillan.

Harris, C. C. (1983), *The Family in Industrial Society*, London: Allen & Unwin.

 (1987), *Redundancy and Recession in South Wales*, Oxford: Blackwell.

Hawkes, Gail (1996), *A Sociology of Sex and Sexuality*, Buckingham: Open University Press.

Hoggart, Richard (1957), *The Uses of Literacy*, Harmondsworth: Penguin.

Klein, Josephine (1965), *Samples from English Culture*, vol. I, London: Routledge and Kegan Paul.

Lasch, Christopher (1977), *Haven in a Heartless World: The Family Besieged*, New York: Basic Books.

Laslett, Peter, with Wall, Richard (1972), *Household and Family in Past Time*, Cambridge University Press.

Mansfield, Penny, and Collard, Jean (1988), *The Beginning of the Rest of Your Life?*, Basingstoke: Macmillan.

Marshall, Gordon, Rose, David, Newby, Howard, and Vogler, Carolyn (1988), *Social Class in Modern Britain*, London: Unwin Hyman.

Morris, Lydia (1990), *The Workings of the Household*, Cambridge: Polity.

Murdoch, Graham, and Day, Jonathon (1993), 'Locality and community coming to terms with places', *Sociological Review*, 41: 82–111.

Oxley, H. G. (1974), *Mateship and Local Organization*, Brisbane: University of Queensland Press.

Pahl, Ray (1984), *Divisions of Labour*, Oxford: Blackwell.

Pahl, Ray, and Wallace, Claire (1988), 'Neither angels in marble nor rebels in red: privatization and working-class consciousness', in David Rose (ed.), *Social Stratification and Economic Change*, London: Hutchinson.

Paine, Robert (1969), 'In search of friendship', *Man* (n.s.), 4: 505–24.

Parsons, Talcott (1949), 'The social structure of the family', in Ruth N. Anshen (ed.), *The Family: Its Function and Destiny*, New York: Harper and Row.

Proctor, Ian (1990), 'The privatisation of working-class life: a dissenting view', *British Journal of Sociology*, 41: 157–80.

Roberts, Robert (1973), *The Classic Slum: Salford Life in the First Quarter of the Century*, Harmondsworth: Penguin.

Rosecrance, John (1986), 'Racetrack buddy relations: compartmentalised and satisfying', *Journal of Social and Personal Relationships*, 3: 441–56.

Saunders, Peter (1990), *A Nation of Home Owners*, London: Unwin Hyman.

Silver, Alan (1990), 'Friendship in commercial society: eighteenth-century social theory and modern sociology', *American Journal of Sociology*, 95: 1474–1504.

Social Trends (1977), *Social Trends No. 27*, London: Stationery Office.

Wallace, Claire (1987), *For Richer, For Poorer: Growing up in and out of Work*, London: Tavistock.

Wellman, Barry (1985), 'Domestic work, paid work and net work', in Steve Duck and Dan Perlman (eds.), *Understanding Personal Relationships*, London: Sage.

Wellman, Barry, Carrington, Peter J., and Hall, Alan (1988), 'Networks as personal communities', in Barry Wellman and S. D. Berkowitz (eds.), *Social Structures: A Network Approach*, Cambridge University Press.

Wellman, Barry, and Wortley, Scott (1990), 'Different strokes from different folks: community ties and social support', *American Journal of Sociology*, 96: 558–88.

Westergaard, John, Noble, Iain, and Walker, Alan (1989), *After Redundancy: The Experience of Economic Insecurity*, Cambridge: Polity.

Williams, Rex (1983), 'Kinship and migration strategies among settled Londoners', *British Journal of Sociology*, 34: 386–415.

Young, Michael, and Willmott, Peter (1973), *The Symmetrical Family*, London: Routledge and Kegan Paul.

5

Rich friendships, affluent friends: middle-class practices of friendship

Kaeren Harrison

Introduction

It has been argued that married women face a number of structural and cultural barriers to the construction of personal relationships outside the domestic sphere, for typically they have much less time, personal space, and access to financial resources than do their husbands (Pahl, 1984; Allan, 1989). It has also been suggested that married women are reluctant to encroach on their quality family time with children and husbands (that is, in the evenings and over weekends) as this in turn inevitably confines both the range of activities wives can participate in, and the number of interactions they could 'conveniently' have (Green, *et al.*, 1990; O'Connor, 1992). This chapter, however, comes to a rather different conclusion. It will be argued below that, while there are a number of effective barriers to the construction, development, and maintenance of close female relationships, these constraints are not always as rigid or as forceful as they might first appear, especially for the particular people at the heart of this study – married, middle-class women.

By focusing on a specific socio-economic group, one of the central themes of this book – that different structural features influence personal ties and organise informal relationships – can be made explicit here. This will be done by addressing a number of connected questions: what is the place of friendship in these married women's lives? What constraints and opportunities do they face in their daily 'doing' of friendship? How are female friendships managed in the context of marriage? In what ways are their friendship practices an indication of their social location? By exploring these issues, it will be shown that, while the friendship patterns of the women in this study were framed within a societal context that retains a firm commitment to the primacy of marriage and a heterosexual couple-based ideology, the women in this study not only preserved and protected established friendships, but also constructed and developed new relationships.

In order to situate this research – indeed, to place this chapter in context – it is important to describe these women in more detail. While no group of individuals could ever legitimately be described as homogeneous, the women focused on in this study did have a number of social characteristics in common. They were all white, middle-class, and, when the fieldwork began, under forty years of age. Nearly all of them were in part-time paid employment outside the home, and had one or more dependent children. Their husbands were well-paid professional men – hospital consultants, television producers, academics – and they themselves were planning to return full-time to their own careers – as GPs, teachers, social workers – at some point in the future. This meant that not only did they have access to a joint income, they also had money of their own. Being relatively affluent, they actively fostered their social lives, for they could afford the occasional cinema and theatre ticket, their health club visits and wine bar excursions, and enjoyed spending money on 'treats'. Buying ready-made meals from Marks & Spencer when their friends came to visit, and 'spoiling' themselves with luxuries from the Body Shop, demonstrated not only their consumption choices and lifestyle practices, but was highly indicative of three significant features. These women valued their leisure and recreational activities, and rated sociability highly, but, most importantly, had time and money to spend on themselves.

This raises an important point: for the women in this study their close female friendships were *not* socially difficult to maintain. Indeed, the constraints that came with marriage, part-time work, motherhood, and household responsibilities also produced a variety of opportunities in which to develop their friendships both individually with close intimates and collectively with larger groups. For example, being married to professional men in full-time employment gave them some status and – as previously mentioned – access to an amount of disposable income and material resources such as a second car. This made entertaining at home, holidaying with family friends, and membership of various health and leisure centres possible, reflecting a comfortable social location and promoting group friendships based around shared activities. Working flexible hours around school days that ended at 3:30 p.m. required co-operation with other employed mothers over reciprocal child-minding, and the ferrying of children to after-school clubs facilitated friendships based around shared responsibilities.

Forging alliances in these ways, shaped as they were by 'relationship symbols' (Baxter, 1987) and routinised interactions (Feld and Carter, this volume), produced group friendships and constructed networks of practical support. There was evidence, too, of more intimate and privatised friendship patterns, although these were typically dyadic rather than group-based. Exchanging gifts, having long telephone conversations, or going for walks in the forest with one or two close intimates were all possible because the women in this study had the time, space, energy, and material resources to do so.

In other words, in spite of living in a patriarchal, capitalist society where persistent gender inequalities in the division of labour, emotion work, power, and status remain firmly entrenched, these women worked hard at both their individual and group friendships, for very often they were the source of their happiest, most fulfilling relationships. By exploring the significant, if not fundamental, role friends played in the personal and emotional lives of these women, this chapter will discuss how, regardless of the barriers married women face in constructing, developing, and maintaining friendships with their close, female friends, they do in fact continue to be committed to these very important relationships.

Methods

This chapter is based on a small-scale, qualitative study of married women's friendships, set in the southeast of England between 1994 and 1997. It draws on two main sources of empirical data. First, multiple in-depth interviews with twelve individual women were conducted by 'snowballing' from a core group of four. In addition, two of the twelve introduced me to some of their own friends, and I was included in a number of 'girls' nights out' and invited to their homes for informal suppers. This gave me the opportunity of observing a variety of friendship pairs and circles at close quarters, and introduced a further ten women to the project, bringing the total number of participants in this part of the study to twenty-two. Extracts of dialogue from both the individual interviews and the collective group social evenings are liberally drawn on and incorporated in the discussion that follows. The second source of data comes from analysing responses to Directive No. 32 on 'Close Relationships', held in the Mass-Observation Archive at the University of Sussex.[1] Since its revival in 1981, this archive has built up a unique bank of written material by sending out three 'directives' a year on specific themes to a national panel of over 600 voluntary correspondents. These directives are not questionnaires as such, but a series of open-ended questions or 'prompts' designed to encourage contributors to express themselves freely and write with as much candour as possible. Each respondent is given a special reference number when they join the project, and all correspondence is anonymised, further ensuring that people can write without being personally identified. Subsequently, material generated in this way provides an extremely rich source of reflexive data – what has been described elsewhere as a 'sort of "free-association" on paper' (Shaw, 1996, pp. 6–7).

While the panel of writers to the Mass-Observation Archive are unrepresentative in categorical terms of the UK population as a whole (i.e., they are disproportionately female, white, and middle-class), this was precisely the socio-economic group I was interested in. Directive No. 32 proved a popular topic, generating 631 responses, from which I found 114 women who were in the same age range as the women being interviewed locally. By integrating quotes from the in-depth interviews and passages from the group discussions with the insights and reflections from the writings of the Mass-Observers (M-Os), it has been possible to explore the contexts in which these married women's friendships develop, and to examine how these contexts influence the form these friendships take.

The following discussion is in three parts. The first section examines 'barriers to friendship', opening with a number of graphic quotes from the data to illustrate the constraints that come with marriage and motherhood. It then goes on to describe how these constraints are managed, arguing that 'strategies of resistance' are employed by the women in this study, which, while hardly transforming the patriarchal structure within which they live, nevertheless undermine and challenge societal and cultural assumptions of female friendship. The second section describes the style and pattern of these women's friendships, and what they do for each other. Here the focus will be on identity construction, and the importance of 'really talking and really listening' (Belenky, *et al.*, 1986). The third and final section tackles contemporary marriage, where women's experience of varying degrees of unfairness in their marital relationship, their perceptions of inequality in the sharing of family work, and the dawning realisation that working outside the home and contributing to the financial income of the family do not necessarily lead to husbands' increased participation in the home in return will be discussed. By looking at how female friendships are managed in the context of marriage, explanations for why their 'friendship practices' take the shape they do should become evident.

Barriers to friendship: husbands blocking the way

Well, yes, I do get out in the evenings with my friends sometimes, once in a while, maybe once every few weeks or so, but it takes a lot of organising – and preparation – you know, in terms of leaving meals ready and sorting out the kids, and checking that Steve *is* actually going to be home on time to take over. When I think of it, I mean, to have a night out with the girls, well . . . it's a bit like staging a bank robbery!   (Teresa)[2]

I was just about to leave, I had one foot out the door, when Annie started to play up, and John said 'Come on, Annie-pie, you know Mummy's going to leave you now, because she's got to go out' [laughs] you know, he said it just like that, 'Mummy's going to leave you now' – playing the blackmail card – and so I said, 'Yes darling, Daddy's right, I'm rather afraid I am . . . but I expect Daddy'll read you a nice long story' [laughs], which was dropping him in it even more I suppose, but I was so cross with him. And I just left. I gave Annie a quick kiss and I left. And I kind of put it to the back of my mind, because I didn't want it to spoil the rest of the evening, but it bothered me, you know? And what bothered me most was not that he seemed reluctant to put Annie to bed on his own for a change – although that was bad enough – it was more that if it had been the other way around – if it had been John who was the one going out – well, he wouldn't have had a child clinging limpet-like to his leg. You know, I wouldn't have made it so difficult for *him* to leave the house.   (Clare)

I said, 'Where have you been? You know I've got to pick everyone up before seven', and he said [laughs] get this, he says, 'I thought, *as I was on my own on a Friday night* [her emphasis], I'd get some beers in.' So he'd been shopping! [laughs] Imagine! 'Well – there's always a first time', says me, thinking, you might have got some bread and milk while you were at it. [Because] he hadn't just bought beer – there were crisps and snacks and all sorts of treats in those bags! He'd never have thought to do that if we'd both been stopping in! [laughs] Anyway, I just left it – he was obviously, you know, making his point, so that I knew, even though we'd talked about it ages ago and he'd said that he didn't mind me going out, that actually, underneath it all, he did.   (Helen)

At first glance the quotes above appear to confirm what previous sociological studies have found: that marital relationships take precedence over friendship relationships, and husbands and children are married mothers' first and foremost concern. That these women appear to have few opportunities to behave spontaneously, for example, is captured quite nicely by Teresa, who claimed that her evenings out with friends had to be organised as if they were 'staging a bank robbery'. While this might seem an extreme analogy to make, the groundwork for a 'night out with the girls' had to be strategically planned well in advance of the proposed date. These women readily concede that they are simply not at liberty to just get up and go: 'it takes a lot of organising . . . and preparation . . . in terms of leaving meals ready and sorting out the kids, and checking that Steve *is* actually going to be home on time to take over'. Teresa has to quite literally 'put her house in order' before embarking on an evening out with friends, despite this event only occurring every 'once in a while'. By feeding and bathing the children before she goes out, and leaving Steve his supper on a tray, the household's established evening routine continues relatively smoothly, with husband and children suffering the minimum of disruption by her absence. Other women in this study were also careful to ensure that their social gatherings were orchestrated around husbands' timetables. By holding their 'get-togethers' in the home of whoever's husband was working away, they reduced potential tension to some extent, but did not remove it completely: 'I thought, *as I was on my own on a Friday night*, I'd get some beers in'.

It could be argued that these examples are indeed illustrative of the structural and cultural constraints married women face in the making and maintaining of friendships that were referred to in the introduction to this chapter. Certainly, if it is believed that married women's friendships take place in a culture where relationships with men and children are thought to be instrumental to women's happiness and well-being, and it is also assumed that marriage and motherhood are women's primary source of identity construction, then it is perhaps not surprising that these relationships have been overlooked in the past and afforded a somewhat secondary status in the literature. This could also go some way to explaining why those studies that have been conducted tend to conclude that married women's friendships with each other reflect and reinforce a system of patriarchy where the primacy of marriage and a commitment to heterosexual couple-based ideology is a powerful method of social control (see O'Connor, 1992). Certainly, friends have been viewed very much as the 'poor relation', which until fairly recently was echoed in much of the sociological literature where female friendships were considered the poor relation*ship*.

It will be argued in this chapter, however, that this position needs re-examining. For instance, if we turn again to the quotes that opened this section, one might initially interpret these expressions of familial obligation as confirming the power and prevalence of society's cultural norms where both the bulk of domestic work and the caring for young children are primarily the responsibilities of wives and mothers. Significantly, however, it is not the women who are expressing these concerns, but is what they are reporting their husbands say and feel. Wives were left in no doubt as to what their husbands thought about them socialising with friends in 'family time'. In spite of advance warning being given, their response to news of a forthcoming night out was often less than enthusiastic. Even when grudging permission had been given, subtle pressures were still exerted by 'playing the blackmail card', or as Helen's husband made clear rather less subtly by 'making his point, so that I knew, even though we'd talked about it ages ago and he'd said that he didn't mind me going out, that actually, underneath it all, he did'.

What is being suggested here is that it could be husbands who are hanging on grimly to the assumption that marriage always take precedence over friendship (for arguably it is in their best interests that these societal norms are reproduced), but there is little evidence to support the claim that these notions are reciprocally held by their wives. For example, when husbands behaved ungraciously, exhibiting, as Clare described above, a certain amount of reluctance in putting their fretful child to bed single-handedly, retaliation was swift. Clare deals with her peevish partner by 'dropping him in it', helpfully suggesting John reads his daughter 'a nice long story'. Significant here is that while her account starts off in good humour – shifting halfway through to express mild irritation with her husband – it ends by reflecting on what she perceives as transparent unfairness in the practice of parenting. What begins as an amusing anecdote comes to an uncomfortable conclusion when she observes: 'had [it] been the other way around – if it had been John who was the one going out – well, he wouldn't have had a child clinging limpet-like to his leg. You know, I wouldn't have made it so difficult for *him* to leave the house.' Daily experiences like this raise questions of marital equity and fairness, but also throw into sharp relief the notion that parenthood is a joint project and marriage a 'negotiated partnership'. These issues will be returned to in the final section.

It is worth pointing out, however, that, while exasperation with their husbands' petulant behaviour might have been these women's first reaction, the overriding feeling was one of amusement. At their husbands' expense, the thwarted attempts to delay their departures were shared with their friends once they all met. Indeed, the quotes above from Helen and Clare came from a social evening at a third friend's house, where one of the rituals of the evening was to begin by swapping stories of how they had all 'managed to escape' – echoing Teresa's 'bank robbery' metaphor that opened this discussion. By laughing with their friends about their husbands' unreasonable demands, and discussing together the constraints they experienced in both marriage and motherhood, the women were in many ways expressing solidarity. Although they shared a number of practical difficulties when it came to leaving the domestic arena, they quite deliberately secured their own personal and emotional space to ensure they had time to spend with friends. This gave them plenty of opportunity to 'do intimacy', which required acts of disclosure, expressions of private thoughts and feelings, and the sharing of common experiences.

Nevertheless, at a number of levels these women recognised that to avoid conflict it was probably a lot easier to fulfil certain 'prerequisites' before going out. Ensuring that their departure was as hassle-free as possible was done in the spirit of appeasement, for skilful diplomacy was needed to legitimise any leisure time spent socialising with friends. This is a complicated issue, for, while the women in this study were beginning to question the gendered division of domestic tasks, child care, and the emotional labour of 'marriage work', they were also unable to resist embroidering their accounts to one another in ways that emphasised the amount of work they had to do before they left the home. Friends, after all, would always appreciate the felt obligations of housework and family life, even if husbands did not. In this way, fulfilling the socially prescribed tasks of wives and mothers performed two functions. By their demonstration of proficiency in 'domestic juggling', it was difficult for husbands to object to wives going out, for, with 'a lot of organising . . . and preparation', all the tasks were done. Most importantly, though, their identities as housewives and primary carers could be validated by their female friends, who understood the worth and work of these roles, even if they went unrecognised and unrewarded by family members in particular and the wider culture more generally. Consequently, should husbands play 'the blackmail card', wives felt justified in following with their trump: contributing so much time and effort to the tasks and jobs around the home, whilst working – and being paid – outside the home, meant they had quite literally earned their time out with their friends. The significance of this sense of entitlement will be returned to below.

The picture here, then, is that while husbands may have thought that they took priority over their wives' friends (and certainly wives did little to persuade them otherwise) this was not always the case. Indeed, partners were not so much prioritised as mollified. On returning home in high spirits from a night out with friends, one of the 'costs' (from the wives' point of view) and 'rewards' (from the husbands') was that sex was more of a viable proposition. Take, for example, Helen's comment towards the close of the evening referred to above, when she said: 'Let's be honest, the only time I ever fancy doing it these days is when I've had a bottle of red wine down my neck!' While this remark was made in jest, it was met with howls of laughter and prompted further revelations. Using humour to gauge friends' responses to serious and personal issues (in this case the frequency of marital sex) was an acceptable way of introducing sensitive topics which could then be discussed more fully or – had the reaction been stony silence rather than knowing laughter – dismissed as 'just a joke'. The power of humour, as has been demonstrated elsewhere, is that 'it allows the unspeakable to enter the discourse' (Crawford, 1995, p. 152).

As women like Clare, Helen, and Teresa will show, it is by interacting with friends – laughing, joking, teasing, talking through problems, sharing news and gossip, expressing beliefs and values using everyday language – that women reflect together on their current positions, construct and create new 'ways of being' and imagine how life could be if things were different. Although the extent to which any long-term difference can be maintained is fairly limited, given the social and cultural context of their marriages, in a number of small, almost unobtrusive ways, strategies of resistance are embarked upon that help undermine dominant discourses of male hegemony, and validate and support women's close relationships with each other. Women do this, as we have seen, with the help of their friends. For having established the principle of evenings out with 'the girls' – perhaps originally inspired by celebrating a friend's birthday or house-move – they quickly gathered a momentum of their own, becoming routine practice, organised 'just for fun' and because 'it had been a few weeks since the last get-together'. In the same way Marks (this volume) demonstrated the inclusive style of women's group friendships in the Hawthorne study, part of the fulfilment of friendship for the women here was in the gathering itself. Unlike the 'Hawthorne women', however, these women also experienced 'exclusive intimacy' with individual friends, by constructing relationships that were special or unique. Similarly, as Oliker (1989, p. 152) notes, 'Women established bonds of best friendship by a mutual self-disclosure and empathy that most found unparalleled even in marriage.' In having inclusive group friendships, and exclusive individual friends, the women in this study were fortunate indeed. The following section will examine the place of friendship in these married women's lives further, focusing in particular on the role friends play in the construction of identity.

The place of friendship in married women's lives

One of the observations made about adult friendships is that for both sexes 'somebody to talk to and confide in' is almost an established principle if not an anticipated outcome of the relationship (Rawlins, 1992, p. 2). For the women in this study, the lived experience of emotional support given to

friends in the form of having 'time and space to really talk' was fundamental to their friendship relationships. Almost without exception, these
women expressed the opinion that friends were people who were 'there for
you' in times of need. This was considered to be not so much a felt obligation of friendship, but more a reciprocal fact. The sentiment 'I hope I give
her back a fraction of what she gives to me' echoed through many of the
answers to the question 'what does friendship mean to you?'; and, while
women give emotional support to their friends on a regular basis, it is
during times of personal crisis that their solidarity is depended on. One
woman voiced her sense of indebtedness to her friends as follows:

> There were times when I thought I was going mad. I was desolate. All I
> could think about was how empty my life was now that he wasn't in it.
> Some days I thought I would die of sadness. Without the support and
> patience of my dear and loving long-suffering friends, I could never have
> got through it. They listened to the same stuff for days on end, putting up
> with long telephone calls in the middle of the night, and – against their
> advice – a humiliating attempt at a reconciliation. When the worst of it
> was over, they hung on in there, remaining constant and steadfast and
> true. They have seen me at my lowest ebb – they know all of my weak-
> nesses and insecurities – and yet in a funny way, this doesn't make me feel
> feeble or foolish. I'd say the reverse – it is my friends who have made me
> strong. (Archive: C3516)

Clearly, while talking and listening can be seen as collaborative 'friendship work', it is not the only thing that is accomplished when friends talk
together. It could be argued in the quote above that listening 'to the same
stuff for days on end' is indicative of friends helping to reinterpret past
events, and offer their counsel. That the reconciliation was 'against their
advice' implies there was some amount of consultation and debate before
the unsuccessful attempt was made, confirming that friends do not always
approve of and condone each other's behaviour. They do however, usually
understand the *motivations* for the behaviour, for, as Orbach and
Eichenbaum (1994) have commented, in commiseration there is identification. While this could very well reinforce feelings of inadequacy – or indeed
as O'Connor suggests in this volume – reduces women's friendships to
'simply a kind of shared victimisation' (p. 122), it could also be interpreted
rather more positively. Hite (1987, 1991), for example, has argued that, in
discussing with friends what range of possible options there are to various
problems in their personal lives,

> women are in fact dealing with philosophical dilemmas central to our
> social culture . . . In other words, these conversations are an important way
> in which women compare their own value system with the dominant
> culture's ideas of who they are and what is going on. (Hite, 1991, p. 722)

Analysing events, reflecting on incidents, making sense of subtle injustices and challenging interpretations – all of these occur in women's conversations and are worked through with their friends. Support given through talking and listening, which can lead to differing and, occasionally, contradictory positions being taken through discussion and debate, helps to challenge beliefs and values and interrogate collective identities. Sharing experiences, making connections, thinking through what may or may not be appropriate responses – this is how women with their friends establish codes of behaviour and accept different 'ways of being' that affirm on some occasions and resist in others socially sanctioned norms of identity as wives and mothers. This 'identity work', like 'emotion work', is one of the achievements of women's talk. It is suggested here that these everyday interactions with the people you call friends not only reinforce the image you present of yourself, but help assemble multiple images of 'self'.

Theorists of identity have suggested that an individual's social identity depends largely on mutual recognition, combined with self-validation of this recognition (Kellner, 1992). In this way, conceptualisations of identity are usually about belonging to, and identifying with, a cause, a group, a community, a family, an organisation, an association, or a union. The list could go on, but being included as a member implies by definition that those who are not members are recognised as different. Somehow they do not belong or 'qualify' with the insiders and are therefore excluded from the group, becoming outsiders. The division becomes one of difference – to put it crudely, into the categories of 'us' and 'them'. It can be useful to think of identity as being marked out through the use of symbols. There is an association between the things a person uses, the things a person does, and the image presented of their personal and collective identities (Woodward, 1997). For example, in a number of ways the women interviewed in this study demonstrated their consumption choices and lifestyle practices, which was reflected in their dress, behaviour, and choice of home furnishings. Wearing clothes from Principles, buying food from Waitrose, and decorating their homes with prints, rugs, and lamp shades from Ikea are all symbols of middle-class status, and demonstrate the kinds of things they value. Similarly, writers to the archive listed listening to Radio 4, reading novels by Dickens and Austen, playing classical music, and going to the theatre and ballet as some of the activities that gave them pleasure (Directive No. 42, spring 1995). Again, these choices are significant in that they indicate membership of a particular socio-economic class.

While a person's structural location in terms of class, occupation, status, and income helps to place individuals in specific socio-economic groups, it is how they perform in their various circumscribed set of roles – and how these performances are recognised by others – that is important. However, while there are still recognisable customs and conventions surrounding various roles (for example, being a student, a teacher, a mother, a wife, etc.), it is argued that there are more possibilities available and increasing choices to be made in modernity over – as Giddens (1991) puts it, the 'what to do, how to act, who to be' question. This can be problematic, for as Kellner observes,

> The modern self is aware of the constructed nature of identity and that one can always change and modify one's identity at will . . . One's identity may become out of date, or superfluous, or no longer socially validated . . . [or] One is tired of one's life, of who one has become. One is trapped in a web of social roles, expectations and relations. There appears to be no exit and no possibility of change. Or, one is caught up in so many different, sometimes conflicting roles that one no longer knows who one is.
>
> (Kellner, 1992, pp. 142–3)

Clearly then, while some aspects of identity are relatively fixed (I am white, I am a woman, I am heterosexual), other aspects are more fluid, open to change and reinterpretation as time goes by. As one of the writers to the archive comments,

> I am not the same person I was at twenty-two when I married. I expect I shall change even more between now (thirty-three) and, say, fifty-five. Yet I am expected to stay with the same man, who is also changing continually. Not only are we expected to stay together, we are expected to remain faithful. (Archive: D1526)

Here then, is a good example of how this woman experiences tension between the social and cultural expectations that marriages should last, and her own awareness that both she and her partner are 'changing continually'. Recognising that they will not be the same people they were when they were first married raises some concerns about the longevity of the relationship, especially when fidelity appears to be one of the conditions.

It has been persuasively argued elsewhere (albeit in another context) that 'One needs the power to imagine and rework both a self and a future; it requires time, aspiration, resources, ambition, energy and confidence' (Hey, 1997, p. 144). Clearly, while these resources are not distributed equally amongst the population at large, the socio-economic group represented by the women here might be said to enjoy a high proportion of these assets. Certainly as the extracts below make clear, with friends they believed they could 'be authentic', find and create new identities, and present a number of alternative aspects of self. While the more discriminating cultural theorists may criticise my reluctance to distinguish between an authentic self and multiple selves, for the women in this study these terms were interchangeable, and holding both positions was not a contradiction:

> Sometimes I think, wouldn't it be nice to go away for a weekend or something . . . you know, I'd like to go off and just be me again, instead of being the children's Mum and John's wife . . . and just go off and be Clare again. I suppose I miss being Clare. And to a certain extent that's what is so special about my friend Jen that I was telling you about, because with her then I am Clare . . . because there, with her, I'm primarily Clare, and then I'm the mother of two children and John's wife second.   (Clare)

> I've been thinking about what you asked about friendship, and really what we're saying is that it's to be known, isn't it? To be really and truly known, for who and what you are – what you really and truly are. It's like those awful 'love is' cartoons [laughs] like, friendship is not having to finish off sentences. So, you're sat with someone, and a word will come up that you both laugh at, or you both know, and so much is going on up here [taps forehead] that you don't always have to verbalise it. And that connection is friendship. You don't have to waste a lot of time explaining things. Because with your friends, you just are.   (Maggie)

> With my husband, I feel I have to tread carefully, as he construes some things as criticism of himself. He doesn't think others are worth talking about, and says so, so I tend to censor what I say – think first, plan a diplomatic way of putting things, i.e., not speak too impulsively. The point is, with friends, all that doesn't matter. With friends, it is much easier to relax and let the 'true self' show.   (Archive: D2360)

> Sometimes I can be more honest about certain issues with my friends. Friends are hugely important because we all have so many different 'sides' to us, and they all need an airing from time to time!   (Archive: D2239)

> So, for me, it's not just all the nice things I've been telling you about Sue that make her special, it's about being really safe with her – being comfortable enough with Sue to really let my hair down. With Sue I can get drunk, you know, say outrageous things, show off – make a complete fool of myself [laughs] but that would be all right. You know, with her, that would be completely all right, and just a laugh. But I don't do that with other people. With some of the people I know, well, you just can't let anything slip, can you? You have to behave yourself, and that's not always . . . well, it doesn't make for a very relaxing evening. I mean, it can be pleasant enough, chatting about house prices and mortgages and what school your kids are going to go to next, but it's not a lot of laughs. Do you know what I'm saying?   (Hannah)

This selection of quotes drawn from the interview transcripts and the archive demonstrates quite convincingly that it was with their friends that these women could 'really let [their] hair down' and 'let the "true self" show'. Clare and Maggie both reveal similar sentiments around the stepping out of ascribed roles: 'To be . . . known, for . . . what you really and truly are', and 'with her, I'm primarily Clare', which is in marked contrast to Hannah's later observation that there are some social occasions where this just cannot happen. Keeping up appearances and not being able to 'let anything slip' with some friends implies that a performance is being acted out, and reflects the tension between being open and honest and the potential risks involved in exposing the self and revealing vulnerabilities, especially if the behaviour does not match the role expectations. At the same time, acknowledging that 'we all have so many different "sides" to us, and they all need an airing from time to time' suggests that the side we choose to reveal not only depends upon who we choose to reveal it to, but that it is perhaps not always feasible to have only one side playing.

One of the aims of this chapter is to illustrate how with friends more than one side is seen. When Maggie says, 'And that connection is friendship', it is intimacy she is referring to. In the company of their friends, women feel comfortable enough ('it's about being really safe with her') to admit that there are conflicting emotions surrounding their various roles and responsibilities. With friends it is acknowledged that not liking your children does not make you a bad mother; complaining about your husband does not mean that your marriage is a complete sham; disapproval of a friend's behaviour does not necessarily end the friendship or stop you being supportive. They are able to do this by sharing the news of their daily events and happenings with their friends. As will be demonstrated below, when women friends meet they talk, and telling the stories of their daily lives, swapping experiences, both positive and negative, is what their friendships are all about (Coates, 1997). Furthermore, while talking and listening are important skills and significant elements of women's friendships, it will be shown that talking with husbands is a very different activity from talking with friends.

'Can we talk?' Speaking freely with friends and husbands

Bryan doesn't have the faintest interest in knowing who said what to who . . . and it's not that I wouldn't talk to him . . . it's just that I'd tell him, but not in as much detail. And his response – well! He just wouldn't have the same enthusiasm for my conversation. It would bore the socks off him! Whereas another woman . . . well, they'd be just as keen to hear as you would be to tell, if not more so. And that's the difference.   (Mary)

There's lots of things he wouldn't really be very interested in – I mean, mundane stuff – so when I get the chance to talk to him, I give him the condensed version. You know – edited, so he doesn't have to listen to me rabbiting on for more than a few minutes! Friends, of course, are different. They want the complete and unabridged edition!   (Clare)

I can see that . . . that husbands are perhaps more available than past generations of husbands might have been . . . But I know for a fact that I do tend to talk more to my girlfriends than my husband, because he wouldn't have the patience to listen to my chitter-chatter. Let's face it, men are *far* too busy to talk – women never are!   (Jenny)

When I need to talk and offload my emotions, I will usually turn to my female friends – ditto the silly trivia that I need to talk about – which would, over a period of time, drive my husband absolutely mad!
                                                        (Archive: K2373)

Well, my friend Rose is very intuitive. I could be telling the exact same story to my husband and he just wouldn't get it, you know? I mean, he would completely miss the point! But Rose would understand – I'd get a much better response from her. She'd give me good, considered advice. And I know that she would be really listening to me, and not just pretending to be listening from behind a newspaper!   (Helen)

What has been termed 'the gender asymmetry in emotional expression' (Duncombe and Marsden, 1993, p. 229) is captured by Stacey Oliker, who observed somewhat dryly that 'Wives talk to husbands, of course . . . however, husbands are not always pleased to do so, whereas friends usually are' (1989, p. 36). Similarly, fundamental differences between talking to friends and talking to husbands are made explicit in the extracts above. Realising it was politic to keep the news of their day 'edited' so as not to 'bore the socks off him', suggests that the women in this study were well aware that whatever they had to communicate to husbands was unlikely to precipitate an animated exchange. In direct contrast to this, however, it was felt that 'Friends, of course, are different.' Clearly, having the time to talk is closely related to the importance attached to the topic under discussion. Not registering 'the faintest interest', feigning slight 'enthusiasm', and having precious little 'patience' for wives' conversations all show how husbands made themselves unavailable and inaccessible in a way that female friends found incomprehensible. Furthermore, friends are always fascinated by specifics: they 'want the complete and unabridged edition' of a story, not simply the quicker (and far less interesting) 'condensed version'. While husbands are kept informed 'but not in as much detail', friends are presented with all the particulars, for it is firmly believed that friends would be 'just as keen to hear as you would be to tell'. In this way, as has been argued elsewhere, it becomes clear that in sharing the details women are in fact 'sharing themselves' (Wood, 1996, p. 155).

By keeping these details down to a minimum with husbands, and being careful not to '[rabbit] on for more than a few minutes', women demonstrate that the style and nature of marital communication is qualitatively different when compared with that of friends. Tailoring the commentary to suit the audience's attention span connects two interrelated beliefs: men have less time 'to spare' than women, and men have much better things to do than talk. One of the consequences of accepting the notion that 'men are *far* too busy to talk' is that most of the topics women would like to discuss at length are then regarded as 'silly trivia' and 'mundane stuff'. By limiting the time there is to talk, and effectively vetoing discomfiting topics, husbands are successfully imposing their definition of what subjects they consider specifically worth responding to. By complying with this – and describing, as we saw Jenny do above, that much of the news she wants to share is merely 'chitter-chatter' – wives perpetuate the stereotype of women's talk being meaningless and unimportant. However, when Helen tells 'the exact same story . . . and [her husband] just [doesn't] get it', it would suggest that the issues being discussed are recognised as highly important by female friends. Indeed, when wives admit that they would 'get a much better response' from friends, they pay tribute to one of the distinctive values of female friendship – undivided attention. Friends 'understand . . . give . . . good, considered advice' and would never 'just [pretend] to be listening from behind a newspaper'.

While Coates (1997) thinks of women's talk as action – a way of 'doing' friendship – and Gouldner and Symons Strong (1987) regard one of the main functions of 'woman talk' as play or entertainment, talk has also been conceptualised as 'the work women do' (Fishman, 1978, p. 397). Thinking of talk as a form of emotional labour is useful in the context of marriage, where it can be demonstrated that wives have 'more responsibility than husbands for monitoring the relationship, confronting disagreeable issues, setting the tone of conversation and moving toward resolution when conflict is high' (Thompson and Walker, 1989, p. 849). Outside marriage, too, women encourage couple-friendships and foster active, joint social lives: 'I have a wide circle of friends, and my husband gets on well with most of them. Probably all of "our" friends are basically "my" friends' (Archive: R2399). Commentators have warned of the potential difficulties this can have for married men: 'Depending on his wife to fulfil his needs for intimate friendship and to co-ordinate their other social contacts, the husband may resent her attention to her own friendships outside of the marriage' (Rawlins, 1992, p. 173). Signs of this can be seen in the following extract from one of the letters to the archive:

> Being married is restrictive in regard to other relationships. My husband gets very jealous of my closeness with my own family, and in particular the friendship I have with my sister and the attention I give to my children. He also resents it if I go out without him. He always prefers me to be home early, and if I am out later than he thinks I should be, tends to sulk!
>
> (Archive: C1356)

This of course, resonates with the segments from Clare, Teresa, and Helen that opened this chapter. It would seem that in a number of ways husbands found it difficult to object openly to wives going out, especially when they had successfully relegated talking 'about emotional things' to the province of friendship, and dismissed idle 'chitter-chatter' as an activity they did not have time for. However, resorting to silent reproaches and sulking tactics might not have been solely about registering disapproval. In ways they could only begin to hazard a guess at, husbands were realising that somehow they were 'missing the point completely'.

Nevertheless, women's sense of entitlement (to having fun, to seeing friends) was a mobilising force of friendship, overriding any qualms they may have felt about socialising without their partners present. Moreover, as talk was a central feature of their friendships (Aries and Johnson, 1983), and as husbands did not appear to be terribly keen to talk, it should come as no surprise to find women reporting somewhat bitterly, 'My friends know more about what's going on in my life than my husband does' (Helen). The point being made here is that, if talking and sociability are closely correlated, and if the criteria for being a good friend include properties that men are deemed to have in short supply, then, while wives may well wish that their husbands were their best friends, it is often their female friends who fit these requirements best (Oliker, 1989). Although husbands recognise how important close friends are for their wives, perhaps even in some instances feeling threatened by these intimate relationships, they nevertheless seem unwilling or unable to break the mould of 'inexpressive male', even when direct appeals are made:

> I sat beside him in the car, tears rolling down my face, and told him that I felt he just wasn't there for me, and that I needed his support. He said, 'What do you mean support? I'm giving you a lift in to work, aren't I?'
>
> (Teresa)

Such a practical demonstration of concern from her husband in the form of a 'lift in to work' was perhaps not, in this instance, what Teresa was looking for. Later, as she struggles to come to terms with what she feels was a pretty inadequate response, she exhibits a certain amount of loyalty to the image of coupledom by remarking:

It's difficult to explain it. Don't get me wrong, we've got what I would call a good marriage. I just don't really know for sure how much unhappiness in my life is down to Steve . . . But I do know what little happiness is generated by being with him. (Teresa)

Describing her marriage as still 'good', whilst simultaneously recognising that 'little happiness is generated by being with him', seems like a hopeless situation and blatant contradiction. And yet this pattern was not uncommon. Many of the women reported that their husbands and partners were frequently uncommunicative and emotionally absent. Interestingly, though, they were reluctant to allocate personal blame for this, speculating instead with their friends that 'He does his best – it's just the way he is', or, 'He can't help it, can he? Let's face it, all men [in other words, all husbands] are the same, aren't they?' Taking this basically essentialist stance – that men behave in particular ways because they are men – was an understandable option. How else could they explain the impasse they found themselves in? On the one hand, the women in this study recognised that they were responsible for maintaining the emotional balance and sustaining happiness in their personal relationships (Cancian and Gordon, 1988). On the other hand, they were only too aware of the reciprocal model of marriage and the companionate, egalitarian ideal. Drawing on these two competing discourses was problematic, for simultaneously there was an appreciation that they were often dismayed with the tenor of their emotional relationship with their husbands, when they were presenting the image of – and living with the ideal of – a husband who was also a best friend. In this way, there was a certain amount of solace gleaned from sharing the belief that other marriages were similar in style and structure to your own, and – as 'men are all the same' – then your husband was likely to be no worse (and no better) than anyone else's.

Practical demonstrations of care and affection – like Steve taking Teresa to work in the example above – illustrate the instrumental roles and tasks with which men seem rather more comfortable than the expressive, nurturant demonstrations of feeling that some women are looking for. While researchers have warned of the danger in conflating 'expressing care' with 'expressing care in a particular way', arguing that, 'if feminized forms of intimacy are the only ones counted, is it any surprise that men are found to be less intimate than women?' (Wood, 1993, p. 43), such theoretical distinction holds little appeal for the women in this study. They operationalised their own measures for assessing the quality of their relationships – using what has been described as a 'feminine rule' (Cancian, 1987, p. 74) – and, as the sharing of everything they do and everything they feel has long been an expectation and function of female friendships, applied this principle to marriage too.

How successful this has been is of some consequence for understanding the way female friendships are managed in the context of middle-class marriage. As such, the 'best friends' and 'equal partners' model of companionate and egalitarian marriage (as exhibited by the women here) is worth discussing in more detail. Throughout this chapter the focus has been on the importance of friends and the significance of friendship for a specific group of married, middle-class women. Now, however, let us briefly examine the nature of marriage and its role in shaping friendships, by analysing the following bleak portrayals of marital love:

> I suppose we have a working relationship or modus vivendi which suits us, even if it is unorthodox or different – whether it's love, I don't know. In my heart of hearts I know I married James because I was scared of being left on the shelf. It isn't the idealised marriage I dreamed of, and I've lost out on much that I've wanted.   (Archive: D1673)

> Although I have never felt that I fell in love with my husband, the quality of our love has sustained us through many difficulties, so I feel that what it may lack in passion and romance, it gains in endurance and mutual support.   (Archive: H1651)

> I still wonder why I married my husband. He has never fired me the way some other men have. He gives me stability and security, but I can never quite admit that I love him.   (Archive: D1526)

> Over the years, we reached calmer waters. We know where we stand. We thrashed out all the rows years ago . . . I believe we're approaching the nature of 'true love' – defined as having a deep concern for the happiness of another without thought for oneself. True love sees how pathetic we all are; compassionate, it can be relied upon . . . A long-term relationship is simply an agreement to put up with each other. If you find you're still friends, so much the better!   (Archive: M2251)

> I have been married for seventeen years, and by now it really is just a matter of established custom and practice. Too many repetitions of the same disappointments have worn away the original relationship.
>   (Archive: R1897)

Feeling love for another, and being 'in love' with another are not synonymous or interchangeable terms (Berscheid and Meyers, 1996). The women make this distinction clear in the extracts above, where qualities like 'endurance and mutual support' and 'stability and security' are predominant. By saying they had a 'deep concern for the happiness of another' and describing their love as something that 'can be relied upon', headier emotions of passion and lust, desire and need are conspicuous by their absence. These elements do not seem to be present in – or at least are not used to describe – their marriages. Arguably, what haunts these letters and unites them all is the air of resignation that seeps through: 'it really is just a matter of established custom and practice'. They have come to terms with the fact that their marriages are a 'working relationship or modus vivendi'. Having 'thrashed out all the rows years ago' – perhaps even feeling they have 'lost out on much that [was] wanted' – they have reached a level of understanding that holds marital success to consist of more than ever-lasting romantic love. In this way, the thesis that couples will remain in partnerships for as long as each member finds them emotionally and sexu-ally fulfilling (Giddens, 1992) is directly challenged. Rewards that come from marriage – economic stability, being joint home-owners, having chil-dren together, sharing mutual family friends – raise the stakes higher, making the investments in marriage far outweigh any despondency over emotional returns.

It is not possible here to explore adequately the changing nature of marital love. Evidence from elsewhere in this study (though not fully quoted here) suggests that most of the direct confrontations and habitual complaints women raised were based around notions of unfairness in the allocation of tasks around the home:

> We had a huge argument this afternoon. Monumental. All about domes-tic stuff, as usual. It's the same thing every time. He thinks he does his fair share, and I'm being totally unreasonable to expect more of him . . . he says that my standards are just too high, and the amount of housework I feel needs doing is just over the top . . . and that neither do I understand the pressure he's under at work. And I think, yes, he's probably right. I don't understand the pressure he's under at work. But you can feel under pressure and still put a plate in the dishwasher, for God's sake!
>
> (Hannah)

It is difficult to speculate how much resentment caused by a partner's reluctance to participate around the home can be directly linked with marital disenchantment. I would suggest, though, that both direct and indirect refusal to take on board some measure of shared responsibility in the home, sustained over a length of time, will almost inevitably lead to an increased irritation with the person one is meant to be having a loving and sharing relationship with. Mansfield and Collard found in their British study of sixty newlyweds that wives conceded that their husbands' role of 'breadwinner' was the explanation for their lack of participation in domestic tasks. What they expressed most disappointment with was that their relationships were emotionally unsatisfying. The women wanted 'a common life with an empathic partner . . . a close exchange of intimacy which would make them feel valued as a person and not just a wife' (Mansfield and Collard, 1988, p. 179). That they experienced blatant inequality in the domestic division of labour was annoying, and potentially the root cause of many disagreements, but not their main concern. What they really wanted their husbands to do was show some appreciation and regard for them, to listen to and talk to them, and spend time with them. This remains the same sentiment, whether you are newly wed, as Mansfield and Collard's sample were, or have been married for fifteen years or so, as the women in this study were:

> He often has to work late and doesn't get in 'til late, you know, long past the time the boys are in bed. And just sometimes I'd like him to say he's sorry about that. I mean, I don't want him to miss a deadline, or be ill prepared for a client or whatever, you know I do realise that he can't just say 'Sod it! I'm going home!' But he could phone me and tell me he'd much rather be at home with me and the kids all eating supper together . . . he could say that he misses me and he misses the boys, and that he thinks I'm brilliant for holding it all together at home. But he never says that kind of thing – I suppose he would say that it goes without saying. But it doesn't really. I mean, you're left with a sinking feeling that maybe he doesn't mind staying on late at work that much after all. Because that way he can avoid all the things he'd much rather not do. Like help with the housework, and talk to me.   (Susan)

The problem of struggling to match the reality of life with a husband whose work schedule dominated to such an extent sits somewhat uncomfortably with promoting the ideal of an equal, sharing, close marital relationship. In the above quote, for instance, Susan might find it difficult to sustain the image of a husband sharing much of her life when he was physically absent from it for most of the time.

The single most important point that is being made in this section is that, for most of the women in this study, it was not their husbands who fulfilled their emotional needs. Expressed differently, and stretching this point further, it has been demonstrated throughout this chapter in a variety of ways that it was certainly not their female friendships that were unsupportive, hollow, and riddled with disappointments. Consequently, given the cultural context of rising divorce, growing single parenthood, and the pessimism surrounding longevity of marriage, for this particular set of women it made sense to invest what resources they had in developing a number of close, personal relationships outside marriage. This is one of the explanations for why their female friendships were important on an individual level, and socially significant on a wider scale.

Conclusion

When friends share essentially similar social positions, hold corresponding beliefs and values, and have broadly equivalent backgrounds, conventional sociological wisdom holds that their friendship patterns will reflect and reinforce existing social and sexual divisions rather than undermine them (Hess, 1972; Jerrome, 1984; Allan, 1996). It has been argued throughout this chapter, however, that, for this particular group of middle-class, affluent women, these distinctions were not so clear cut. Whilst acknowledging that these married women did encounter a number of barriers to the construction of personal relationships outside the domestic sphere, it was established that their close female friendships were *not* socially difficult to maintain. Working full- or part-time, having a wide range of friends and interests outside the home, and the frequent expression of feminist beliefs concerning women's equality suggested they enjoyed a degree of power and control that was consonant with the notion of 'equal partnership', but incompatible with 'traditional' marital roles. Certainly, this sense of entitlement – to having fun, to making choices, to expressing opinions – was strongly articulated when they were with their friends, and allowed these women a degree of validation and self-esteem that was often difficult to find elsewhere.

By focusing on the friendship patterns of a specific group of individuals, this chapter – and the study it is based on – has questioned societal and cultural assumptions about married women's friendships and challenged the description of these relationships as secondary and unimportant. While it was accepted that the 'strategies of resistance' employed by these women could hardly transform the patriarchal structure within which they lived, these women were shown to be capable of constructing and developing their friendships – both individually with close intimates and collectively with larger groups – because they had the time, energy, space, and material resources to do so. Furthermore, a number of distinctive features around the style and practices of middle-class friendships were highlighted: the importance of individual friends in terms of emotional support and identity construction was one; that larger group friendships were significant sites of pleasure, recreation, and fun was another. Perhaps most importantly, though, it was demonstrated that talking with friends was qualitatively different from talking with husbands. The failure of husbands to communicate in ways the women in this study valued compounded their dissatisfaction with other aspects of their marital lives and accentuated the significance of their close female friends.

The purpose of this chapter, then, has been to turn from a theoretical discussion of the context of friendship to an exploration of the practice of friendship in context. By illustrating the contexts in which these married women's friendships developed it has been possible to show how these contexts influence the form these friendships take. In examining a specific socio-economic group, the aim has not been to make generalisations about the population as a whole. However, it could be suggested that the organisation of these friendship ties, the level of commitment these women have to their friends, and the significant role they play in their lives reflect not only wider social change but question too our understandings of contemporary marriage and coupledom in Britain today.

Notes

1. The Mass-Observation project was initiated in 1937 and conceived of as a 'people's anthropology' of life in Britain before and after World War II. Men and women were recruited as volunteers to write social commentaries about events they observed around them in their communities, and record aspects of their own daily lives. This phase lasted until 1950. Since its revival in 1981, the archive has been sending out three directives a year containing up to three themes in different sections. The Mass-Observers can then decide which topics they want to tackle – some indeed address them all – and these responses are all filed in alphanumeric sequence. The archivist, Dorothy Sheridan, designs the directives based on ideas from outside researchers or suggestions from the correspondents themselves. Past topics have included holidays, growing old, shopping, the royal family, and menstruation, to name but a few, and occasionally the archive requests special 'one-day' diaries for specific days.

   Directive No. 32 on 'Close Relationships' was sent to the M-O panel in the summer of 1990. The extract that follows (taken from the directive's introductory preamble) illustrates how the archive gathers its rich and fascinating material:

   > This directive . . . focuses specifically on close adult relationships. You may feel that this is a subject which is too intimate to write about . . . If you do feel uncomfortable about answering, please tell us. I do want to stress, however, that your replies remain anonymous. In any case, it is always up to you how much you wish to say. You can if you wish confine your reply to your opinions rather than your experiences, but as we have often said before, it is personal experience and insight which have a way of bringing your directives to life. The franker you can be, the more valuable your contribution. This is what makes our project so unique.

   With the emphasis on joint collaboration, the promise of confidentiality, and the tactful way the archivist acknowledges that for some people this may be a delicate topic to write about, the ground is laid for an almost confessional style of reply. The direct appeal to write about personal experiences and feelings encourages correspondents to be highly reflective, which makes the M-O records very different from any other form of letter or diary writing.

Directive No. 32 was of particular interest to me as some of the areas the panel were invited to respond to were similar to the research questions I was asking my respondents in the one-to-one interviews. Here are some of the more obvious links:

* If you are married, or in a close relationship with one other person, how do you feel it affects your other relationships?
* Are several close relationships compatible?
* Are there rewards to be experienced from friendships which are not available in marriage?
* What makes for a 'good' marriage?

Such direct questions prompted candid and heartfelt replies. This article, and the research it is based on, would not have been possible without the contributions of the Mass-Observers. Their voices are reproduced here, with the kind permission of the Trustees of the Mass-Observation Archive.

2. The names used in this chapter are all pseudonyms.

References

Allan, Graham (1989), *Friendship: Developing a Sociological Perspective*, Hemel Hempstead: Harvester-Wheatsheaf.

(1996), *Friendship and Kinship in Modern Britain*, Oxford University Press.

Aries, Elizabeth, and Johnson, Fern (1983), 'Close friendship in adulthood: conversational content between same-sex friends', *Sex Roles*, 9: 1183–96.

Baxter, Leslie A. (1987), 'Symbols of relationship identity in relationship cultures', *Journal of Social and Personal Relationships*, 4: 261–80.

Belenky, Mary, Clinchy, Blythe, Goldberger, Nancy, and Tarule, Jill (1986), *Women's Ways of Knowing*, New York: Basic Books.

Berscheid, Ellen, and Meyers, Sarah (1996), 'A social categorical approach to a question about love', *Personal Relationships*, 3: 19–43.

Cancian, Francesca (1987), *Love in America: Gender and Self-Development*, Cambridge University Press.

Cancian, Francesca, and Gordon, Steven (1988), 'Changing emotion norms in marriage: love and anger in US women's magazines since 1900', *Gender and Society*, 2: 308–42.

Coates, Jennifer (1997), *Women Talk: Conversation Between Women Friends*, Oxford: Blackwell.

Crawford, Mary (1995), *Talking Difference: On Gender and Language*, London: Sage.

Duncombe, Jean, and Marsden, Dennis (1993), 'Love and intimacy: the gender division of emotion and emotion work', *Sociology*, 27: 221–41.

Fishman, Pamela (1978), 'Interaction: the work women do', *Social Problems*, 25: 397–406.

Giddens, Anthony (1991), *Modernity and Self-Identity: Self and Society in the Late Modern Age*, Cambridge: Polity.

(1992), *The Transformation of Intimacy: Sexuality, Love, and Eroticism in Modern Societies*, Cambridge: Polity.

Gouldner, Helen, and Symons Strong, Mary (1987), *Speaking of Friendship: Middle-Class Women and Their Friends*, New York: Greenwood.

Green, Eileen, Hebron, Sandra, and Woodward, Diana (1990), *Women's Leisure, What Leisure?*, Basingstoke: Macmillan.

Hess, Beth (1972), 'Friendship', in Martha W. Riley, Marilyn Johnson, and Anne Foner (eds.), *Aging and Society*, vol. III, *A Sociology of Age Stratification*, New York: Russell Sage Foundation.

Hey, Valerie (1997), *The Company She Keeps: An Ethnography of Girls' Friendship*, Buckingham: Open University Press.

Hite, Shere (1987), *The Hite Report: Women and Love*, London: Penguin.

(1991), *The Hite Report on Love, Passion and Emotional Violence*, London: Macdonald Optima.

Jerrome, Dorothy (1984), 'Good company: the sociological implications of friendship', *Sociological Review*, 32: 696–718.

Kellner, Douglas (1992), 'Popular culture and the construction of postmodern identities', in Scott Lash and Jonathon Friedman (eds.), *Modernity and Identity*, Oxford: Blackwell.

Mansfield, Penny, and Collard, Jean (1988), *The Beginning of the Rest of Your Life?*, Basingstoke: Macmillan.

O'Connor, Pat (1992), *Friendships Between Women*, Hemel Hempstead: Harvester-Wheatsheaf.

Oliker, Stacey (1989), *Best Friends and Marriage: Exchange Among Women*, Berkeley: University of California Press.

Orbach, Susie, and Eichenbaum, Luise (1994), *Between Women: Love, Envy and Competition in Women's Friendships*, London: Arrow Books.

Pahl, Ray (1984), *Divisions of Labour*, Oxford: Blackwell.

Rawlins, William (1992), *Friendship Matters: Communication, Dialectics and the Life Course*, New York: Aldine de Gruyter.

Shaw, Jenny (1996), 'Surrealism, Mass-Observation and researching imagination', in E. Stena Lyon and Joan Busfield (eds.), *Methodological Imaginations*, Basingstoke: Macmillan.

Thompson, Linda, and Walker, Alexis J. (1989), 'Gender in families: women and men in marriage, work and parenthood', *Journal of Marriage and the Family*, 51: 845–71.

Wood, Julia (1993), 'Engendered relations: interaction, caring, power and responsibility in intimacy', in Steve Duck (ed.), *Social Context and Relationships*, London: Sage.

(ed.) (1996), *Gendered Relationships*, Mountain View, Calif.: Mayfield Publishing Company.

Woodward, Kathryn (ed.) (1997), *Identity and Difference*, London: Sage.

6

Women's friendships in a post-modern world

Pat O'Connor

Introduction

It has become almost a cliché to observe that we are living in a post-modern world – a world where identity, truth, and rationality are all equally problematic. The implications of this for personal relationships in general, and for women's friendships in particular, have tended to be ignored. Nevertheless, there have been suggestions that, where discourses are relativistic, where power at many levels is diffuse, and where women are becoming an important economic and political constituency, their friendships with each other could play an important part in shaping their identities.

This theme will be explored first in the context of a discussion of the attractiveness of friendship as a relational form. It will be argued that friendships in a post-modern world are attractive because they offer a definition of self which is very much under the control of the individual participants. In addition, women's friendships with other women potentially offer an alternative definition of identity – or at least one which enables women to critique the dominant definition of themselves as 'the Other'.

The second issue which the chapter takes up is the question of the variability of friendship as a relational form. It is argued that the preoccupation with intimate relationships obscures the importance of such relationships in maintaining the very real structures created by capitalism and patriarchy. Thus, it is suggested that it is unhelpful to dismiss the kind of inarticulate solidarity which sometimes characterises men's relationships, since it constitutes a kind of ego support, but one which is at the positional rather than the personal level. Such positional ego validation plays an important part in maintaining the structural and cultural *status quo*. It is suggested that the depiction of friendship as a residual social structure is essentially misleading and reflects a preoccupation with the private, and particularly with intimate confiding in friendship. Indeed, it is argued that cultural definitions of otherness are reflected in and reinforced by ideas about the kinds of similarities which are most important in friendship.

It is suggested that the social structure in a particular society at any one moment in time is reflected in the absence/presence of foci of activity within which relationships are embedded, and in the resources available to individuals to create or maintain such relationships. Women's position is interesting in so far as the very fluidity and cultural instability of friendship and the dominance of heterosexuality as an institution challenge the appropriateness of investing resources in them (although this type of perspective has been challenged by the women's movement). As has been widely noted (Smith-Rosenberg, 1975; Oliker, 1989), there is no cultural ideal of friendship between women, and the cultural and social space for women's friendships is limited. The boundaries between such relationships and lesbianism are much more permeable than heretofore – a phenomenon which Faderman (1987) suggested was not unrelated to women's increasing economic independence and the economic viability of a lifestyle not involving men. In this context, depicting women's close ties with each other as sexual, and stigmatising them, acts as a further cultural inhibitor of these relationships.

Paradoxically, then, although women's relationships with each other have enormous possibilities as regards self-validation, these are the very relationships which have been constructed in such a way as to be culturally problematic and socially difficult to maintain. These issues are explored in the final section of this chapter dealing with the process of creating and maintaining friendships.

The attractiveness of friendship as a relational form

Friendship in Western society is a voluntary relationship between peers. With marriage being less stable, and with the number of children falling, peer relationships potentially become increasingly important. Friendship offers a way of inventing and re-inventing the self in an authentic way throughout one's life. As such, it is potentially particularly important to women whose idea of themselves is typically rooted in social relationships. Wiseman (1986) has noted that, in contrast to marriage, friendship is a relationship which can be terminated by those involved, because it is not legally or societally regulated in any way. Its essence is typically interwoven with its continued existence. Within a post-modern world, in which there is increasing disenchantment with institutional structures which are seen as irrelevant, unrepresentative, and illegitimate, friendship relationships are attractive. Simmel (1971, p. 392) early on recognised the basic contradiction implicit in cultural life, viz., the idea that social forms make our life meaningful, and that yet these very forms 'in their rigidly individual shapes, in the demands of their imprescriptable rights', contradict 'the essence of life itself, with its weaving dynamics'. Friendships appear to avoid this dilemma. They are relationships which can be chosen and re-chosen throughout one's life in a way which allows for a high degree of self-definition. Parents and siblings are inherited. Husbands can be changed only so often. Lovers can be more numerous, but even today conventions about respectability arguably have some effect. Of course, as will be argued later, to some extent this open-endedness is an illusion, since it has been widely noted that friendships reflect and reinforce the stratified nature of the society, with friends typically being made with people from the same class, race, educational background, level of income, recreational interests, etc.

Yet, paradoxically, part of the attractiveness of friendship as a relational form lies in its ability to generate alternative definitions of self, ones which, particularly in the case of dyadic friendship, are peculiarly under the control of those involved. Within Western society, women have typically been viewed as 'the Other' (De Beauvoir, 1972 [1949]). Friendship is thus a particularly attractive form to women who are enmeshed within a patriarchal culture. In a world where knowledge is filtered through a male lens, it is impossible to know what it is to be a woman since a woman enters 'into a system of values that is not hers, and in which she can "appear" and circulate only when enveloped in the needs/desires/fantasies of others, namely men' (Irigaray, 1985, p. 134). As Irigaray sees it, in this situation, it is only when women are together that a new and different way of being is possible: 'In suffering but also in women's laughter. And again: in what they "dare" – do or say – when they are among themselves, in these places of women, among themselves, something of a speaking [as] woman is heard' (ibid., pp. 134–5).

Irigaray is not suggesting that interaction between women will be harmonious, but rather that it offers the possibility of defining a self which transcends the place accorded to it within a male language and culture. Indeed, these same ideas emerged in Jerrome's (1984) study of a group of elderly women who, when they were together, were able to escape from what they saw as one aspect of conventional femininity – the need to be acceptable to men. In the company of other women, they were able to be strong and enterprising, but also child-like and unconcerned with sexual attractiveness. By their very existence, they undermined the idea that women could find pleasure and identity only in their relationships with men. They created arenas where men became the objects – where they were present, but defined through women's eyes (Gullestad, 1984).

However, within a social and cultural context where heterosexual units are seen as 'natural' and desirable, where women remain the main care-givers (of children, elderly people in need, etc.), and where they remain partially or totally financially dependent on men, there is a constant ambivalence about challenging the centrality of men in their lives. Baker Miller (1988, p. 89) suggested that in Western society the only forms of connection that have been available to women are 'subservient affiliations'. The problem as she sees it is that women have been seeking connections that are impossible to attain under the present arrangements. Prioritising their relationships with men, they have continued to look to such relationships for validation, for intimacy, and for those kinds of interaction which it has been shown men are least likely to be able or willing to give.

Within a post-modern world where the inevitability of the identities and discourses generated by the hegemonic institutions (Foucault, 1980) becomes more problematic, the possibilities as regards the identity-defining characteristics of friendship become heightened. The first and second women's movements have contributed to a recognition of the reality and importance of women's friendships. Nevertheless, there are limits to the extent to which such relationships can be valued without undermining the assumptions implicit in a heterosexual society where women are defined by their relationships with men, who are seen as providing them with their identity and their most important emotional experiences. Rubin (1985, p. 167) captures part of the dilemma women face in this situation:

> It is a vicious circle for women, as it is for any devalued group in a society. They internalise the social definition of self as inferior, then turn to those who formulated that definition and who now have a stake in maintaining it, for reassurance that it isn't true. In doing so, they help to increase the power of the powerful.

Women's relationships with each other cannot, of course, dissolve that world. They can provide women with a status or power within the world of women which is denied to them within a predominantly male public arena where the aristocracy of sex predominates. Such status may be based on a variety of sources, such as their skills and their contribution to a group, whether at the level of tending, leadership, or conversational ability. Through such relationships they can maintain an idea of self which transcends other stigmatising characteristics (such as those related to age or race). They can validate those identities which are required of women but not valued by the wider culture (e.g., motherhood, housewifery). They can provide diversion.

Oliker (1989, p. 38) noted that the women in her study found a willingness amongst their women friends to enter the 'inner life', to understand the constrained nature of their situation, and to appreciate those priorities and values which were not seen as important in the wider culture: 'children and personal problems in marriage and motherhood'. Through these friendships and the discourses they created, it is clear that the women in Oliker's study acquired validation and a positive definition of self – and in particular one which validated aspects of their identity which were not valued by the dominant (male) culture.

It has been widely assumed that women's friendships have little impact in the public arena. Increasingly, however, it has been recognised that women do have power, for example as voters, consumers, viewers, and readers – power that they have been slow to recognise and to utilise collectively on behalf of other women (Wolf, 1993). Typically, as Wolf noted, women are more comfortable arguing on others' behalf, and so they have the power to cross-target. They are the kin-keepers and community-creators, and so they have the ability to use these existing networks to promote women's interests. It has been shown that even in the nineteenth century women, as members of the American Female Moral Reform Society, organised themselves in an attempt to change values and behaviour within the society as a whole (Ryan, 1979, p. 73). However, women have been slow to recognise and utilise their power in what we think of as the public arena. This arguably reflects their tendency not to think of themselves as women, as having value and interests other than those deriving from their connections with men (a pattern which can be seen as itself a mechanism of patriarchal control (O'Connor, 1995)). Paradoxically, women in Western society today value friendship for its intimacy – a relational form which reflects and reinforces their position of powerlessness in the public arena (Cancian, 1986; O'Connor, 1992). The issue of the variability of friendship as a cultural form and the implications of this are explored in the next section.

The variability of friendship as a cultural form

Oliker (in this volume) has argued that the stress on intimacy within friendship (and indeed also within marriage) reflected the culture of individualism, and the structural context which generated this. Interestingly, she makes no reference to gendered power relationships as part of that wider context. In Western society we have become accustomed to think of friendship as a personal attachment to people who are not socially defined as kin. Wright (1978) suggested very early on that, in so far as one has to identify a single characteristic of friendship, it is the extent to which it provides self-affirmation. It is perhaps not coincidental that, in a society where the self is increasingly seen as problematic, the most important characteristic of friendships will be the extent to which they provide ego support, in the sense of enabling people to maintain a positive concept of themselves.

Typically ego support has been construed in terms of the level of intimacy in the relationship – such intimacy being defined in terms of the level of confiding about personal, potentially damaging topics. From the mid-1980s onwards, there was increasing recognition of the limitations of this kind of approach. Thus Cancian (1986) noted that it implicitly prioritised a feminised style of relating. Intimacy for women typically involved admitting dependency, sharing problems, and being emotionally vulnerable – a style which reflected and reinforced their disempowered situation. Indeed, Cancian (1986, p. 701) noted that the only area of personal experience about which women confided less than men was their victories and achievements. Other work showed that men were equally capable of intimate confiding but that either they preferred to do it less often than women (Reis, *et al.*, 1985) or, if they did do so, they preferred to confide in women rather than in men (Derlega, *et al.*, 1985).

What seemed to be happening was that a style of relating which reflected and reinforced powerlessness, and which was peculiarly characteristic of women's friendships, was being seen as an indicator of close, freely chosen, and highly desirable personal relationships. It has been increasingly recognised that intimate confiding between women, which has been seen as the epitome of closeness, is simply a kind of shared victimisation and that a stronger and more enduring kind of solidarity must be based on shared strengths and resources (Raymond, 1986; O'Connor, 1992). It is, however, also increasingly recognised that such solidarity can occur only when 'differences' between women are recognised – whether these be in terms of class, race, or sexual identity (Hooks, 1992).

The question of the kind of cultural context which stressed intimacy as the key defining characteristic of friendship has typically not been discussed (Allan, 1989). It has, however, increasingly been recognised that this concept of friendship is highly culturally specific. Indeed, it is perhaps not coincidental that, as the self becomes problematic within a post-modern world, this feminised concept of friendship has acquired currency. Evidence on the cultural specificity of this pattern has come from a variety of different sources. Hannan (1972, p. 176) noted that in Ireland the 'concept of friend as a freely chosen confidante and intimate to whom one is joined in mutual benevolence' was still used by the older people in rural areas to refer to kin. A similar pattern existed in France in the high medieval period (Contarello and Volpato, 1991). Allan's early work (1979) highlighted the fact that, in Britain, working-class respondents were more likely than their middle-class counterparts to define friendship in terms of kinship or work-based relationships. There was evidence that in a variety of different cultures (including Chile: Adler Lomnitz, 1988) friendship as a cultural form transcended the private world entirely. This has also emerged in Shlapentokh's (1984) work. Zeldin (1995, p. 210) noted that historically, in most societies, friendship had nothing to do with affection; a friend was 'a protector or someone useful to whom one sold one's allegiance in return for favours, for as long as the favours lasted'. Because of our preoccupation with intimacy, such a concept of friendship appears very cynical indeed.

In Western society, relationships which are related to 'the concrete motives bound up with life goals' are typically not seen as friendship (ibid., p. 210). Yet they facilitate access to resources which are necessary for the performance of key roles and the attainment of key objectives. As noted by Allan (1990, p. 5), studies of elites have consistently adverted to the importance of friendship ties in influencing access to information and other resources. There is a great deal of ambivalence about recognising their reality because of their obvious implications as regards corruption and the implicit undermining of a belief in a meritocratic and democratic society.

It is plausible to suggest that a social reality constructed by patriarchy and capitalism still exists. It may be a less convincing reality than heretofore, and one which is not sufficient at the level of identity or meaning. Nevertheless it provides structures through which resources are allocated and tasks undertaken. Within it, men's relationships with other men provide them with access to economic and political resources and validate their identity as men. It has been increasingly recognised that relationships play an important part in maintaining these structures. Indeed, men's relationships with each other have been seen by Hartmann (1981, p. 14) as a key element in patriarchy, which she defines as 'a set of social relationships between men, which have a material base, and which, though hierarchical, establish or create interdependence among men that enable them to dominate women'. It has been recognised that men's relationships with other men within organisations play an important part in 'opening opportunities for some and closing them for others' (Allan, 1990, p. 5). The importance of these relationships has also been adverted to by Kanter (1993). Within this context, who you have coffee or lunch with reflects and reinforces your place within the hierarchical organisational structure, with those who are upwardly mobile seeking to associate with higher-status individuals so as to increase their own status within the organisation. In this context the other is valued, but this is defined more in terms of pragmatic usefulness, rather than in terms of depth or the extent of intimate confiding. Such ties are typically described as mentoring and are seen as providing self-affirmation, and furthering the economic and political interests of the mentored. It seems plausible to suggest that, in so far as confiding occurs in such relationships, it is more likely to be about achievements than about failures and inadequacies. These relationships can be seen as personal in the sense that the individuals involved react to each other as 'genuine, unique, and irreplaceable individuals' (Wright, 1978, p. 201). They do so, however, from a position (as male, manager, etc.) which is part of their idea of themselves and which the other person validates and empowers. This kind of relationship is typically seen as involving men, although it is of course possible that it may exist amongst women (Gouldner and Symons Strong, 1987). Typically, however, women in organisations exist within a predominantly male structure and are not integrated into these powerful (male) informal networks (Eckenrode and Wethington, 1990).

The tendency within the literature on friendship to underplay the importance of such relationships can be seen as reflecting a continued acceptance of the distinction between 'private' and 'public'. This distinction has increasingly been seen as problematic, implying as it does that the public area is peopled by 'depersonalised automatons' whose relationships with each other are purely instrumental. Once we accept that 'staff bring their personal interests into organisations, and that these shape the way they discharge their functions, we must also accept that gendered perceptions, practices and attitudes will be present too' (Halford, 1992, p. 172).

In this situation it becomes obvious that friendships may exist in the public arena and that these play an important part in maintaining the system, and in reflecting and reinforcing men's identity as men. It seems unhelpful to exclude these relationships from a discussion of friendship – or indeed to view them as in some way an inferior kind of friendship relationship. The exclusion of such ties from a concept of friendship can thus be seen as part of a wider phenomenon which involves the obscuring of the gendered reality of the public arena and the idealisation of the private arena as a source of emotional satisfaction.

Equally, it does not seem useful to dismiss relationships involving a kind of inarticulate solidarity which is reflected in routinised activity. In the case of these relationships, identity comes from being part of a particular 'scene'. Rubin (1985, p. 69) suggests that this sort of solidarity is reflected in 'the shared experience of maleness – of knowing its difference from femaleness and affirming those differences through an intuitive under-standing of each other that needs no words'. This kind of sociation is stereotypically seen as reflecting and reinforcing a general bond between men – and as being characteristic of a traditional male pub culture (Hunt and Satterlee, 1987). The image is one of almost silent men seated on bar stools, part of a tenuous but identity-defining and undemanding group. This kind of relationship is arguably another face of friendship.

Implicit in Marks's work (in this volume) is the idea that in certain situations (e.g., amongst the five women operators in the Relay Assembly Test Room) friendships between women may be somewhat similar in so far as they are deeply embedded in social structures, and reflect and reinforce cat-egorical identities. Such relationships, although less taciturn than their male counterparts, are characterised by the construction and telling of stories about the behaviour of the group members, rather than about their innermost thoughts and feelings. They reflect a similar sort of categorical solidarity – the essence of which is the structural affirmation of the 'world', so to speak, within which these relationships are located. Thus, as noted by Marks, closeness was best expressed in group activities such as singing or telling stories in large family-like groups rather than in intimate confiding in dyadic relationships. It was reflected in ties of 'sociability' – a playful form of sociation where 'the concrete motives bound up with life goals fall away', where sociability is an end in itself (Simmel, 1971, p. 136).

Similarly, it seems unhelpful to dismiss relationships which involve a caring component, whether this is reflected in emotional concern or in more practical tending (Lynch and McLaughlin, 1995). This kind of relation-ship, which is often thought of as a kin relationship, has also been docu-mented amongst 'real' friends (see O'Connor, 1992). Jerrome (1990) also suggested that those who provide extensive help and support are frequently seen as 'special' quasi-kin – 'a true friend', 'like a sister to me'. This kind of support is not exclusive to such relationships but has also been documented amongst, for example, assembly-line workers (Green, *et al.*, 1990). Like intimate relationships, these may be seen as ones where the main resource available to those involved is their own time and energy, and where they utilise this in the interests of those to whom they feel close and/or with whom they identify. It is possible to argue that such relationships are par-ticularly characteristic of women because they are more likely to have access only to such resources. However, by focusing exclusively on intimate friendships (which typically only require such resources), and by seeing them as the epitome of friendship, such resource issues become further obscured.

Friendship as a residual social structure in Western society

It is one of the paradoxes of Western society that friendship relationships are not institutionalised. Momentary reflection highlights the fact that key areas of social life are typically institutionalised – whether, for example, these relate to paid employment, education, marriage, or family life. Such institutions can be seen to have an important social significance. However, it is equally clear that friendship has an important social and personal reality – particularly for those such as elderly people whose lives are outside the dominant institutional structures. Furthermore, friendship relationships are structured (O'Connor, 1992). Yet the creation of such relationships is very much a matter of personal initiative and social chance. It has been recognised that individual women will vary in terms of the extent and nature of their needs for friendship depending on their life-stage and other social or personal characteristics (Duck, 1988). Such individual variation is in a sense neither here nor there. Thus, for example, a society does not abandon structures to control sexuality or to educate people simply because some people at particular times have a desire for neither.

Within a capitalist society, the importance of relationships which appear to be unrelated to the cash nexus is inevitably questionable (Allan, 1989; Lynch, 1989). Within a patriarchal society, the importance of women's relationships with each other is even more questionable. Thus in a sense it is not surprising that friendship is a residual social structure in Western society, and that friendship between women in particular has been neglected and ignored, or at the very least taken for granted. It has arguably been inhibited by the ideological dominance of heterosexuality as an institution, although it has been argued that the women's movement has played an important part in rehabilitating such relationships (Rose and Roades, 1987). It is perhaps not surprising that, in so far as attention has been paid to friendship, it has occurred in the context of a discussion of social support (see O'Connor, 1992). Such a focus implicitly ignores issues related to the wider social and cultural context. It thus leaves the whole status of friendship as a residual social structure unexamined.

As previously mentioned, friendship, although it is typically not thought of as a social institution, is socially patterned, and is unlikely to occur between those who are socially perceived as different. Indeed, it has been suggested that:

> Patterns of friendship interaction provide one social indicator of the character of the status system operating. In terms of mapping out who is accepted by whom as a social equal, who is seen as occupying a different position, of investigating how permeable or otherwise the boundaries drawn around social groups are, informal networks of sociability in general, and friendship choices in particular can provide information just as crucial as marriage selection, education background and the like.
>
> (Allan, 1990, p. 9)

Implicit in this is the idea that friendship is a relationship between equals. Hence, the social identity of those who are chosen as friends reflects assumptions about status. Thus, other than in young people, and to a lesser extent amongst the old (O'Connor, 1993), friendships tend to be gender-specific. Amongst women, they tend to be between those who are similar in social class, race, marital status, maternal status, and participation in paid employment. In this sense, they can be seen as relationships which reflect and maintain structural realities.

It is clear that similarity is socially constructed within particular contexts. By asking about 'best friends', one is implicitly asking respondents to prioritise what are seen as the most important kinds of social similarity. This stress on similarity in close ties in particular situations is taken a stage further in so far as one's 'best friends' are chosen from amongst kin relationships (O'Connor, 1992; Gouldner and Symons Strong, 1987). This pattern has been observed within highly ascriptive societies (such as Ireland up to the early 1970s). Allan (1989) observed it amongst his working-class respondents, as I did (O'Connor, 1992) amongst my lower middle-class respondents. It is arguable that, amongst these respondents, similarity of early experiences is key and thus only kin can 'qualify'.

Implicit in the notion of such similarity as an important element in friendship lies the idea that friendships are likely to be differentially available to women who are in some way 'out of synch' with the normal lifestyle and/or with the wider social context (young widows, single women in their forties and fifties, etc.). A further implication of the stress on similarity as a basis for friendship is that changes in key attributes (such as divorce or unemployment) inevitably challenge the basis of the friendship (Allan and Adams, 1989). The implication of this is that, although 'true' friendship is implicitly assumed to be unaffected by such vicissitudes, such events may erode the similarity on which these relationships are based. Yet this dilemma has not been recognised, in so far as social institutions have been slow to develop what Gouldner and Symons Strong (1987) have called new forms of organised social life to deal with this tension.

Allan (1979, p. 23) early on noted that there was nothing in the nature of friendship that required it to be equal, but he went on to note that the 'economic and social divisions within the society certainly encourage this'. It has been noted that homogeneity in friendship ties was particularly likely to exist in the case of those who had power or status in the society. Less attention has been paid to the role of men's friendships in reinforcing men's concept of themselves as men, and hence indirectly maintaining concepts of masculinity. Connell (1987) has argued that these ties are essential to the maintenance of patriarchy. Thus, in so far as men support each other in their belief that their position relative to women is natural, inevitable, and what women want, they can feel comfortable maintaining that system. The stress on similarity in friendships thereby facilitates not only the strengthening of ties amongst those with power or status generally, but it also facilitates the strengthening of ties between men. They are thus a very important but insufficiently recognised element in maintaining the *status quo* in a society.

However, it has also been noted that 'numerous exceptions' do occur (Allan and Adams, 1989). Thus, for example, if interaction mainly revolves around shared interests (such as bridge or golf), then it is arguable that similarity in this area is likely to be key. There are few limits to social ingenuity as regards the construction of similarity/difference. Thus, for example, limiting the kinds of interaction settings or activities undertaken can obscure differences in friends' wealth, status, or lifestyle (Allan, 1989, and in this volume). On the other hand, differences can be identified amongst those who appear to be similar. Thus Hochschild (1973) noted that amongst the elderly women she studied distinctions were made on the basis of, for example, health or closeness to children amongst this apparently homogenous group.

In a sense, then, the stress on similarity as a characteristic of friendship tells us more about the cultural context within which friendship relationships arise than it does about the relationship itself. The dimensions that are seen as important as regards similarity are culturally and socially constructed. Thus, in a society where religious difference is seen as critically important, it is highly likely that similarity in this area will be seen as important in friendship. Similarly, in an age-stratified society, friendship will be most likely to occur amongst those of similar age, while, in a class-stratified society, this will be a crucial axis in terms of friendship. On the other hand, within a society where place of birth is seen as socially irrelevant, similarity in this area will not be seen as important in terms of friendship.

Thus, what is being suggested here is that structural realities are maintained by cultural definitions of 'otherness' and that these are in turn reflected in individual perceptions of the types of people who are 'like them' and so who could be appropriately defined as friends within a society where friendship is seen as involving identity-validation and support from people who are similar. Yet, paradoxically, the very real social and cultural consequences of such relationships are obscured by a stress on an essentially personal, individuated concept of friendship. The creation and maintenance of friendships also reflect the very real situational parameters of women's lives – the topic to which I turn in the next section.

Creating and maintaining relationships

It has been noted that the question of how relationships are created and maintained – both interactionally and ideologically – is a key issue that needs to be explored (Duck and Perlman, 1985). It is increasingly recognised that relationships are embedded in social life, in the sense that they involve co-ordinating the social activities of those involved: 'Friendships do not start until people do friendly things in friendly places: they are not created merely by friendly talk' (Duck, 1988, p. 56). Implicit in this is the idea that the day-to-day rhythm of women's lives, the type of areas in which they meet others, and the kinds of activities in which they are involved, their access to resources such as time, money, and personal space, and the networks into which they are already embedded by 'ties of love and duty' will all affect their ability to create and/or maintain friendship relationships. This creates potential problems as regards the creation and maintenance of women's friendships.

A variety of studies have shown that husbands typically have greater access to personal spending money than their wives (see Rottman, 1994) and they typically have more free time (Green, *et al.*, 1990). Their access to non-home-based areas for social interaction (e.g., the pub) tends to be seen as more acceptable and less dependent on subtle negotiating tactics (ibid.; Harrison, in this volume). Women's activities – including their friendships – outside the home may also be limited by their fear of male violence and the perceived appropriateness of women being under an individual man's protection. It has been noted that friendships become interwoven with daily chores with, for example, conversations being interrupted to distract, soothe, or reprimand children, to prepare food, or to answer doors. Nevertheless, 'Women's capacity to develop and maintain friendships at school, in the workplace, outside the school gates and in any number of other unpromising leisure venues where women meet regularly has long been noted by observers' (Green, *et al.*, 1990, p. 143).

Feld (1981; Feld and Carter, in this volume) has captured this reality by the concept of 'focus of activity'. He defines this as 'any social, psychological, legal or physical entity around which joint activities are organised'. He includes in such foci interactional arenas, such as neighbourhoods, workplaces, and voluntary organisations, as well as family and local ties which bring people together in repeated interactions involving particular activities. In so far as structural realities become weak, such foci may become less common and/or less institutionalised. This can be seen as the reality of a post-modern world, where individuals increasingly construct their own lives and identities, and where the only ties that persist when the focus of activity is lost are those that the individual is strongly motivated to maintain. Typically these are not re-embedded in new foci and become structurally disconnected, thereby requiring the expenditure of individual effort to sustain.

It has been increasingly recognised that such friendships, like all relationships, need to be maintained. Very much less attention has been paid to these processes than to those involved in initiating romantic relationships (Duck, 1988). They require the expenditure of time, effort, and other resources. Lynch (1989) has referred to this as 'love labour'. Cheal (1987) and Lynch (1989) have noted that this is typically carried out by women. The work involved includes, for example, visiting, writing letters, answering phone calls, sending presents and cards, and organising Christmas and holidays. Cheal noted that, in a capitalist society, the social construction of these ties is tied up with the money economy. Buying gifts requires money, as does participation in a variety of interaction venues (even having people in for coffee in your own home requires some financial expenditure). However, until very recently, there was a tendency not to see this type of activity as work (Lynch, 1989).

Of course, the need for such work may be ignored. Gouldner and Symons Strong (1987), and O'Connor (1992) noted that there were some women in their studies whose concept of friendship was very much in the realm of 'make-believe'. They expected wonderful new friends to emerge and they expected these relationships to persist without any maintenance. Indeed, the sheer absence of day-to-day interaction with them enabled such relationships to be constructed, without any reference to reality: 'a romantic conception of the perfect friend and confidante died hard in friendships, just as it did in marriage' (Gouldner and Symons Strong, 1987, p. 124).

It has also been increasingly recognised that part of the maintenance of friendship (like romantic relationships) also involves the creation of what Baxter (1987, p. 278) has called 'relationship symbols'. She suggested that in the case of friendship such symbols were likely to involve behaviours, outputs, and events. Implicit in Baxter's work is the idea that routinised interaction with friends was both a way of embedding friendship within day-to-day life and a way of signalling that they were a 'unit' (Campbell and Tesser, 1985). Of course, there are clear limits to the extent to which such a unit can be recognised.

Potential tensions between conflicting obligations can be avoided or minimised by routine social practices. Thus Gullestad (1984) noted that potential tension between friendship and spousal ties was reduced by visits to friends occurring while the husband was at work. Oliker (1989) also noted that the prioritisation of their family ties and responsibilities meant that women avoided committing resources (such as family time, space, or money) which they did not see as exclusively theirs. She argued that 'women's culture of friendship' (ibid., p. 100) encouraged ties but within the context of and limited by family responsibilities. The impact of such responsibilities varied since women differed, for example, in terms of their social and geographical mobility, the extent and nature of their responsibilities for housework and child care, their husband's attitudes and presence in the home, and in the kinds of networks in which they were embedded.

The very existence of friendships between women sits somewhat uneasily in capitalist patriarchal societies where the 'reality' is the pursuit of power and profit in the public area and the existence of a heterosexual family-based unit in the private area. In Western society, although men are brought up to be independent and separate, there is the assumption that women will be available to meet their emotional needs, without these even having to be spelt out. On the other hand: 'girls absorb early on that in the most profound sense they must rely on themselves, there is no one to take care of them emotionally. They cannot assume – as does the man – that there will be someone for them to bring their emotional lives to' (Orbach and Eichenbaum, 1984, p. 22).

In so far as women need such a relationship, within Western society it is up to them to create it for themselves. The importance of such relationships is heightened by the fact that many activities which are central to women's idea of themselves (e.g., child-rearing) receive little or no validation in dominant discourses. There are inevitable tensions involved in maintaining heterosexual relationships within a context where they are not providing the expected emotional support (Hite, 1987). To a degree to which Western society has only begun to appreciate, these tasks have been performed by women's friendships. Yet the creation of foci of activity to maintain such relationships, and their cultural valuation, is by no means unproblematic.

Conclusion

As Restivo (1991) has noted, sociologists have tended to psychologise love and to ignore the fact that who we love, how we love, even what is seen as love are socially constructed. This is just as true of friendships as of other kinds of close relationships. The wider social and cultural context in Western society within which women's friendships occur both inhibits and facilitates them. It is a world where, on the one hand, women's dependency needs are typically not met, where they are defined as 'the Other' by a patriarchal culture, where close ties with other women are seen as problematic, and where their entitlement to resources to create relationships with such women is, to varying degrees, socially and culturally limited. On the other hand, it is also a world where dominant discourses are fracturing; where women are becoming more visible and where the women's movement has legitimated women's voices and women's relationships. In this world friendship has usually been defined as a personal relationship, typically involving intimate confiding. Within this perspective women's friendships, rooted in victimisation, are seen as the epitome of friendship. Men, lacking such intimate ties, are seen as in some way less emotionally expert, deficient, less able, or unwilling to construct a personal identity. Within this perspective the realities of a patriarchal capitalist system are ignored. Mentoring, taciturn solidary relationships, and affable sociable relationships which perpetuate the *status quo* and provide positional and gender affirmation are ignored. The qualities which are valued in this feminised view of friendship arguably tell us more about the qualities which are missing in the wider social and cultural context than they do about friendship.

Nevertheless, friendships between women, in so far as they affirm women's identity as women, are still in some ways potentially at odds with a patriarchal culture. At the very least they undermine the idea that women's only source of identity and pleasure lies in a relationship with a man. In so far as they validate submerged discourses (such as the value of love labour), they are also in tension with the 'received wisdom'. Like all relationships, they are emotionally costly to create and maintain, and the legitimacy of the commitment of resources to them is problematic within a patriarchal society. Because of the stress on equality in such relationships and the salience of class as an indicator of equality, their ability to transform the class structure is potentially limited. However, in Western society where there is a high level of marital breakdown and lone motherhood, the stability of women's class position is questionable. In this context the possibility of women's cross-class identification and action cannot be eliminated. In any event, in so far as such relationships exist, and particularly in so far as they are not confined to the 'therapism' of the private arena, their transformative potential cannot be underestimated.

References
Adler Lomnitz, Larissa (1988), 'Informal exchange networks in formal systems: a theoretical model', *American Anthropologist*, 90: 42–55.
Allan, Graham (1979), *A Sociology of Friendship and Kinship*, London: Allen & Unwin.
  (1989), *Friendship: Developing a Sociological Perspective*, Hemel Hempstead: Harvester-Wheatsheaf.
  (1990), 'British studies in the sociology of friendship: a review of the past decade', paper given at the Fifth International Conference on Personal Relationships, July, Oxford, England.
Allan, Graham, and Adams, Rebecca G. (1989), 'Ageing and the structure of friendship', in Rebecca G. Adams and Rosemary Blieszner (eds.), *Older Adult Friendship: Structure and Process*, Newbury Park: Sage.
Baker Miller, Jean (1988), *Toward a New Psychology of Women* (2nd edn), Harmondsworth: Penguin.
Baxter, Leslie A. (1987), 'Symbols of relationship identity in relationship cultures', *Journal of Social and Personal Relationships*, 4: 261–80.
Campbell, Jennifer D., and Tesser, Abraham (1985), 'Self-evaluation maintenance processes in relationships', in Duck and Perlman (eds.).
Cancian, Francesca M. (1986), 'The feminization of love', *Signs*, 4: 692–709.
Cheal, David J. (1987), 'Showing them you love them: gift giving and the dialectic of intimacy', *Sociological Review*, 35: 150–70.
Connell, Robert W. (1987), *Gender and Power*, Cambridge: Polity.
Contarello, Alberta, and Volpato, Chiara (1991), 'Images of friendship: literary depictions through the ages', *Journal of Social and Personal Relationships*, 8: 49–75.
De Beauvoir, Simone (1972 [1949]), *The Second Sex*, Harmondsworth: Penguin.
Derlega, Valerian J., Winstead, Barbara A., Wang, Paul T. P., and Hunter, Susan (1985), 'Gender effects in an initial encounter', *Journal of Social and Personal Relationships*, 2: 25–44.
Duck, Steve (1988), *Relating to Others*, Milton Keynes: Open University Press.
Duck, Steve, and Perlman, Dan (1985), 'The thousand islands of personal relationships: a prescriptive analysis for future explorations', in Duck and Perlman (eds.).

(eds.) (1985), *Understanding Personal Relationships: An Interdisciplinary Approach*, London: Sage.

Eckenrode, John, and Wethington, Elaine (1990), 'The process and outcome of mobilizing social support', in Steve Duck with Roxane C. Silver (eds.), *Personal Relationships and Social Support*, London: Sage.

Faderman, Lillian (1987), *Surpassing the Love of Men*, London: Junction Books.

Feld, Scott L. (1981), 'The focused organization of social ties', *American Journal of Sociology*, 86: 1015–35.

Foucault, Michel (1980), *Power/Knowledge*, New York: Pantheon.

Gouldner, Helen, and Symons Strong, Mary (1987), *Speaking of Friendship: Middle-Class Women and Their Friends*, New York: Greenwood.

Green, Eileen, Hebron, Sandra, and Woodward, Diana (1990), *Women's Leisure: What Leisure?*, Basingstoke: Macmillan.

Gullestad, Marianne (1984), *Kitchen Table Society*, Oslo: Universities Forlaget.

Halford, Susan (1992), 'Feminist change in a patriarchal organisation', in Mike Savage and Anne Witz (eds.), *Gender and Bureaucracy*, Oxford: Blackwell/ Sociological Review.

Hannan, Damian (1972), 'Kinship, neighbourhood and social change in Irish rural communities', *Economic and Social Review*, 3: 163–87.

Hartmann, Heidi (1981), 'The unhappy marriage of marxism and feminism: towards a more progressive union', in Lydia Sargent (ed.), *Women and Revolution*, London: Pluto.

Hite, Shere (1987), *The Hite Report: Women and Love*, London: Penguin.

Hochschild, Arlie R. (1973), *The Unexpected Community*, Englewood Cliffs, N.J.: Prentice Hall.

Hooks, B. (1992), 'Sisterhood: political solidarity between women', in Janet A. Kourany, James P. Sterba, and Rosemarie Tong (eds.), *Feminist Philosophies: Problems, Theories and Applications*, Englewood Cliffs, N.J.: Prentice Hall.

Hunt, Geoffrey, and Satterlee, Saundra (1987), 'Darts, drink and the pub: the culture of female drinking', *Sociological Review*, 35: 575–601.

Irigaray, Luce (1985), *This Sex Which Is Not One*, New York: Cornell University Press.

Jerrome, Dorothy (1984), 'Good company: the sociological implication of friendship', *Sociological Review*, 32: 696–718.

——— (1990), 'Frailty and friendship', *Journal of Cross-Cultural Gerontology*, 5: 51–64.

Kanter, Rosabeth M. (1993), *Men and Women of the Corporation* (2nd edn), London: Basic Books.

Lynch, Kathleen (1989), 'Solidary labour: its nature and marginalisation', *Sociological Review*, 37: 1–14.

Lynch, Kathleen, and McLaughlin, Eithne (1995), 'Caring labour and love labour', in Patrick Clancy, *et al.* (eds.), *Irish Society: Sociological Perspectives*, Dublin: Institute of Public Administration.

O'Connor, Pat (1992), *Friendships Between Women*, Hemel Hempstead: Harvester-Wheatsheaf.

——— (1993), 'Same-gender and cross-gender friendships amongst the elderly', *Gerontologist*, 33: 24–31.

(1995), 'Tourism and development in Ballyhoura: women's business?', *Economic and Social Review*, 26: 369–401.

Oliker, Stacey J. (1989), *Best Friends and Marriage: Exchange Among Women*, Berkeley: University of California Press.

Orbach, Susie, and Eichenbaum, Luise (1984), *What Do Women Want?*, London: Fontana.

Raymond, Janice (1986), *A Passion For Friends*, London: Women's Press.

Reis, Harry T., Senchak, Marilyn, and Solomon, Beth (1985), 'Sex differences in the intimacy of social interaction: further examination of potential explanations', *Journal of Personality and Social Psychology*, 48: 1204–17.

Restivo, Sal (1991), *The Sociological World*, Oxford: Blackwell.

Rose, S., and Roades, L. (1987), 'Feminism and women's friendships', *Psychology of Women Quarterly*, 11: 243–54.

Rottman, D. B. (1994), 'Allocating money within households: better off poorer', in B. Nolan and T. Callan (eds.), *Poverty and Policy in Ireland*, Dublin: Gill and Macmillan.

Rubin, Lillian B. (1985), *Just Friends: The Role of Friendship in Our Lives*, New York: Harper & Row.

Ryan, Mary P. (1979), 'The power of women's networks: a case study of female moral reform in antebellum America', *Feminist Studies*, 5: 66–85.

Shlapentokh, Vladimir (1984), *Love, Marriage and Friendship in the Soviet Union*, New York: Praeger.

Simmel, Georg (1971), *On Individuality and Social Forms*, University of Chicago Press.

Smith-Rosenberg, Carroll (1975), 'The female world of love and ritual: relations between women in nineteenth-century America', *Signs*, 1: 1–29.

Wiseman, Jacqueline (1986), 'Friendships: bonds and binds in a voluntary relationship', *Journal of Social and Personal Relationships*, 3: 191–211.

Wolf, Naomi (1993), *Fire with Fire*, London: Chatto and Windus.

Wright, Paul H. (1978), 'Towards a theory of friendship based on a conception of self', *Human Communication Research*, 4: 196–207.

Zeldin, Theodore (1995), *An Intimate History of Humanity*, London: Minerva.

7

Foci of activity as changing contexts for friendship

Scott Feld and William C. Carter

Friendship is the most voluntary type of personal relationship. People generally understand that whether two people are neighbours, co-workers, or kin is largely determined by the surrounding institutional arrangements, but they also believe that whether they are friends is a matter for the individuals themselves to decide. People expect that many of their activities and interactions as neighbours, co-workers, and kin are determined by the circumstances: for example, neighbours interact while coming and going from their homes; co-workers interact as part of their jobs; and kin encounter one another at family functions. In contrast, people feel that they determine their own friendship activities and interactions. Nevertheless, this entire volume is devoted to showing that, even though friendship is *relatively* voluntary and self-determined, social context has important effects on who become friends and how those friends act towards one another.

The 'context' of a friendship includes everything apart from the most immediate characteristics of the relationship itself (see Allan, 1989; Blieszner and Adams, 1992; Adams and Allan in this volume). Our present task is to suggest the value of taking account of one particular aspect of the social context that is captured in the concept of a 'focus of activity' (Feld, 1981, 1982, 1984). A focus of activity is defined as any 'social, psychological, legal or physical entity around which joint activities are organized' (Feld, 1981, p. 1016). Foci of activity take varied forms, including families, work-places, voluntary organisations, and neighbourhoods, but all have the common effect of bringing a relatively limited set of individuals together in repeated interactions in and around the focused activities. Most importantly, each friendship that is formed in the context of a focus of activity is embedded within a relatively dense web of other relationships (some friendships and some not) that are derived from the same focus of activity.

Many of the relationships that develop around foci of activity do not become friendships; for example, everyone has neighbours and co-workers whom they do not consider to be their friends. However, most friendships do originate in one focus of activity or another: e.g., neighbourhoods, work-places, families, schools, teams, and clubs (Feld, 1982; Allan, 1989). Many friendships outlive the particular focus of activity in which they originate, as when people remain friends after one of them moves out of their previously shared neighbourhood, or changes jobs and leaves their previously shared work-place. Even so, people can generally trace each friendship back to at least one shared focus of activity at some point in the past. While it is possible for a friendship to develop out of an isolated encounter between two people (as in a shop or on a bus), it is much more likely that a friendship will emerge when two people come into repeated contact with one another in the course of their ongoing activities. Furthermore, while individuals may take it upon themselves to develop and maintain a friendship, ongoing focused activities greatly facilitate the meeting, interacting, and communicating that are needed for the maintenance and development of a friendship. Finally, foci of activity often include many people who are similar to one another in respects that facilitate friendships (e.g., age, gender, socio-economic status, religion, and life-stage). Thus, while it is possible for friendships to develop from encounters outside repeated focused activities, the large majority of friendships are derived from some sort of ongoing focused activities.

The crucial aspect of context captured in the idea of a 'focus of activity' is whether a relationship between two people is accompanied by relationships of those two people to many others who are themselves related to one another. A friendship that is heavily embedded (Granovetter, 1985) within such a set of relationships among the others is inevitably affected by the entire set of relationships. The others may have, express, and enforce expectations for the nature of the friendship, and may support or impose costs upon the friendship itself and/or each of the individuals involved.

In addition, the particular set of norms and expectations that is enforced by a dense social network derived from a focus of activity may be largely determined by the particular focus of activity from which the entire set of relationships emerges. For example, adolescent relationships that derive from a church youth group are likely to be subject to a set of collective norms different from those that derive from a local video arcade. Thus, it is important to recognise that relationships derived from a focus of activity are inevitably embedded in a dense web of other relationships, and that the particular norms and expectations of the focus of activity may have important effects on the nature of the friendships that exist in that context (see, for example, Marks in this volume).

In this chapter, we include four major sections. In the first section, we provide a very general discussion of how a friendship is affected by being embedded in a particular set of other relationships, regardless of how the friendship comes to be embedded in this way. In the second section, we describe how each friendship drawn from a particular focus of activity is inevitably embedded within the set of other relationships drawn from the same focus of activity. We emphasise that the nature and extent of the embeddedness of any particular relationship are largely determined by the focus of activity that was the source of that relationship. In the third section, we discuss how experiencing a particular life transition can have dramatic effects on the nature and extent of a person's participation in particular foci of activity. In particular, we use divorce as an example of a life transition that changes a person's set of relationships, and also changes the embeddedness of the relationships that continue. Finally, in the fourth section, we suggest that the increasing frequency of divorce in recent years exemplifies a general tendency for various types of foci of activity to be less stable than in earlier historical periods. We discuss some direct and indirect effects of the increasing rate of change in foci of activity in society on the social networks and the relationships embedded within those social networks in society.

Implications of embeddedness for personal relationships

The 'embeddedness' of a relationship is important, irrespective of its source. The primary effect of embeddedness is that it facilitates and encourages communication among shared associates. The more two people associate with a set of interrelated other people, the more those other people can somehow become involved and influential in the relationship between the two people (Milardo, 1988). One effect of this communication and involvement is increased enforcement of norms. Bott's (1957) classic research on married couples showed that the extent to which couples were embedded in shared social networks was closely associated with the nature of their relationship with one another. Couples who were highly embedded tended to have traditional gender-segregated marital roles, presumably because traditional gender role norms were more effectively enforced upon them by their closely knit social networks. Festinger, *et al.*'s (1950) classic community study illustrated the process by showing that individuals who were embedded in groups with dense social networks were less likely to be deviant from the group norms than those who were less embedded in dense group networks. In general, personal relationships that are highly embedded are subject to follow the norms of the group in which they are embedded.

Social embeddedness may be burdensome to a relationship in so far as social pressures limit the free choices of the people involved. However, the embeddedness also benefits the relationship by increasing the effective normative pressures on the others in the dense network. Thus, if the individuals and/or the relationship is in need of support, the embeddedness makes it more likely that the others will become aware of the problem and will become involved in trying to help solve the problem.

In addition to providing support for a troubled relationship, the embeddedness may increase the likelihood that others provide social pressure and means for individuals to resolve conflicts that arise within their relationship. In Evans-Pritchard's (1950) description of conflict resolution among the Nuer of southern Sudan, he shows how dyads are inevitably embedded within larger sets of interrelated ties in the community. The consequence of the immediate embeddings of the two separate individuals involved in a dispute is the possibility that their separate factions may expand their simple dispute into a much larger feud between the entire factions. However, the further embedding of all possible factions within larger interconnected sets of interrelated individuals dampens the potential for large-scale conflict. The common others are highly motivated to pressure the parties and their factions to settle their differences without violence (or further violence, as the case may be), and ritual procedures to settle the dispute peacefully are available and expected to be followed by the aggrieved parties. Thus, most disputes, even those that involve the killing of one person by another, are peacefully resolved without any serious long-term disruptions of the relationships in the community.

The social networks and ritual conflict resolution processes of the Nuer provide an unusually vivid example of how social embeddings help to resolve conflicts within dyadic relationships. It is easy to think of examples of situations where friends who are embedded within a larger context (e.g., in a family or at work) tend to be pressured by their shared associates to resolve their dispute with minimal overall social disruption. In contrast, when a dyad does not have an effective common embedding, their separate individual embeddings may exacerbate and escalate a conflict between them. Thus, when friends have only minimally overlapping networks, their few mutual friends may be ineffective at bringing them together. Meanwhile, their separate friends, each hearing only one side of the story, caring about only one member of the dyad, and having little or no stake in the maintenance of the relationship, may encourage the aggrieved parties to seek further redress and/or sever the relationship. Such conditions can easily encourage escalation of a dispute and the ending of a relationship. Because of both social pressures and social support, friendships that are more embedded are more likely to persist over time (Feld, 1997). The present discussion concerns effects of network *embeddedness*; see Surra (1988) for a discussion of how various other patterns of networks (e.g., centrality) may affect relationships.

Foci of activity as the primary sources of embeddedness

The concept of a focus of activity reflects the assumption that most relevant social embeddedness derives from shared social activities that are organised independently of particular dyadic relationships. For example, a work-place is generally created for the purposes of facilitating the accomplishment of organisational tasks by many people whose work requires some degree of interaction with one another. Once a work-place exists, the routine activities there create frequent occasion for interaction among the participants. Repeated interaction among individuals, even initially of a passive sort, tends to develop personal relationships over time. To the extent that many different dyads within a work-place experience repeated passive contacts and develop personal relationships, those relationships arise and continue as embedded within the web of personal relationships among the others. The work-place is the 'focus of activity' underlying the embeddedness of all of the relationships arising there. Each particular focus of activity has characteristics that affect all of the dyadic relationships embedded within the dense web of interrelationships. Each focus of activity tends to include people with certain types of traits (e.g., particular common educational levels in a work-place: Feld, 1982, 1984), and activities involving certain types of norms (e.g., who has authority over whom in the work-place, and which outside social activities are expected or disallowed).

To the extent that a particular focus of activity from which a friendship is derived generally determines the set of relationships in which the friendship is embedded, it may also influence the norms that guide friendships and other behaviour in that context. There may be norms for behaviour, norms for social support among the participants, and norms for friendships. Foci of activity can vary in the extent to which they create a 'group' in the sense of having its own relatively clearly defined shared norms. When there are group norms, a dense set of relationships would tend to enforce those particular norms. If the focus of activity does not have its own norms, any co-ordinated efforts among the interrelated individuals would tend to enforce norms that are generally shared by the type of people in this type of context. As mentioned earlier, the norms applying to friendships arising out of an adolescent church group are likely to be substantially different from those arising out of a video arcade. Similarly, friendships arising in a work-place are subject to different norms from those that emerge in connections with a neighbourhood coffee house. In general, the nature of the norms and the extent to which the norms are enforced depend upon the underlying focus of activity.

As long as friendships within a group comply with norms, network members will be likely to co-ordinate their efforts to provide support for the relationship when necessary. Similarly, when conflict arises within a dyadic relationship, the set of interrelated others may exert pressure on one or the other to alter their behaviours towards one another. As with the Nuer described earlier, a pair of friends may disagree about something to the extent that the disagreement is straining their relationship. The others may pressure the individuals to follow normative prescriptions for resolving a dispute; for example, disputants may be expected to bring their problem to a group leader. More often, there may be informal ways of resolving relationship conflicts. As others become aware of a dispute, those others may reach agreement about a resolution that is consistent with the norms, and then pressure one or both parties to the dispute to accept that resolution. In general, when there are more interpersonal relationships that arise from focused activities, each dyadic relationship will be more closely monitored by others, and each relationship will be subject to greater pressure to conform to shared expectations through a combination of rewards and sanctions from the others.

An awareness that a relationship may be heavily influenced by its social embedding, and that the social embedding of a relationship is largely determined by its origin in focused activities, leads us to pay more attention to the foci of activity that underlie particular relationships. Looking for foci of activity defines the relevant source as a 'work-place', not just 'work', and as a 'family group', not just being 'kin'. Also, it suggests that referring to a personal relationship as a 'friendship' is often missing its primary structural connection to other relationships of the individuals involved.

In some cases, old friendships outlive the focused activities from which they were initially derived and come to involve new activities which are not always organised around foci of activity (e.g., one might continue to interact with a particular friend only in the context of deliberately arranged dyadic activities). Nevertheless, we suggest that the nature of the embeddedness of most personal relationships is primarily determined by the foci of activity in which the relationships originated and secondarily determined by later shared involvements in foci of activity. Thus, we suggest that most embeddedness can be understood as arising from one or another shared focus of activity, and that understanding the underlying foci of activity is crucial for understanding friendships and other personal relationships.

Individuals move in and out of involvement with foci of activity throughout the life-course. In contemporary Western societies, people are generally born into families, sent to schools, domiciled in neighbourhoods, etc. Later, they may join teams and clubs, seek and accept jobs, marry into other families, and choose places to live. In older age, changed circumstances, interests, and capabilities may lead people to retire from jobs and withdraw from certain activities. While some join new clubs and move into new communities with more suitable activities, many participate less in the types of activities that bring them into contact with others (Patterson, 1996; Kelly, 1993). It is apparent that the structure of society in terms of foci of activity is inevitably highly determining of the friendships that are possible and likely. The effects of participation in foci of activity are most evident at those times when individuals move in and out of involvements with particular foci of activity.

In some cases, people anticipate that becoming associated with a particular focus of activity may facilitate their making certain types of friends, and they may even join a club or move into a neighbourhood partly because of the types of people who would be likely to become their friends in those situations. However, people are generally aware of many other benefits and costs of associations with foci of activity, and take those into account in choosing a particular club, home, or job: e.g., the facilities and convenience of the club, the appearance and price of the home, and the salary and career prospects of the job. So we suggest that social considerations constitute only one small piece of an inseparable package of consequences of being associated with a particular focus of activity.

Even if individuals anticipate and take account of some social consequences, it does not make those consequences any less real or important. Friendships that exist within the contexts of foci of activity are not entirely subject to the definition and control of the dyad directly involved, but inevitably reflect the entire network of other relationships associated with that same context. As we have discussed, friendships that arise in the context of a particular focus of activity are affected by the patterns of communication, specific norms, norm enforcement, social pressures, and social support associated with the entire cluster of personal relationships derived from that focus of activity.

Effects of divorce as an example of changes in foci of activity over the life-course

As people move in and out of foci of activity over the life-course, their changes in foci of activity have profound effects for the formation, mainte-nance, and ending of friendships (Stueve and Gerson, 1977). When people go to and leave schools, take and leave jobs, marry and divorce, have chil-dren, move into and out of neighbourhoods and towns, and join and leave churches and other organisations, they inevitably change their associations with different foci of activity. Some changes in foci of activity are the direct result of a life transition, as taking a new job inevitably brings a person into a new work-place. Other changes in foci are the indirect result of a life transition; the life transition may result in changed needs or responsibilities that, in turn, lead to changes in associations with foci of activity. For example, having a child may make it less likely that the new parents will spend time at their former evening hangouts, and more likely that they will spend time around a local playground.

To illustrate the significance of various types of direct and indirect changes in foci of activity, we consider the implications of divorce for changes in foci of activity, and the effects of these changes in foci of activ-ity on social relationships. When a woman divorces, she typically loses most of her contact with her husband's family, his work colleagues, and the bulk of his set of childhood and school friends (Ambert, 1988; Nelson, 1995). In the most typical pattern where the husband leaves the wife in the marital home with the children, the husband tends to reduce his participation in the neighbourhood, in the children's school and other child-centred activity groups, and in the wife's family, work, and childhood friendship groups. In addition, as former spouses become less involved in one another's foci of activity, each of the parent–child relationships become less embedded in intertwined relationships to others.

To be more analytical about the changes in foci of activity, we examine various effects of divorce on foci of activity and the resulting changes in personal relationships from the perspective of a married working mother who stays in the home with the children while her husband establishes res-idence elsewhere. For the purpose of this particular discussion, we consider the full range of personal relationships rather than confining our attention only to those that would be considered 'friends'. Specifically, most people explicitly exclude kin from being considered as 'friends' (Fischer, 1982b), presumably because kin relationships are obligatory, and do not have the essentially voluntary nature that is crucial for friendship. However, the amount of obligation is often a matter of degree that is determined by the embeddedness of the relationship within a web of family relationships. For example, it is apparent that non-custodial fathers (and certainly their kin) have enormous discretion concerning whether or not to interact at all with their children. Thus, instead of making a qualitative distinction between friendships and other relationships, we discuss foci of activity and their effects on relationships more generically.

First, and most evidently, a divorce changes the composition of the household itself as a central focus of activity by removing the husband from the household. From the perspective of the wife, the most direct effect of removing the husband from this focus of activity is removing their joint activities from her daily rounds. Removing the husband from the household also removes or reduces his relationships with the other household members (the children), which had previously been important parts of the embedding of his relationship with his wife. In this same way, each of the relationships in the household become less embedded than before. While the former spouses may continue some level of communication concerning the children, it is likely that the husband will know less and have less influence on the interactions between the wife and children than previously. She is freer to change her parenting style, judgements, and activities. At the same time, the influence of the husband over the children is less subject to her knowledge or control, which can have indirect effects on her relationships with her children.

Secondly, the wife may be largely removed from the husband's family of origin. While there may be some ongoing contact with in-laws, especially his parents and occasionally his siblings, those contacts are likely to be relatively isolated and unsupported by repeated contact with many interrelated others in that family. Nelson (1995) found that, apart from including or excluding the husbands themselves, the most systematic difference between the network size and composition of separated and married women was that the majority of married women included their husbands' parents in their active networks, while only 13 per cent of the separated women did so. Ambert (1988) found that 46 per cent of ex-wives had no contact at all with their former in-laws. As with the loss of the husband in the household, the loss of this branch of the extended family affects the surviving relationships in the household. The paternal grandparents are likely to have less influence over the mother–child relationships. In some cases, paternal grandparents may deliberately counteract the usual tendencies towards loss of extended family relations by becoming *more* involved in the household activities following divorce. However, such involvement requires extensive efforts in the absence of the more institutionalised extended family activities (Cherlin and Furstenberg, 1986).

Thirdly, the former wife is removed from her auxiliary participation in her ex-husband's foci of activity. For example, a wife may become involved with the set of her husband's co-workers' families as a result of repeated interactions at parties (e.g., Christmas parties, company picnics) and in smaller groups that typically involve co-workers and their spouses. Spouses tend to be included in one another's circles of old friends, but a divorce would remove a wife from these groups. The pattern of involving a wife in coupled activities with the friends and associates of the husband (and vice versa) is particularly characteristic of middle-class families (Benjamin, 1988).

Fourthly, participation 'as a couple' may be crucial for many, especially middle-class social activities; for example, neighbourhood get-togethers, cooking or tennis groups, and even church events may be organised around 'couples'. In that case, both the husband and the wife may be effectively removed from participation in these foci of activity. Spanier and Thompson (1987) found that 70 per cent of their respondents reported seeing less of their 'shared' friends after the separation. Those who had shared more friends in marriage lost more friends when the marriage was ended. To the extent that being coupled was the essential feature of participation in certain social groups, an individual might effectively rejoin the group if and when she becomes recoupled. However, in some cases, the history of the old couple and its dissolution might interfere with the acceptance of the new couple and so preclude her ever rejoining this particular group.

Fifthly, participation in particular foci of activity may depend upon resources, especially money, that may be lost in divorce. A wife might no longer be able to afford a country club or recreation centre. In the extreme, she might no longer be able to afford to live in the same neighbourhood, or have her children involved with the same schools. These may be the most drastic and overwhelming effects on the lifestyle and social relationships of the entire family.

Sixthly, divorce may allow or require change in the participation in other foci of activity by a wife on her own. A wife who has refrained from taking another job, moving to another place, or participating in a church or club, in deference to her husband's preferences, could now move in the directions that she would have preferred all along. On the other hand, divorce may create new needs for a job (a need for higher income or for insurance coverage) or for leisure activities that lead to participation in new foci of activity.

We have just described six different types of effects of divorce on a wife's participation in various foci of activity. In addition, the divorce may also change the form of her participation in those foci of activity that she continues. For the same types of reasons as discussed above (importance of coupling, financial loss, change in needs, loss of constraint from her husband, etc.), the change in marital status may change the former wife's attitude and motivation to participate in certain activities, and make her more or less welcome in certain subgroups.

Overall, divorce may produce dramatic change in the nature and extent of a woman's participation in many of her foci of activity. While much research has focused on changes in motivation and circumstances following divorce, there has been relatively little work on the changes in the extent and nature of embeddedness in different sectors of social networks. Changes in participation in particular foci of activity affect the amount and nature of social embedding in each aspect of a person's life. There may be different sets of people who are aware of and who are in a position to influence an individual's behaviour. A full analysis of the effects of divorce requires studying not only how changes in participation in foci of activity lead some relationships to end and others to start, but also how each of the continuing relationships is affected by the changes in the nature and extent of their embedding within webs of other relationships.

Wilcox (1981) found that people with denser networks did not adjust to divorce as well as those with sparser networks. However, each network can be decomposed into parts drawn from and maintained in various different foci of activity. Overall network density is primarily a function of the number of different focus sources underlying the network – more sources means lower density (Feld, 1981; Fischer, 1982a). Thus, the finding that high density is associated with poorer adjustment may mean only that people who depend upon one or two specific foci of activity (e.g., their own families of origin) do not adjust as well as people who have access to more different sources of support (Feld, 1984; Wellman and Wortley, 1990). It is crucial that one looks beyond the overall density to the number and nature of the continuing foci of activity to understand how participation in each of those particular foci of activity facilitates or hampers adjustment.

Divorce is primarily the breakup of the immediate household, and secondarily the breakup of the extended family. It has direct implications for the relationships among the participants in the household, the husband, the wife, and the children. As discussed above, it also has indirect implications for relationships between the participants and others (including extended family and friends). In some sense, all of these relationships are weakened, because the extent of their embedding is reduced by the breakup of the family. However, many of the relationships persist after the divorce in one form or another even in their weakened state. As families are reconstituted, new families re-embed some of the relationships in newly constituted focused sets. Ironically, the total number of relationships in society may actually be increased by divorce if the weakened relationships continue to be counted and new relationships are also introduced. However, many of the surviving relationships, especially those between children and non-custodial parents and their extended families, are likely to be substantially weakened because of their lack of traditional embedding (e.g., children and their non-custodial grandparents are unlikely to have much interaction with many of the same other family members).

In some sense, divorce is an example of a more general trend in the modernisation of societies. Where traditional marriages generally lasted for the lifetimes of the spouses, fewer modern marriages continue until the death of one of the spouses. Instead, many people pass through marriages and accumulate more non-embedded relationships than people in the past. While some relationships associated with former marriages effectively disappear (as many relationships between the ex-spouses), others persist as shadows of their former selves and are supplemented by new embedded relationships.

Breakups of foci of activity, modernisation, and the reduction of social embedding

Other types of foci of activity are experiencing increasing frequencies of such deconstitution. For example, it is becoming less common for people to have jobs that last their full working lifetimes. Instead, people move on to jobs in other work-places in other firms. Some of the relationships formed in those work-places may disappear, while others may continue in severely weakened states, to be supplemented by new embedded relationships in other work-places. People are less likely to live out their lives in the same neighbourhoods, because of unstable marriages and jobs, and because of lesser attachment to houses, neighbourhoods, and communities.

When a focus of activity is lost, the relationships among the participants are no longer supported by ongoing focused activities and become less embedded in networks of other ties. Many of those relationships fall away, and the only relationships that tend to survive are those that are strong enough to motivate the participants to take deliberate efforts to maintain them. As a result of a life history of gaining and losing foci of activity, people tend to have accumulated several strong relationships that have survived the breakup of the foci of activity from which they were derived. These relationships are in addition to many more recent and generally weaker relationships that are currently supported by ongoing foci of activity. Ironically, even though currently embedded ties may involve frequent interaction, they may be relatively weak in emotion and motivation compared to the surviving non-embedded ties.

The separation of strong committed ties from the ongoing embedding in focused activities reduces the extent of social control and social support in society. Even strong relationships tend not to exert much social control over the individuals in that relationship when those relationships are not effectively embedded within larger sets of interrelated ties. Ties that are strong in the minds and hearts of the individuals that are not structurally embedded may not be as effectively activated as if they were structurally embedded.

Meanwhile, ties that *are* socially embedded are unlikely to provide support if these ties are not strong enough to motivate the particular individuals involved. Individuals can avoid social control either by avoiding relatively unimportant contacts or by disengaging from the potentially controlling focus of activity. For example, it is common to find that couples that engage in family violence make frequent residential changes, presumably to avoid the social control that may arise from being embedded in an ongoing dense neighbourhood network (Straus, *et al.*, 1980). Whether it is deliberate or not, mobility in and out of various foci of activity is likely to undermine effective social control and permit increased deviance.

Some of these types of modern changes were anticipated by Simmel (1955 [1922]) in his descriptions of modern society as increasingly consisting of intersecting rather than overlapping social circles. His classic argument could be readily framed in the present terminology as follows. When an individual is surrounded by concentric overlapping social circles, as in traditional society, then each of that individual's relationships is embedded in many dense webs of interrelationships among others. For example, a current neighbour may well be a co-worker and have been a childhood schoolmate. That tie is then embedded within sets of current neighbours, current co-workers, and childhood schoolmates, and these sets are likely to overlap with one another to a considerable extent.

However, in contrast, when an individual is at the intersection of many different social circles, as in modern society, each relationship is largely embedded within a single social circle, and the embeddedness of that relationship is derived largely from that single social circle. In that case, a current neighbour is probably not a co-worker nor a childhood schoolmate and may not share any focus of activity other than the neighbourhood. In contrast to traditional society, each tie in modern society is typically embedded within a smaller set of ties all drawn from a more specific setting. Simmel expected that the central implication of this type of social change would be a breakdown of social control and social support for these less-embedded relationships. He saw such changes as having costs and benefits; while the loss of social control would involve a loss of support and control over the general social environment, it would also involve an increase in personal freedom.

Even as Simmel described the reduction in overlapping social circles, he could not have anticipated the accelerated rate of social network change that has become common with the increasing frequency of breakup of such foci of activity as marriages, work-places, neighbourhoods, etc. The increasing rate of change in the foci of activity themselves has further reduced the network embeddedness of valued social ties. While modern friendships still originate in one or another focus of activity, many of the strongest ties may survive longer than the focus of activity of their origin and continue with relatively little subsequent embedding. Meanwhile, a friendship that arises when an individual enters into a new focus of activity is typically embedded within a set of other relationships that have been recently formed and may not last long. Thus, in the context of more frequently changing foci of activity, friendships may be less constrained by their social embeddedness than in the past. While observers have always tended to exaggerate the extent to which two individuals can define their own personal relationship, societal changes seem to be moving in the direction of not only allowing people more freedom to define their own relationships, but also forcing them to do so in the absence of the traditional forms of embeddedness that provided and enforced norms of traditional relationships.

It is useful to distinguish the present predictions of the significance of modernisation for network change from the most common predictions. Concern with the 'decline of community' has motivated much of this research, where researchers have addressed the social concern that the decline of community may leave individuals without support from others. Wellman (1979), Wellman and Wortley (1990), and Fischer (1982a) have alleviated some of that concern by reporting their findings that, even though many people living 'modern' lives have relatively low density in their personal networks, most of them report receiving considerable amounts of day-to-day social support.

However, our concern is with the embeddedness of the ties, which is only indirectly related to overall density of personal networks. An individual can have many ties that are embedded within dense sub-networks of ties, even though that individual has a personal network with low overall density. A friendship can be embedded in a dense set of interconnections among people associated with one particular focus of activity. If that individual draws ties from many different foci of activity, then the overall personal network would have low density even though each of the ties is embedded within its own focus of activity. We suggest that it is the extent of local embeddedness that is the most important determinant of social support and constraint on friendships. Thus, research is needed on whether the embeddedness of friendships is declining as we expect, not just whether overall density of personal networks is declining, and whether those relationships that are less embedded receive less support and constraint than other ties.

We consider recent findings (Wellman, 1979; Fischer, 1982a; Wellman and Wortley, 1990) encouraging in showing that dissatisfaction with social support is not widespread even in the most modern reaches of contemporary society. However, these findings may hide real declines in social support if many people have realistically lowered their expectations so as not to be disappointed by the actual lower levels of support that they receive. We expect to find that embeddedness is declining and that the less-embedded relationships provide a lower overall level of objective support. Increasing rates of homelessness and poverty as well as family violence and divorce (a consequence as well as a cause of declining social embeddedness) may reflect the fact that families and friends are less likely to accept responsibilities to support and sanction their friends and kin than they had been in previous times. Of course, these types of large social problems have complex causes, but we believe that declines in the embeddedness of personal relationships may contribute.

While it is most difficult to isolate the effects of different social changes over different historical periods, it is more possible to make comparisons among places within the same current time period. Whatever the extent of increasing rates of breakdown of marriages, neighbourhoods, and long-term work relationships overall in modern society, there remain wide variations in these rates over different positions in society. We hope that further research on foci of activity as contexts for social relationships will make further comparisons between urban and rural places, among countries, between social classes, and between ethnic groupings, which will reveal the extent to which different rates of change in foci of activity have different effects on the common patterns of personal relationships in each of these different types of situations.

In conclusion, once one recognises the nature of foci of activity as contexts for the development, maintenance, and form of personal relationships, it becomes necessary to attend to the foci of activity surrounding particular relationships, including friendships. Even when individuals may no longer be aware of the social origins of their friendships, the embeddedness arising from those origins may continue to affect the form of the relationships. Also, even if someone thinks of a particular relationship as primarily a 'friendship', the fact that it is embedded in a neighbourhood, work-place, church, social club, or family can have important effects on the form it takes. We hope that our general discussion of the effects of embedding on relationships will lead to further specific research to investigate how particular types of foci of activity affect friendships, how changes in foci of activity affect friendships over the life cycle, and how historical changes in the make-up and longevity of foci of activity have systematic implications for social networks and their effects in society.

Acknowledgements
We would like to thank Jill Suitor and Rebecca Carter for their support in the writing of this chapter.

References
Allan, Graham (1989), *Friendship: Developing a Sociological Perspective*, Boulder: Westview Press.
Ambert, Anne-Marie (1988), 'Relationships with former in-laws after divorce: a research note', *Journal of Marriage and the Family*, 50: 679–86.
Benjamin, Esther R. (1988), 'Social relations of separated and divorced men and women: a class comparison of the effects of marriage on the middle- and working-class divorce experience', Ph.D. dissertation, Northwestern University, Evanston, Ill.
Blieszner, Rosemary, and Adams, Rebecca G. (1992), *Adult Friendship*, Newbury Park: Sage.
Bott, Elizabeth (1957), *Family and Social Network*, London: Tavistock.
Cherlin, Andrew J., and Furstenberg, Frank F. Jr. (1986), *The New American Grandparent*, New York: Basic.
Evans-Pritchard, Edward E. (1950), 'The Nuer of the southern Sudan', in M. Fortes and Edward E. Evans-Pritchard (eds.), *African Political Systems*, Oxford University Press.
Feld, Scott L. (1981), 'The focused organization of social ties', *American Journal of Sociology*, 86: 1015–35.

(1982), 'Structural determinants of similarity among associates', *American Sociological Review*, 47: 797–801.

(1984), 'The structured use of personal associates', *Social Forces*, 62: 640–52.

(1997), 'Structural embeddedness and the stability of interpersonal relations', *Social Networks*, 19: 91–5.

Festinger, Leon, Schachter, Stanley, and Back, Kurt (1950), *Social Pressures in Informal Groups*, New York: Harper.

Fischer, Claude S. (1982a), *To Dwell Among Friends: Personal Networks in Town and City*, University of Chicago Press.

(1982b), 'What do we mean by "friend"? An inductive study', *Social Networks*, 3: 287–306.

Granovetter, Mark S. (1985), 'Economic action and social structure: the problem of embeddedness', *American Journal of Sociology*, 91: 481–510.

Kelly, John R. (1993), *Activity and Aging: Staying Involved in Later Life*, Newbury Park: Sage.

Milardo, Robert M. (1988), 'Families and social networks: an overview of theory and methodology', in Milardo (ed.).

(ed.) (1988), *Families and Social Networks*, Newbury Park: Sage.

Nelson, Geoffrey (1995), 'Women's social networks and social support following marital separation: a controlled prospective study', *Journal of Divorce and Remarriage*, 23: 149–69.

Patterson, Ian (1996), 'Participation in leisure activities by older adults after a stressful life event: the loss of a spouse', *International Journal of Aging and Human Development*, 42: 123–42.

Simmel, Georg (1955 [1922]), *Conflict and the Web of Group Affiliations*, translated by Reinhard Bendix, from the German *Soziologie* (1922), New York: Free Press.

Spanier, Graham B., and Thompson, Linda (1987), *Parting: The Aftermath of Separation and Divorce*, Beverly Hills: Sage.

Straus, Murray A., Gelles, Richard J., and Steinmetz, Suzanne K. (1980), *Behind Closed Doors: Violence in the American Family*, Garden City, N.Y.: Anchor Press/Doubleday.

Stueve, C. Ann, and Gerson, Kathleen (1977), 'Personal relations across the life-cycle', in Claude S. Fischer (ed.), *Networks and Places*, New York: Free Press.

Surra, Catherine A. (1988), 'The influence of the interactive network on developing relationships', in Milardo (ed.).

Wellman, Barry (1979), 'The community question: the intimate networks of East Yorkers', *American Journal of Sociology*, 84: 1201–31.

Wellman, Barry, and Wortley, Scott (1990), 'Different strokes from different folks: community ties and social support', *American Journal of Sociology*, 96: 558–88.

Wilcox, B. L. (1981), 'Social support in adjusting to marital disruption', in B. H. Gottlieb (ed.), *Social Networks and Social Support*, Beverly Hills: Sage.

8

The demise of territorial determinism: online friendships

Rebecca G. Adams

New social forms and processes emerge and old ones change and sometimes disappear with technological change. In this chapter, I consider the state of development of transportation and communications technologies as a context for the structure and content friendship. The focus of this discussion is therefore on how technology affects relationships, rather than on how society shapes technology (see Meyrowitz, 1985, for a discussion of the latter topic). None the less, the position taken here is not technologically deterministic (see McLuhan, 1964, and Innis, 1951, for examples of this approach), but rather social constructivist. Participants use technology to form and maintain friendships and, as a consequence, encourage technology to develop in ways that serve this purpose (see Couch, 1989, 1990, for an examination of the role of human agency in using technology for relationship work). This chapter is focused on the social construction of relationships instead of on the social construction of technology, and thus the discussion considers only one side of the process. For the purposes here, the question of technological versus social determinism is inconsequential, because technological determinists, social constructivists, and those who see technology and society as dialectically interdependent (e.g., Castells, 1996) agree that social relationships are different depending on the technological context in which they are formed and maintained. Of interest here is how friendships might be different now and in the future than they were 200 years ago, before the recent, rapid developments in communications and transportation technology.

Research has repeatedly verified Homans's (1950) proposition that increased interaction leads to increased liking (e.g., Hays, 1984, 1985). This suggests that any change in technology that facilitates increased contact among friends would contribute to the solidarity of relationships. It is common knowledge that technological changes during the past 150 years have made contact between the members of both physically proximate and long-distant friendship pairs less expensive, faster, and easier. Although numerous studies have been conducted on the social impact of previous technological developments (e.g., Pool, 1983; Fischer and Carroll, 1988; Martin, 1991), the effects of the most recent developments in electronic communications on friendship have not been studied (see Parks and Floyd, 1996, for an exception).

The purpose of this chapter is to examine what we know about how the electronic context affects friendships and to suggest directions for future research. Before examining the consequences of electronic communication for friendship, it is useful to examine the extent and variety of changes in the technological context of friendship and the state of the research literature on interaction between friends. Examining the changes in technology serves as a reminder of how dramatically the context of friendship has changed, and surveying the literature on interaction among friends serves to demonstrate how slowly sociologists have changed their perspectives on relationships to reflect these developments.

After documenting the existence of this scholarly lag, I use an integrative conceptual framework for friendship research (Adams and Blieszner, 1994) to organise a summary of what we know and do not know about the structure and process of a newly emergent social form, electronic friendship. In the process of doing this, I will elaborate on the notion of 'context' to incorporate dimensions relevant to the electronic environment and on the interpretation of the elements of the framework to demonstrate its suitability for use in examining online and other non-proximate friendships.

Changes in the technological context

A mere 200 years ago, communication across distance was dependent on transportation. Messages could be sent only via animals or people who were travelling. Letters were sent when someone happened to be going in a certain direction. Although postal systems existed in Egypt in about 2,000 BC and in China about 1,000 years later, the efficiency of these systems did not improve dramatically until extensive road building made the introduction of the stage coach possible in the eighteenth century ('Postal system', 1997). Although as early as 1860, messages could be sent between St Joseph, Missouri, and Sacramento, California, in ten days via the Pony Express, normally letters were delivered much more slowly ('Pony Express', 1997). Dependent on air delivery, the first regular international delivery service started between Paris and London in 1919, and in the United States regular transcontinental service began in 1924. Regular air-mail delivery across the Atlantic was initiated just prior to World War II ('Postal system', 1997).

When the telegraph was developed, communication was no longer dependent on transportation. For the first time, messages could be sent without someone travelling, and they could be sent faster than someone could carry them (Carey, 1983). Morse sent the first intercity telegraph message on 24 May 1844. By 1861, the Pony Express had ceased operation and the transcontinental telegraph system had been fully established (Klein, 1993; 'Pony Express', 1997). On 12 December 1901, forty years after the first transatlantic telegraph cable had been laid, Marconi sent a message by wireless telegraph across the Atlantic. Although the wireless was used mainly to send commercial messages, amateur enthusiasts, forebears of the current Internet junkies, began communicating socially with one another (Warthman, 1974; Reynolds, 1977–9).

During this century, both communications and transportation have become faster, more efficient, and more accessible. In 1876, Bell invented the first telephone transmitter and patented it. Within a decade the Bell Telephone system had begun to develop (Warthman, 1974). The diffusion of the telephone started out slowly; by 1900, only two out of every hundred Americans had telephones, and even most of these were instruments of convenience and commerce rather than tools for friends to use in keeping in touch (Fischer and Carroll, 1988), By 1915, transcontinental telephone service was possible (Warthman, 1974). According to Fischer and Carroll (1988), on the eve of the Great Depression, 41 per cent of all homes in the United States were equipped with a telephone, and it had become firmly established as a social instrument, at least among the middle class. Full saturation did not occur until the 1960s.

Transportation technology developed rapidly over this same period. In the early nineteenth century, commercial steam ships began operation in the United States and Britain and shortly thereafter steam locomotives were available as transportation ('History of technology', 1997). Then came automobiles and aeroplanes. In 1895, there were 3,700 car owners in the United States; by 1900, there were 8,000. In 1903, both the first flight by the Wright brothers and the first continental crossing by automobile occurred (Hokanson, 1988). The Lincoln Highway opened in 1915, making it possible for people to cross the United States by car relatively easily (ibid.). In 1918, the first airline was formed in Germany. By the 1930s, three airlines were developing world-wide flight patterns, and one-fifth of all Americans owned automobiles ('Formation of airlines', 1997; Fischer and Carroll,

1988). By the 1960s, most people in the United States owned cars and air transportation was easily available to passengers who could afford it.

By the 1970s, it was thus relatively easy for people with adequate financial resources to talk and visit with people who lived all over the globe. With the development of the Internet, communication with large numbers of people world-wide could take place almost instantly and more easily than before. According to Castells (1996), there were only twenty-five computers on the Internet in 1973. As late as the 1980s, there were only a few thousand Internet users. By the mid-1990s, the Internet 'connected 44,000 computer networks and about 3.2 million host computers world-wide with an estimated 25,000 million users, and it was expanding rapidly' (ibid., p. 345). Experts predict that one day the Internet could connect 600 million computer networks. Although most electronic communication is currently mainly text-based, multimedia applications for online communication are being developed (Paccagnella, 1997). We are now hearing about the possibilities of virtually projecting people to another location, once again blurring the distinction between transportation and communications (Rheingold, 1991). This time, though, rather than communication being dependent on transportation, transportation-like experiences will be dependent on communications technology.

Scholarly responses to changes in technology

With each technological development, forecasters predicted its social impact. With the development of the telegraph, telephone, automobile, aeroplane, and now electronic communication, scholars have debated whether the effect would be increased social isolation or integration (e.g., Pool, 1983), have discussed inequality of access (e.g., Fischer and Carroll, 1988; Martin, 1991), and have considered how technological change alters spatial and temporal boundaries of relationships (e.g., Carey, 1983). Whatever the net effect of the most recent technological developments, current theoretical assumptions regarding friendship clearly need examination now that interaction can so easily take place between people who are not currently in the same geographic location and now that travelling long distances to be with friends is relatively easy. Current theory is not so easily adapted to the new technological environment, however (see Lea and Spears, 1995, for a discussion of the theoretical issues regarding relationships raised by recent technological changes). Early studies (e.g., Festinger, *et al.*, 1950) showed that friendships were more likely to form when people live near one another, because the cost of establishing and maintaining long-distance contacts was so high that they were unlikely to be offset by any emotional rewards. Most researchers thus have assumed that relationships form between people who are in each other's physical presence, at least in the beginning and intermittently thereafter. This has led researchers to focus on local relationships rather than on relationships that form between people who live at a distance from each other.

Social psychological theory regarding relationships has developed from this starting point. For example, in sociology, the concept of primary groups, those most important in linking the individual with society and helping with socialisation, assumes proximity and face-to-face contact (see Litwak and Szelenyi, 1969). The examples of primary groups that Cooley (1983 [1902]) listed included family, neighbours, and the play groups of children, all of which involve repeated, intimate, face-to-face contacts. Psychologists who study interpersonal attraction also assume that people are physically co-present. For example, some of them have emphasised the importance for relationship development of visual cues, including phenomena such as gazing into a lover's eyes or being attracted to someone because of their physical appearance, as well as gestures, facial expressions, tie-signs, and how people space themselves and orient themselves to each other (see Short, *et al.*, 1976).

The assumption of physical co-presence made some sense in the technological context in which these territorially bound theories developed. Although people have maintained long-distance relationships for a very long time with people they had previously met face to face, it was relatively unusual until recently for a relationship to develop between people without them being initially physically co-present. When there was little possibility of travelling regularly to another geographic location or communicating easily with people who lived at a distance, friendships could form only between people who lived physically proximate to each other, at least for the period during which the relationship was being established. Even maintaining already established relationships across distances was difficult, because contact was infrequent, expensive, or unsatisfying. As transportation and communications technology developed, however, it became increasingly possible to maintain and even establish friendships across distances. It took the recent radical developments in electronic communications, however, to call the attention of scholars to how inadequate their theoretical approaches assuming physical proximity are. Now that relationships more frequently develop and are maintained without any face-to-face interaction, theorists must consider what functionally substitutes for physical co-presence in long-distance or virtual interactions and whether it was physical co-presence or frequency of interaction that was important after all. Recent researchers have also demonstrated that it is not merely the quantity of interaction that matters, but the form and content of relationships as well. Understanding how the current technological context shapes the qualities of relationships makes the task facing scholars more complex.

Representatives of various disciplines have begun to map out intellectual agendas. Biocca (1992) discussed questions of interest to communications scholars; Taha and Caldwell (1993) examined issues relevant to work environments; and Escobar (1994) articulated an approach to the anthropology of 'Cyberia'. In some senses, sociologists interested in the study of close relationships have been slow to respond to the implications of these recent developments. Special sessions devoted to online culture and communities were scheduled at the American Sociological Society meetings for the first time as late as 1995. Only recently have special issues of sociological journals and books appeared which examine the impact of new communications technologies on social life (Cerulo, 1997).

In some ways, though, sociology has been responding to these technological developments gradually over a sixty-year period. Perhaps one of the earliest commentaries, or at least one of the most frequently cited, was Lynd and Lynd's (1929) chapter on the social impact of the automobile on life in *Middletown*. The authors quoted one observer who asked them why they needed to do a study of what was changing in the United States. This observer reportedly said: 'I can tell you what's happening in just four letters: A-U-T-O!' (p. 251). In the chapter in which this quotation is included, the Lynds described the effects the automobile had on Middletown: people no longer had to live in town to keep in touch with their friends; families dispersed in the evening, rather than spending time together; and residents participated in more leisure activities away from home. The authors observed that neighbours did not know each other as well anymore, but spent their time visiting people who lived elsewhere. Up until World War II, writers followed the Lynds' example and continued to bemoan loss of local community.

Perhaps in response to this lament, sociologists in the 1950s and 1960s spent a great deal of intellectual energy documenting the existence of communities in both slums (e.g., Gans, 1962; Liebow, 1967; and William F. Whyte, 1943) and suburbs (e.g., Gans, 1967; William H. Whyte, 1956). Although the ethnographic descriptions depicted rich interactions among friends, they did not include discussions of long-distance relationships. This is particularly interesting in the case of the ethnographies of suburbs occupied by now famous transients, such as organisation men and

Levittowners. For example, in *The Organization Man* (William H. Whyte, 1956), 'The web of friendship' is about the importance of proximity to local relationships, 'The transients' is on the topic of the separation of organisational families from their past lives, and 'The new roots' includes a passing reference to old friends only in the last paragraph, as people whom 'you can pick up with . . . where you left off when you meet again' (p. 329). Although at the time Parsons (1949) argued that the nuclear family was most adaptive in contemporary society because geographic mobility was common and long-distance connections were so difficult to maintain, these migratory families surely maintained relationships with people left behind in their communities of origin and in other neighbourhoods they had occupied temporarily. Rather than examining how people were maintaining long-distance relationships and the nature of these relationships, researchers focused attention on the new local communities they created.

While ethnographers focused on local communities, survey researchers relied mainly on global questions regarding frequency of face-to-face interaction with friends to measure social integration (e.g., Zena Smith Blau, 1961; Pihlblad and McNamara, 1965; Rose, 1965). Researchers asked questions such as: 'On the average, how often do you see each of your friends?', or 'How many times did you visit a friend last week?' (see Adams, 1989, for a discussion of measurement issues in friendship research). Long-distance friendships were not treated separately from local ones, and most questions were designed to measure face-to-face contact specifically and thus asked how frequently the respondents 'visited' or 'saw' friends. Some scholars even defined friendship as a local phenomenon and eliminated non-local contacts from consideration (e.g., Williams, 1959; Rosow, 1967). The assumption seemed to be either that people did not have very many non-local friendships, or that once friends were no longer proximate, they ceased to play an active role in each other's lives.

Subsequently, in an important series of articles, Litwak demonstrated that changes in technology had led to new forms of primary group structure, but that 'contacts among extended family kin can be maintained despite breaks in face-to-face contact; neighbourhoods can exist despite rapid membership turnover; and friendships can continue despite both of these problems' (Litwak, 1960a, 1960b, 1965; Litwak and Szelenyi, 1969, p. 465). In response to Litwak's astute observations, some survey researchers began to ask specifically about telephone communication and letter-writing or at least about contact in general without including wording that specified only face-to-face encounters. Technological developments were finally affecting the questions researchers were asking.

In the 1970s, urban sociologists began discussing the impact of technological developments in communications and transportation on settlement patterns. Although these urban scholars discussed friendship only in passing, their forecasts regarding changes in communities are important when thinking about the relationships embedded within them. In a classic article, Webber (1973, p. 297) discussed the erosion of localism and argued that 'Cities develop only because proximity means lower transportation and communication costs for those interdependent specialists who must interact with each other frequently or intensively.' With advancements in technology, he noted, 'For the first time in history, it might be possible to locate on a mountain top and to maintain intimate, real-time, and realistic contact with business or other associates' (ibid., p. 301). He observed that, since these developments had occurred, rather than being loyal and bound to a residential community, it was possible to emphasise communities based on beliefs and interests.

Shortly after Webber's classic piece appeared, other scholars began addressing the topic of communities without shared territory (see Effrat, 1974, for a discussion of this literature). In particular, social network scholars began examining 'personal communities':

> To recapitulate, while neighborhood communities do exist, for most urbanites they exist as only one of a multiplicity of communities in which they claim membership. The study of urban communities, therefore, must proceed from questions about the nature of interpersonal linkages, and the structural characteristics of networks. The spatiality of any given community then becomes an empirical problem . . . [D]espatialized communities can cross city – and national – boundaries.
>
> (Craven and Wellman, 1974, p. 78)

Wellman and other researchers (e.g., Fischer, 1982) have since spent two decades demonstrating that the community has not only been 'saved', but has been 'liberated' from neighbourhood and kinship boundaries. (See Wellman, 1996, for a critique of research in this tradition.)

Perhaps in response to network analysts, survey researchers interested more in friendship than in community in general began asking how far away friends lived and stopped eliminating non-local friends from inclusion in research. None the less, very few researchers have focused specifically on how these ties are maintained or on their qualities. One exception is research conducted by Rohlfing (1995) on the long-distance friendships of women. She found that the telephone was the primary channel of communication between long-distance friends, and that they did not write or visit each other much. As part of the Andrus Study of Older Adult

Friendship Patterns, Blieszner and I collected data on a probability sample of older adults in Greensboro, North Carolina, that confirm these findings (Adams and Blieszner, 1993). We asked each respondent to list their friends according to their own definition and then asked them detailed questions about their most geographically distant emotionally close friend and about the geographically nearest emotionally close friend. Of the long-distance friends, 40.7 per cent lived outside the South, and another 18.5 per cent lived outside North Carolina. Most (92.6 per cent) saw their long-distance friends occasionally; 81.5 per cent talked to them by telephone; and 44.4 per cent wrote to them. Similar to Rohlfing's study, the Greensboro data show that when long-distance friends come together, it is often because one friend happens to be in the other's area or for some special purpose such as a wedding, funeral, or reunion. The time long-distance friends spend together is primarily spent reminiscing and bringing each other up to date rather than creating new memories. Although long-distance friends are often very close to each other, they do not often have the opportunity to share details about their everyday lives or to help each other when problems arise. Shea, *et al.* (1988) referred to these as 'latent friendships', relationships that are psychologically important, but not developing further.

By the time researchers began to focus attention on long-distance relationships, the Internet and electronic communication were beginning to diffuse throughout the upper echelons of Western society and to a lesser extent into other social strata and regions of the world as well. In the 1990s, researchers have begun to turn their attention to electronic relationships and online communities, but they have little material on which to build. Although much literature exists on the way in which face-to-face dyadic relationships are formed and maintained (see Blieszner and Adams, 1992, and Fehr, 1996, for reviews of this literature), and on how territorial communities operate as a context for friendship (see Adams and Blieszner, 1993, for a discussion of this literature), researchers collected very little information before the electronic revolution on how long-distance relationships are different from face-to-face relationships and on how communities form without shared territory.

Additional information on how long-distance relationships are different from proximate ones would actually be of little use to researchers interested in relationships that develop online, because they are a different social form altogether. The long-distance friendships that people maintained before the electronic revolution were primarily with people who had previously met face to face and had often lived nearby. The basis of their relationship was often the experiences they had shared in the past. In an article based on my doctoral dissertation research on elderly women in a Chicago suburb, I reported that their emotionally close friends tended to be long term and long distant, and their casual friends tended to be neighbours and constant companions (Adams, 1985–6). The results from the Greensboro data are similar: the respondents' long-distance friends were emotionally closer and longer-term friends than the ones who lived near to them, but the respondents saw their proximate friends more frequently. When the respondents discussed the difference between long-distance friends and proximate friends in the abstract, they generally assumed that the interviewers were asking about the difference between long-term friends and new friends. Although it would be interesting to know how the introduction of e-mail and other online exchanges into already existing long-distance friendships transforms them, apparently researchers have not conducted such a study. At this point in history and unlike old-fashioned long-distance friendships, those formed online have generally not endured for long (Parks and Floyd, 1996), are not primarily based on experiences shared in the past, and are not held together by long-standing affection. Furthermore, people who meet online do not typically live near each other when they initiate a friendship.

An integrative framework for the study of friendship

Although the findings from the Andrus Study on Older Adult Friendship Patterns are not particularly useful in understanding online relationships, the framework that Rosemary Blieszner and I (Adams and Blieszner, 1994) used in designing the instrument is useful as a starting point for assessing what we know about them. We developed this framework to summarise what had been written about friendship in general and to identify gaps in the literature. Similarly, this framework can be used to identify unexplored topics regarding electronic relationships and online communities. Examining the scant literature on online friendships will also suggest ways to elaborate this framework and to make it more suitable for addressing issues regarding non-proximate relationships.

The framework (see figure 1) posits that the social structural and dispositional aspects of individual characteristics such as age and gender interact with each other to shape a person's behavioural motifs, defined as the constellation of the routine and unpredictable aspects of daily activities. Behavioural motifs then influence friendship interaction patterns. These patterns consist of the phases, structure, and processes of friendship networks and of the dyadic relationships embedded within them.

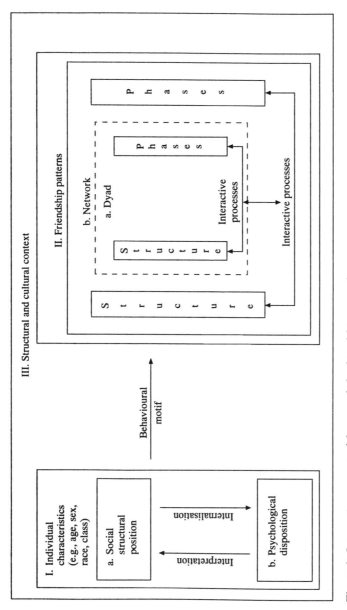

Figure 1: *Integrative conceptual framework for friendship research*

Reprinted by permission of Sage Publications Ltd from Rebecca Adams and Rosemary Blieszner, 1994, Figure 1 from 'An integrative conceptual framework for friendship research', *Journal of Social and Personal Relationships* 11(2): 166.

Note that, although from the inception of the framework Blieszner and I (Blieszner and Adams, 1992) realised that it, its elements, and the connections among them would vary by context, we did not discuss what contextual characteristics might be important in shaping friendship. In the Andrus Study on Older Adult Friendship Patterns, which operationalised the original framework as completely as was practically possible, we asked questions regarding the foci of activities from which the older adults' friends were derived (see Feld, 1981, and Feld and Carter, this volume). These data suggested that cultural as well as structural characteristics of context are important in shaping the friendships that are formed and maintained within them. By examining the empirical literature on electronic relationships and thinking theoretically about the effects of an electronic environment on elements of this framework, I will develop this notion of 'context' further.

Individual characteristics

The majority of friendship researchers have examined the connection between individual characteristics (e.g., sex and age) and some aspect of friendship patterns (see Blieszner and Adams, 1992, for a summary of these findings). Each of these characteristics has implications for the structural opportunities available to people for friendship formation and maintenance and for their psychological dispositions, whether learned or physiologically determined, that might affect their behavioural motifs and thus their propensities to form certain types of relationships. When using these characteristics as predictors of friendship patterns, researchers have failed to distinguish between structural and dispositional effects, and thus we know little about the mechanisms that lead men and women and people of various ages to have different friendship patterns (Adams and Blieszner, 1994).

Although we know that computer users are relatively affluent (Castells, 1996; Dyrkton, 1996) and more often male than female (Castells, 1996), we do not know very much about the individual characteristics of people who have online friendships as opposed to those who use the Internet but do not establish personal connections. In one of the only examinations of this topic, Parks and Floyd (1996) reported that women were more likely to develop personal relationships online than men were and that age did not have an effect. They hypothesised that friendships develop more as a result of experience than as a consequence of demographic or personality factors. The difference between men and women they reported does not support this interpretation, though. Researchers have repeatedly found that women are more likely to establish relationships based on verbal exchanges than men are (Wright, 1982), which seems to be reflected in Parks and Floyd's (1996) finding regarding gender differences.

One aspect of the framework presented in figure 1 that needs elaboration becomes obvious when considering how it might operate in the context of electronic environments. Sociologists view externally imposed expectations regarding the behaviour of people with different characteristics as social facts. Not only is it difficult for people to resist living up to these expectations, when they do depart from them, they are sanctioned (Durkheim, 1964 [1938]). As Goffman (1959) has observed, although misrepresentation occurs, people expect others to act as members of their social category are expected to behave – it is part of the social contract. Although online participants generally also operate in the 'real' world where the social contract is generally enforced, the electronic world has different rules. Although some online participants might continue to expect the same consistency between appearance and reality that is acceptable to assume in the face-to-face world, the norms are distinctly different on the Internet. When people interact online, their gender, race, rank, and other features of their normally public identity are not obvious. It remains for the participants to reveal their characteristics, honestly or otherwise. Although more attention has been paid to gender-switching than to other online deceptions (Lea and Spears, 1995; Parks and Floyd, 1996), it is possible for people to move in and out of other social roles and characters (Jones, 1995). Participants can experiment with the effects of social structure by assessing how they are treated when they present themselves with different characteristics. Although the framework as it is currently constituted allows for the social construction of these characteristics, the underlying assumption was that individuals did not change their identities, but that they interpreted them differently and internalised different aspects of them. In order to accommodate online culture, the notion of interpretation has to be expanded to include manipulation and deception, and the notion that these identities are not necessarily internalised at all has to be recognised. Dimensions of context that become important include how relevant social structural location is to interaction and how visible the social characteristics of participants are.

Phases of friendship

Friendship phases reflect the developmental status of the relationship, whether in the formative or dissolution stage, or someplace in between

(Blieszner and Adams, 1992). Through the course of a friendship, its internal processes and structural characteristics change. Researchers have only recently begun to pay attention to dyadic friendship development (e.g., Fehr, 1996) and have not yet studied how friendship networks unfold. Only sparse information is available specifically on the trajectory of dyadic electronic friendships (see Parks and Floyd, 1996, for an important exception), and, as I will discuss below, no information is available on the developmental course of electronic friendship networks. Although researchers have been examining online interactions for some time, early theoretical approaches suggested that personal relationships would not be likely to develop online. Researchers who used a social presence perspective (Short, *et al.*, 1976) argued that, because electronic communications are asynchronous and text-based, they are not perceived to be as intimate as face-to-face exchanges are. Others (e.g., Siegel, *et al.*, 1986) argued that, due to the reduced variety of social cues available for interpretation by participants, electronic communication is more negative and impersonal. Possibly because these theories predicted that personal relationships would not be likely to develop online, researchers did not bother to study them.

However, it has become clear that close friendships do develop online. Parks and Floyd (1996) reported that, like face-to-face relationships, those that are initiated electronically develop over time. They increase in interdependence, breadth, depth, understanding, and commitment; the style of communication between partners changes; and the networks of the participants converge. Other recent research has suggested that online relationships none the less develop more slowly (Walther, *et al.*, 1994) or at least in qualitatively different ways (Lea and Spears, 1995) than face-to-face relationships. Even less information exists on the maintenance phase of electronic relationships, though evidence suggests that, when participants interact with each other privately by e-mail (Korenman and Wyatt, 1996) or face to face (Harrington and Bielby, 1995), their relationships increase in solidarity. Although accounts of negative exchanges are common in the literature (e.g., Lea and Spears, 1995), the dissolution of electronic friendships has not been studied.

Researchers need to pay more attention to the notion of friendship development in general and to the importance of behavioural motifs in shaping relationships. Although it is generally acknowledged that friendships do develop over time, measures of that development tend to be confounded with measures of various aspects of friendship structure and process (e.g., solidarity, feelings of intimacy). By studying friendship in a distinctly different context where new forms of personal relationships can emerge, researchers will have an opportunity to construct abstract notions of behavioural motifs and development that apply equally well in online and offline settings.

For now, in light of the paucity of information on the development of online friendships and the potential limited relevance of most information on friendships initiated though face-to-face contact, it is useful to consider conclusions from a study I conducted on how friendships form in the context of a community without a shared territory (Adams, 1998). Although I could have accomplished the same theoretical agenda by studying business people who frequent trade shows, storm chasers, dog and horse show enthusiasts, or even academics who attend professional conferences, I studied Deadheads, fans of the defunct rock band, the Grateful Dead. Participants in the Deadhead community formed friendships with others who had never lived near them and who came together with them only periodically at concerts. Many of them also participated in online Deadhead communities, but what interests me here is that even offline Deadhead friendships often formed between people who did not share local residence. The peculiar characteristics of the online environment and electronic communications technology certainly have different and additional effects on friendships, but some insight can be gained by examining offline friendship formation in this intermittently territorial community.

After initial observations of the Deadhead community, I asked myself how Deadheads met one another repeatedly despite their large numbers and lack of shared territory, how these interactions led to friendship, and what accounted for the seemingly high level of solidarity of Deadhead relationships. In summary, I asked myself how friendships formed and developed between people in this intermittently territorial context. These same questions could be asked by someone studying an online community, which instead of being intermittently territorial is not necessarily territorial at all. In both the Deadhead community and online, however, spatial metaphors are socially constructed to describe movement from one social setting to another. This makes observations of the Deadhead community particularly useful in thinking about online communities as a context for friendship. The Deadhead Project suggests that friendships will be more likely to develop in communities without a shared territory that (1) facilitate repeated interactions between participants, (2) have differentiated meeting places reflective of the diversity of the participants, (3) encourage contact among participants outside the setting, (4) allow for shared experiences that lead to increased solidarity, (5) are characterised by norms and beliefs that encourage pleasant interactions among participants, (6) have members with values, beliefs, and lifestyles distinct from those of the mainstream or at least similar to each other's, and (7) create an atmosphere of trust and respect.

Although researchers have not done comparative studies of online communities to determine whether participants are more likely to develop in electronic contexts with these characteristics, scant evidence at least suggests that some of these effects operate online. Korenman and Wyatt (1996) showed that online friendships increase in solidarity after an exchange of private e-mail which is an online equivalent of interaction outside the setting. In her description of interactions in a virtual fantasy world, Reid (1995) described how a woman met her husband in the process of playing an online game. They built a castle together and were treated as an online couple. They eventually met face to face and married. This suggests that it is possible for online participants to share experiences that contribute to the solidarity of their relationships. Argyle (1996) similarly observed the development of solidarity after a real death of an online participant. Although early inhabitants of the Internet were hoping a normless frontier-like society would emerge (Rheingold, 1991), standards of acceptable conduct have developed (McLaughlin, *et al.*, 1995). These norms make it more likely that interactions will be pleasant and conducive to the formation of friendships. Harrington and Bielby (1995) reported that the stigma of being soap opera fans increased the solidarity of relationships of bulletin board participants, as did face-to-face gatherings. Finally, because control and surveillance of interaction are easier on the Internet than offline, it is possible that people are more reluctant to form friendship in online communities in general. To determine how fully the effects observed in the Deadhead study operate online and how they vary across communities, researchers need to conduct more observational studies of online communities and compare findings across different types of them (see Paccagnella, 1997, for a discussion of strategies for ethnographic research on virtual communities).

Internal processes

Internal processes of friendship include affective, cognitive, and behavioural aspects of interactions – the way participants feel, think, and behave (Blieszner, 1995). Perhaps more research has been conducted on the effects of the electronic environment on these aspects of friendship patterns than on any others. None the less, current theory and research only predict and document the existence of various processes rather than examining the relationships among them, how they are connected to structural aspects of friendship, or what effects they have on the individual or the context in which the relationships are embedded. Moreover, the current literature concerns only the internal processes of dyadic relationships rather than the affective, cognitive, and behavioural exchanges in friendship networks as a whole.

Most of the discussion of affective processes in online friendships has focused on whether and how fully it is possible to express emotions online. As mentioned earlier, proponents of both the social presence and the reduced cues perspectives have argued that, because participants in online interactions cannot see, hear, or feel one another and can maintain their anonymity, electronic interactions are less personal and more negative than face-to-face exchanges (e.g., Sproull and Kiesler, 1991). Extremists (e.g., Heim, 1992) have even argued that, without face-to-face interaction, exchanges become amoral and participants indifferent. In contrast, social constructivists (e.g., Lea and Spears, 1995) have demonstrated that the social cues perspective does not predict the variability in online interactions and that a wide variety of emotions, both negative and positive, are expressed online. Wilkins (1991) discussed how people interacting electronically express emotions by using keyboard characters (e.g., typing ' :-)' to indicate a smile) and inserting words in sentences to convey affect (e.g., 'grin', 'sob'). The next step will be documenting the range of emotions expressed, their sincerity, and the consequences of these affective exchanges.

When researchers discuss the behaviours in which friends engage, they generally make a distinction between talking and participation in other activities. Often, for example, it is noted that women tend to spend more time talking and men spend more time doing things with their friends (Wright, 1982). Generally, data are not examined at a more detailed level than this. When examining online behaviour, this distinction is not very useful, because all behaviour is text-based and thus the electronic equivalent of talking. What people talk about and the activities in which they perceive themselves to be engaged thus become important in distinguishing types of online behaviours. Documented activities range from creating virtual worlds (Reid, 1995) or participating in virtual sex (Deuel, 1996), to mourning the death of an active community participant (Argyle, 1996). Further research into the variety of online behaviours is needed as well as studies examining the likelihood of friendships developing as an outgrowth of these activities.

Cognitive processes are the internal thoughts that friends have about themselves, each other, and their relationships (Blieszner, 1995). For example, a friend might assess the stability of a relationship, evaluate the performance of each partner as a friend, and interpret events, behaviours, needs, and so on. Research has shown that online participants make a variety of attributions regarding their online exchanges. For example, participants can perceive exchanges to be co-operative or conflictive (Kolluck and Smith, 1996), supportive or argumentative (Parks and Floyd, 1996), work or play (Reid, 1995), and realistic or fantastic (Harrington and Bielby, 1995). Although there has been some discussion of the general effects that using electronic media has on the form and content of thought (Biocca, 1992), researchers have not paid much attention to how online participation makes people think differently specifically about their friendships. Most of the discussion of cognitions regarding friendships have focused on whether people distinguish between their face-to-face and virtual relationships. Most of the evidence suggests that people do not make sharp distinctions between them (Parks and Floyd, 1996) and often take online identities very seriously (e.g., Shapiro and McDonald, 1992). The consequences of defining online situations and relationships as real need to be examined. In addition, other attributions people make about online friendships need to be documented.

Internal structural characteristics

Structural characteristics are the form of the ties linking an individual's friends, such as the power or status hierarchy and solidarity or closeness among them, the similarity of their social positions, the number of friends, the proportion of them who know each other, and the pattern of connections among them (Blieszner and Adams, 1992). Researchers have not paid nearly as much attention to the structural characteristics of online friendships as they have to their processes. The lack of attention to the structural characteristics of online friendships probably has resulted because scholars who focus on dyadic relationships typically examine processes and those who study networks generally are more interested in structural characteristics (see ibid. for a discussion of the connections between unit of measurement and theoretical perspective). As Garton, *et al.* (1997) observed, most of the research on computer-mediated communication has focused on individual users, dyadic interactions, and small groups rather than on networks. It is odd that researchers have been slow to examine networks of ties on the Internet, because the medium lends itself to being studied from this perspective. The World Wide Web itself is a network, consisting of loosely knit home pages connected by hypertext hot buttons. Similarly, connections among computer users themselves can also be better described as networks than as groups which are denser and have definite boundaries. Online friendships supplement or sometimes are substitutes for offline relationships. Online networks thus affect the overall structure of people's friendship networks, either by being added to them or by changing the offline relationships themselves. Here I will draw on the scant literature on the structural aspects of online relationships and speculate about how the size, density, homogeneity, and internal hierarchy of friendships and friendship networks might be altered by the electronic revolution.

Initially it would seem obvious that access to the Internet would allow people to maintain many more ties than they could have maintained previously. The effects on size would be not only due to the addition of online relationships to their networks, but also because of the opportunity to interact with friends already known offline easily and more frequently than might have been possible without electronic communication. Before it is possible to predict the effects that access to online communication will have on the size of friendship networks, two important questions must be answered. First, researchers must determine what proportion of online relationships actually develop into friendships and whether these relationships supplement or replace those acquired offline. It is possible that online interactions increase the number of acquaintances, but not the number of friends. Secondly, researchers need to examine how much online interaction contributes to or detracts from the solidarity of relationships that also exist offline. Does the opportunity for frequent interaction increase the solidarity of these relationships, creating friendships out of casual acquaintances? It is also possible that access to online interaction could diminish the solidarity of some friendships, prompting them to fade away. For example, it is possible that old friends who live at a distance from each other are able to remain friends because they are not aware of how much they have grown apart. Exchanging routine messages about their daily lives could increase that awareness and make them less likely to continue to consider each other to be friends. Similarly, having the capability of interacting and not taking advantage of it could also transform some long-distance friendships into ex-friendships.

Density of online networks is another topic that researchers have not explored. Discussion must start at the definitional level. If density is a measure of 'the extent to which links which could exist among persons do in fact exist' (Mitchell, 1969, p. 18), the question becomes: what constitutes a link? Are two people linked if they recognise each other's Internet addresses, or do they have to have exchanged private e-mail? Perhaps they have to acknowledge each other as friends. Studying online relationships introduces yet another measurement wrinkle. It is possible for people to participate in some online contexts without revealing their presence. 'Lurkers' can acquire a great deal of information about people merely from reading their postings. Are lurkers linked to the people they observe? Before answering 'definitely not', think about how previous studies of egocentric networks have been conducted. Researchers have rarely verified the reciprocity of relationships. In my own research, for example, many of my elderly respondents have listed formal service providers as friends. I suspect many of these 'friends' would not even have known the elderly respondents' names (Adams, 1985). This suggests that a lurker could identify an online relationship with another participant that the other participant does not even know exists. Furthermore, relying on information posted by the other participant, the lurker could report on other relationships the participant has. As in studying offline relationships, the concepts of density, solidarity, and reciprocity become hopelessly intertwined. Because e-mail addresses can change frequently and one person can use many of them simultaneously, measurement issues become even more complex. In order to find out if someone 'knows' someone else online, a researcher would have to present a respondent with a complete list of their aliases. This measurement problem would probably contribute to the underestimation of network density and possibly to the overestimation of network size.

Measurement issues aside, predicting the effects of the electronic context on network density is still complex. Participation in an online setting is generally public and thus everyone who participates has an opportunity to 'meet' all other participants. This suggests that density within a foci of activity (see Feld and Carter, in this volume) could be quite high. On the other hand, people can participate in a variety of unrelated online settings, thus contributing to lower network density overall. The effects of the electronic context on density will largely depend on what behavioural motifs individuals adopt and how loyally they participate in specific online settings. If people tend to drift from online location to online location, this would contribute to lower network density for the drifters and for the loyalists alike. The drifters would acquire new network members in each new setting they enter, and the loyalists would acquire new members as others drift into the settings in which they loyally participate. If, on the other hand, network inhabitants tend to be loyalists, homesteading certain areas of the Internet and participating in them to the exclusion of others, network density might be higher. Information on the behavioural motifs of Internet inhabitants as well as on the stability of online ties is thus needed before the effects of the online context on network density can be predicted.

The question of how electronic communications contribute to the homogeneity of friendship networks is also an interesting one. One of the most repeated findings in the friendship literature is that friends tend to share gender, race, age, and other social structural characteristics (e.g., Fischer, 1982; Jackson, 1977; Laumann, 1973; Verbrugge, 1977). Presumably the explanation for this finding is both social structural and dispositional. Although access to certain aspects of the online world is limited by age and wealth, once people are online, these characteristics cease to limit interaction in the same way as they do in the face-to-face world. If one assumes that people have been limited in their choices by social structural constraints, this would suggest that homogeneity of friendship networks might be reduced by online communication. Some evidence suggests online friendship networks are less homogeneous, at least in terms of gender; Parks and Floyd (1996) reported that 51 per cent of the online friendships their respondents reported were with members of the opposite sex, which is considerably less homogeneous than is typical of offline relationships.

One can equally imagine the opposite effect, however. One of the clear advantages of online communication is that people with similar interests and values can find each other. For example, Harrington and Bielby (1995) describe those who participate in constructing fantasies derived from soap operas as people with unusual interests who manage to find each other only because of the Internet. Clearly people who participate on the Internet might have networks of friends who more closely share their interests and values than people who do not. If these interests and values are tied to socialisation which is different for people in different social structural locations, then there might be *de facto* homogeneity of friendship networks even when they develop online. Thus, the effects of the electronic context on the homogeneity of friendship networks will depend on whether social structure has been mainly affecting the choices people make indirectly through socialisation or directly by creating barriers to interaction.

Scholars have treated external social location (e.g., race, gender, class) as conceptually independent from the internal status and power hierarchies that develop in relationships (see Blieszner and Adams, 1992, for a discussion of this literature). For example, though in a context external to a relationship men might have more status than women, within a specific cross-sex relationship the woman partner might be of higher status than the male partner. Of course, researchers have documented empirical correlations between external status and status within relationships. In the online world, however, where external structural characteristics are often not revealed and can even be misrepresented, it is possible that these concepts are empirically as well as conceptually independent. Several researchers have concluded that participation in discussions is more evenly distributed online (Walther, 1992) and that women and minorities have more opportunity to express their views even when their gender and racial identities are known (Baron, 1984). As in other contexts, status emerges based on who has the most valued information and on how well and reliably they express it over time (Harrington and Bielby, 1995). If access to information is not determined by the social structure external to the online environment, then internal status might be independent of it. On the other hand, it is possible that power and status are still associated with these external social characteristics, but that the difference is that, online, these external social characteristics can be borrowed when someone wants to exercise power. For example, Lea and Spears (1995) discuss how women can fend off unwanted attention from men and exploit the power associated with being male by assuming online male identities. Similarly, men can give up their relatively powerful identity and experience harassment.

Conclusion

In the first chapter in this volume, Allan and I described 'context' as 'the conditions external to the development, maintenance, and dissolution of specific friendships' (p. 4). We acknowledged that contexts are multidimensional and consist of structural and cultural elements as well as their spatial and temporal organisations. Furthermore, we mentioned that contexts are not static and can be studied on many levels. This definition was intentionally broad, because we wanted to allow the contributors to this volume to develop their notions of context with minimal constraint. When Blieszner and I developed our Integrative Conceptual Framework for the Study of Friendship (Blieszner and Adams, 1992; Adams and Blieszner, 1994), we were equally indefinite about what dimensions of context might be useful to examine in relation to friendship, reflecting the state of the literature at the time. Despite our lack of specificity thus far, however, my two collaborators and I agree that, in order for researchers to reach an understanding of how contexts shape friendship, we must begin to develop an understanding of what dimensions of context are salient.

Examining what researchers know and do not know about online friendships suggests some ways that the notion of 'context' can be usefully elaborated. Although thinking through the implications of any context for friendship form and process would probably have yielded some results, considering the online context has the advantage of being different enough from the contexts sociologists are accustomed to studying to eliminate any sense of complacency. Reflecting on technology as a context thus forces an open and broad examination of what context entails.

Although the review of the literature suggested many details about the electronic context that are relevant to friendship formation and maintenance, several dimensions stand out as particularly generic and important:

(1) How relevant is external social structure to interaction within the specific context?

(2) How aware are participants of the presence of specific others in the context and of their qualities?

(3) What contextual forces facilitate and undermine the formation and development of friendships?

(4) What limits does the context impose on the structure and process of friendship dyads and networks?

(5) What impact does interaction within a context have on other aspects of the participants' lives?

Although these questions were derived from the scant literature on the electronic context, they could easily be applied to contexts of other types. Think, for example, about the lack of relevance of external social status to interaction within certain religious orders or how secrecy regarding the full membership roster in underground social movements serves to prevent interaction with certain participants. Similarly, consider the solidarity which develops among team members in competitive sports, or the problems that hierarchies within work organisations create for the formation and development of friendship between status-dissimilars. Ponder also the way that selection criteria for Greek fraternal organisations encourage homogeneity of the friendship networks that develop within them. Reflect on how important personal contacts made in elite colleges can be for future careers and how law enforcement officials and criminals alike often insulate their families and friends from the consequences of their vocational activities. All of these are examples of ways in which the contextual dimensions outlined here shape the relationships that form within them.

Although this review of the literature on online relationships does not suggest substantive changes in the way the Integrative Conceptual Framework is configured, it does suggest some expanded interpretations of concepts. First, individual characteristics are not only interpreted, but also manipulated, and not all statuses are necessarily internalised. Secondly, it is clear that more precise conceptualisations of behavioural motif, the phases of friendship development, and network link need to be developed.

These conceptualisations need to be freed conceptually from grounding in face-to-face contexts so that they can be applied equally as productively to non-proximate contexts. Finally, the notion of 'behaviour' needs to be freed from territorial constraints and defined more abstractly and broadly than what people do 'together'.

Understanding the ways in which the technological context affects friendship becomes more important in light of the post-modernist discussion regarding the development of the relational self. Post-modernists such as Gergen (1991) have argued that new technologies make it possible to maintain relationships with countless others and that these relationships pull people in myriad directions, enticing them to become social chameleons and leading them to reconstruct themselves in each new situation. They form symbolic communities, which Bauman calls 'neotribes'. Whether these groups are conceptual rather than actual groups, as Bauman (1992) argues, membership in them affects self-definition. The result is a self populated by multiple identities, what Gergen (1991, pp. 146–7) calls a 'relational self':

> In this era the self is redefined as no longer an essence in itself, but relational. In the postmodern world, selves may become the manifestations of relationship, thus placing relationships in the central position occupied by the individual self for the last several hundred years of Western history.

Friendship plays a particularly critical role in the development of the relational self, because as O'Connor discusses (in this volume, p. 119), it is possible to generate alternative definitions of self within friendships that are 'peculiarly under the control of those involved'.

Sociologists, beginning with Simmel (1955 [1922]) have predicted twin consequences resulting from these changes in the form of social circles – a decline in the effectiveness of social control and an increase in personal freedom. Like post-modernists, Simmel saw modern society as increasingly consisting of intersecting rather than overlapping social circles. From Simmel's perspective, individuals are thus sociologically determined by the intersection of these groups within them. Elsewhere in this volume, Feld and Carter point out that it is unlikely that Simmel anticipated how much the rate of network change would accelerate. I would add that I doubt he foresaw how common it would become for only one person to occupy the intersection of a set of social circles. Given these developments, one has to ask how complete sociological determination is in the electronic context. With the rate of change in group affiliations and the lack of witnesses to multiple group membership, individuals might have more choice about which groups they allow to affect who they are and are expected to be (Bauman, 1992). Individuals might define what takes place in some encounters as pure sociability, as interaction as an end in itself (Simmel, 1949 [1910]). These relationships, as such, might not affect their conception of self. In the absence of others who are integrated into their relational selves, these purely sociable relationships might not affect their perceptions of whom significant others perceive them to be.

Although the electronic context allows for myriad relationships and very well may contribute to the development of relational selves, it is not clear that the rest of Gergen's predictions necessarily follow. He says that, in the post-modern context, people lose their capacity for intimacy and commitment and that genuine friendship is slowly vanishing. Although this consequence is a compelling theoretical consequence of his argument, this literature review provides no evidence to support it. In order to document the effects of these recent technological developments, more research is needed on the structure and process of relationships that form within this context and on how individuals incorporate them into their self-conceptions and everyday lives. Feld and Carter (in this volume) have suggested that local embeddedness has consequences for the support people receive and for social control. If this is the case, the effects that virtual lives have on territorially grounded ones is perhaps more important than virtual lives and relationships themselves. This is an empirical question.

The development of online friendships inevitably has consequences for society as well as for individuals. Previous research has shown the importance of informal ties for decision-making in organisations and communities (e.g., Peter M. Blau, 1955; Gouldner, 1954). These same effects certainly operate on a societal level, though documenting them would be more difficult than documenting the effects of friendship ties on more immediate contexts. As the electronic age unfolds, people previously separated by social stratification barriers could form unexpected alliances and information could be transmitted in less predictable directions. These social changes would have wide-ranging consequences. Before the extent of these possibilities and others can be realised, however, more research on the electronic friendships themselves must be conducted.

Acknowledgements
I would like to thank Graham Allan, Kenneth Allan, Rosemary Blieszner, and Scott Feld for comments on an earlier draft of this chapter and Koji Ueno for assisting with the bibliographic research.

178   *Rebecca G. Adams*

References

Adams, Rebecca G. (1985), 'People would talk: normative barriers to cross-sex friendships for elderly women', *Gerontologist*, 25: 605–11.

—— (1985–6), 'Emotional closeness and physical distance between friends: implications for elderly women living in age-segregated and age-integrated settings', *International Journal of Aging and Human Development*, 22: 55–76.

—— (1989), 'Conceptual and methodological issues in studying friendships of older adults', in Rebecca G. Adams and Rosemary Blieszner (eds.), *Older Adult Friendship: Structure and Process*, Newbury Park: Sage.

—— (1998), *Deadheads: Community, Spirituality, and Friendship*, unpublished.

Adams, Rebecca G., and Blieszner, Rosemary (1993), 'Resources for friendship intervention', *Journal of Sociology and Social Welfare*, 20: 159–75.

—— (1994), 'An integrative conceptual framework for friendship research', *Journal of Social and Personal Relationships*, 11: 163–84.

Argyle, Katie (1996), 'Life after death', in Shields (ed.).

Baron, Naomi S. (1984), 'Computer-mediated communication as a force in language change', *Visible Language*, 18: 118–41.

Bauman, Zygmunt (1992), *Intimations of Postmodernity*, London: Routledge.

Biocca, Frank (1992), 'Communication within virtual reality: creating a space for research', *Journal of Communication*, 42: 5–22.

Blau, Peter M. (1955), *The Dynamics of Bureaucracy*, University of Chicago Press.

Blau, Zena Smith (1961), 'Structural constraints on friendships in old age', *American Sociological Review*, 26: 429–39.

Blieszner, Rosemary (1995), 'Friendship processes and well-being in the later years of life: implications for interventions', *Journal of Geriatric Psychiatry*, 28: 165–83.

Blieszner, Rosemary, and Adams, Rebecca G. (1992), *Adult Friendship*, Newbury Park: Sage.

Carey, James W. (1983), 'Technology and ideology: the case of the telegraph', *Prospects*, 8: 302–25.

Castells, Manuel (1996), *The Rise of the Network Society*, Oxford: Blackwell.

Cerulo, Karen A. (ed.) (1997), 'Toward a sociology of cyberspace: a symposium', *Newsletter of the Sociology of Culture Section of the American Sociological Association*, 2: 2–3.

Cooley, Charles H. (1983 [1902]), *Social Organizations*, New Brunswick, N.J.: Transaction.

Couch, Carl J. (1989), 'Oral technologies: a cornerstone of ancient civilizations?', *Sociological Quarterly*, 30: 587–602.

—— (1990), 'Mass communication and state structures', *Social Science Journal*, 27: 111–28.

Craven, Paul, and Wellman, Barry (1974), 'The network city', in Effrat (ed.).

Deuel, Nancy R. (1996), 'Our passionate response to virtual reality', in Herring (ed.).

Durkheim, Emile (1964 [1938]), *The Rules of Sociological Method*, New York: Free Press.

Dyrkton, Joerge (1996), 'Cool runnings: the coming of cybereality in Jamaica', in Shields (ed.).

Effrat, Marcia P. (1974), 'Approaches to community: conflicts and complementaries', in Effrat (ed.).

—— (ed.) (1974), *The Community: Approaches and Applications*, New York: Free Press.

Escobar, Arturo (1994), 'Welcome to Cyberia: notes on the anthropology of cyberculture', *Current Anthropology*, 35: 211–23.

Fehr, Beverley (1996), *Friendship Process*, Newbury Park: Sage.

Feld, Scott L. (1981), 'The focused organization of social ties', *American Journal of Sociology*, 86: 1015–35.

Festinger, Leon, Schacter, Stanley, and Back, Kurt (1950), *Social Pressures in Informal Groups*, New York: Harper.

Fischer, Claude S. (1982), *To Dwell Among Friends: Personal Networks in Town and City*, University of Chicago Press.

Fischer, Claude S., and Carroll, Glenn R. (1988), 'Telephone and automobile diffusion in the United States, 1902–1937', *American Journal of Sociology*, 93: 1153–78.

'Formation of airlines' (1997), *Britannica CD*, Encyclopaedia Britannica, Inc.

Gans, Herbert (1962), *The Urban Villagers*, New York: Free Press.

—— (1967), *The Levittowners*, New York: Pantheon.

Garton, Laura, Haythornthwaite, Caroline, and Wellman, Barry (1997), 'Studying on-line networks', *Journal of Computer-Mediated Communication*, 3 (1): http://jcmc.huji.ac.il/vol3/issue1/.

Gergen, Kenneth J. (1991), *The Saturated Self*, New York: Basic Books.

Goffman, Erving (1959), *The Presentation of Self in Everyday Life*, Garden City, N.Y.: Doubleday.

Gouldner, Alvin W. (1954), *Patterns of Industrial Bureaucracy*, New York: Free Press.

Harrington, C. Lee, and Bielby, Denise D. (1995), *Soap Fans: Pursuing Pleasure and Making Meaning in Everyday Life*, Philadelphia: Temple University Press.

Hays, Robert B. (1984), 'The development and maintenance of friendship', *Journal of Social and Personal Relationships*, 1: 75–98.

—— (1985), 'A longitudinal study of friendship development', *Journal of Personality and Social Psychology*, 48: 909–24.

Heim, Michael (1992), 'The erotic ontology of cyberspace', in Michael Benedikt (ed.), *Cyberspace: First Steps*, Boston: MIT Press.

Herring, Susan C. (ed.) (1996), *Computer-Mediated Communication: Linguistic, Social and Cross-Cultural Perspectives*, Amsterdam: John Benjamins.

'History of technology' (1997), *Britannica CD*, Encyclopaedia Britannica, Inc.

Hokanson, Drake (1988), *The Lincoln Highway: Main Street Across America*, Iowa City: University of Iowa Press.

Homans, George C. (1950), *Social Behavior: Its Elementary Forms*, New York: Harcourt, Brace, and Jovanovich.

Innis, Harold (1951), *The Bias of Communication*, University of Toronto Press.

Jackson, Robert M. (1977), 'Social structure and process in friendship choice', in Claude S. Fischer, Robert M. Jackson, C. Ann Steuve, Kathleen Gerson, and Lynne McCallister Jones, with Mark Baldassare (eds.), *Networks and Places*, New York: Free Press.

Jones, Steven G. (1995), 'Introduction: from where to who knows?', in Jones (ed.).

(ed.) (1995), *Cybersociety: Computer-Mediated Communication and Community*, Newbury Park: Sage.

Klein, Maury (1993), 'What hath God wrought?', *American Heritage of Invention and Technology*, 8: 34–43.

Kolluck, Peter, and Smith, Mark (1996), 'Managing the virtual commons: cooperation and conflict in computer communities', in Herring (ed.).

Korenman, Joan, and Wyatt, Nancy (1996), 'Group dynamics in an e-mail forum', in Herring (ed.).

Laumann, Edward O. (1973), *Bonds of Pluralism*, Chichester: John Wiley.

Lea, Martin, and Spears, Russell (1995), 'Love at first byte? Building personal relationships over computer networks', in Wood and Duck (eds.).

Liebow, Elliott (1967), *Tally's Corner*, Boston: Little Brown.

Litwak, Eugene (1960a), 'Geographic mobility and extended family cohesion', *American Sociological Review*, 25: 385–94.

(1960b), 'Occupational mobility and extended family cohesion', *American Sociological Review*, 25: 9–21.

(1965), 'Extended kin relations in an industrial democratic society', in Ethel Shanas and Gordon Streib (eds.), *Social Structure and the Family: Generational Relations*, Englewood Cliffs, N.J.: Prentice Hall.

Litwak, Eugene, and Szelenyi, Ivan (1969), 'Primary group structures and their functions: kin, neighbors, and friends', *American Sociological Review*, 34: 465–81.

Lynd, Robert S., and Lynd, Helen M. (1929), *Middletown*, New York: Harcourt, Brace.

McLaughlin, Margaret L., Osborne, Kerry K., and Smith, Christine B. (1995), 'Standards of conduct on Usenet', in Jones (ed.).

McLuhan, Marshall (1964), *Understanding Media*, New York: McGraw-Hill.

Martin, Michèle (1991), 'Communication and social forms: the development of the telephone, 1876–1920', *Antipode*, 23: 307–33.

Meyrowitz, Joshua (1985), *No Sense of Place*, Oxford University Press.

Mitchell, James C. (1969), 'The concept and use of social networks', in James C. Mitchell (ed.), *Social Networks in Urban Situations*, Manchester University Press.

Paccagnella, Luciano (1997), 'Getting the seats of your pants dirty: strategies for ethnographic research on virtual communities', *Journal of Computer-Mediated Communication*, 3 (1): http://jcmc.huji.ac.il/vol3/issue1/.

Parks, Malcolm R., and Floyd, Kory (1996), 'Making friends in cyberspace', *Journal of Communication*, 46 (1): 80–97.

Parsons, Talcott (1949), 'The social structure of the family', in Ruth N. Anshen (ed.), *The Family: Its Function and Destiny*, New York: Harper and Row.

Pihlblad, C. Terrence, and McNamara, Robert L. (1965), 'Social adjustment of elderly people in three small towns', in Arnold Rose and Warren A. Peterson (eds.), *Older People and Their Social World*, Philadelphia: F. A. Davis.

'Pony express' (1997), *Britannica CD*, Encyclopaedia Britannica, Inc.

Pool, Ithiel de Sola (1983), *Forecasting the Telephone: A Retrospective Technology Assessment*, Norwood, N.J.: Ablex.

'Postal system' (1997), *Britannica CD*, Encyclopaedia Britannica, Inc.

Reid, Elizabeth (1995), 'Virtual worlds: culture and imagination', in Jones (ed.).

Reynolds, George F. (1977–9), 'Early wireless and radio in Manitoba, 1909–1924', *Transactions of the Historical and Scientific Society of Manitoba*, 34–5: 89–113.

Rheingold, Howard (1991), *Virtual Reality*, New York: Summit Books.

Rohlfing, Mary E. (1995), '"Doesn't anybody stay in one place anymore?" An exploration of under-studied phenomenon of long-distance relationships', in Wood and Duck (eds.).

Rose, Arnold M. (1965), 'Aging and social interaction among the lower classes of Rome', *Journal of Gerontology*, 20: 250–3.

Rosow, Irving (1967), *Social Integration of the Aged*, New York: Free Press.

Shapiro, Michael A., and McDonald, Daniel G. (1992), 'I'm not a real doctor, but I play one in virtual reality: implications of virtual reality for judgments about reality', *Journal of Communication*, 42: 94–114.

Shea, Laurie, Thompson, Linda, and Blieszner, Rosemary (1988), 'Resources in older adults' old and new friendships', *Journal of Social and Personal Relationships*, 5: 83–96.

Shields, Rob (ed.) (1996), *Cultures of the Internet: Virtual Spaces, Real Histories, Living Bodies*, Newbury Park: Sage.

Short, John, Williams, Ederyn, and Christie, Bruce (1976), *The Social Psychology of Telecommunications*, Chichester: John Wiley.

Siegel, Jane, Dubrovsky, Vitaly, Kiesler, Sara, and McGuire, Timothy (1986), 'Group processes in computer-mediated communication', *Organizational Behavior and Human Decision Processes*, 37: 157–87.

Simmel, Georg (1949 [1910]), 'The sociology of sociability', *American Journal of Sociology*, 55: 254–61.

  (1955 [1922]), *Conflict and the Web of Group Affiliations*, translated by Reinhard Bendix, from the German *Soziologie* (1922), New York: Free Press.

Sproull, Lee, and Kiesler, Sara (1991), *Connections: New Ways of Working in the Networked Organization*, Boston: MIT Press.

Taha, Lilas H., and Caldwell, Barrett S. (1993), 'Social isolation and integration in electronic environments', *Behaviour and Information Technology*, 12: 276–83.

Verbrugge, Lois M. (1977), 'The structure of adult friendship choices', *Social Forces*, 56: 576–97.

Walther, Joseph B. (1992), 'Interpersonal effects in computer-mediated interaction', *Communication Research*, 19: 52–90.

Walther, Joseph B., Anderson, Jeffrey F., and Park, David W. (1994), 'Interpersonal effects in computer-mediated interaction: a meta-analysis of social and antisocial communication', *Communication Research*, 21: 460–87.

Warthman, Forrest (1974), 'Telecommunication and the city', *Annals of the American Academy of Political and Social Science*, 412: 127–37.

Webber, Melvin M. (1973), 'Urbanization and communications', in George Gerbner, Larry P. Gross, and William H. Melody (eds.), *Communications Technology and Social Policy*, Chichester: John Wiley.

Wellman, Barry (1996), 'Are personal communities local? A Dumptarian reconsideration', *Social Networks*, 18: 347–54.

Whyte, William F. (1943), *Street Corner Society: The Social Structure of an Italian Slum*, University of Chicago Press.

Whyte, William H. (1956), *The Organization Man*, Garden City, N.Y.: Doubleday.

Wilkins, Harriet (1991), 'Computer talk: long-distance conversations by computer', *Written Communication*, 8: 56–78.

Williams, Robin (1959), 'Friendship and social values in a suburban community: an exploratory study', *Pacific Sociological Review*, 2: 3–10.

Wood, Julia T., and Duck, Steve (eds.) (1995), *Understudied Relationships: Off the Beaten Track*, Newbury Park: Sage.

Wright, Paul H. (1982), 'Men's friendships, women's friendships, and the alleged inferiority of the latter', *Sex Roles*, 8: 1–20.

9

Reflections on context

Graham Allan and Rebecca G. Adams

If nothing else, the chapters in this book have demonstrated that friend-ships take a variety of different forms. More importantly, they have illus-trated that these various forms do not arise haphazardly nor solely as a result of individual motivation. Like all personal relationships, even when they appear to those involved to be dyadic constructions – an expression of their own personalities, interests, and creativity – they are none the less shaped by contextual factors that lie outside the direct control of particu-lar individuals. Thus, the close friendships analysed by Oliker in chapter 2 not only differed from those Marks examined in chapter 3 and the ones Harrison considered in chapter 5, but did so in ways which become understandable once they are located within the contexts in which they were developed. Each of these forms of friendship involved women sharing intimacies, but the ways in which this was done and the character of the intimacies shared varied as a result of the different worlds these women occupied.

More generally, the papers in this collection highlight the degree to which friendships are contextually embedded. How friendships are organised, their content, and the boundaries implicitly placed around them are all shaped by the characteristics of both the individuals and their interactional locations. Not only does the historic social and economic context inform the patterning of friendship, but so too the friendships people generate are indubitably influenced by their own structural positions. This point, first developed by Hess (1972), is an important one. As writers like Jerrome (1984) and Oliker (1989) have further argued, one of the key aspects of friendship is the way it allows individuality to be expressed while at the same time confirming the significance of social status. In this, it mediates between the individual as a person and the individual as the occupier of a set of varied role positions.

Thus, one of the key aspects of friendships is the way they serve to integrate individuals structurally. That is, by offering an avenue for distancing individual identity from the cumulative set of role positions a person holds, whilst simultaneously confirming the routine significance of those roles within that individual's identity, friendships can be seen as mediating between self and social structure. Many of the chapters in this volume develop this theme, particularly those by Oliker, Harrison, and O'Connor. But if friendships play a part in integrating individuals structurally, they are in turn circumscribed by contextual factors. They cannot be socially significant without also being moulded by both the immediate and more abstracted environments in which they are developed and sustained. To develop these arguments further, let us return to the elements we identified as constituting the continuum of context in the first chapter.

Personal environment

As many of the chapters in this volume have emphasised, gender plays a key part in patterning people's experiences of friendship. But exactly how gender impacts on the forms of friendship which are developed, and more generally on the organisation of sociability, varies widely. For example, while, as noted, there are evident similarities between the close ties which Oliker and Harrison analyse in chapters 2 and 5, there are also significant differences. Both are concerned principally with married middle-class women, yet the contexts within which these women's lives are framed and their femininities constructed ensure that their solidarities with close friends are expressed in quite different ways. Patterns of employment, domestic organisation, marital responsibility, and gender relations, together of course with major technological change, result in different patterns to their expressions of friendship. Similarly Marks's chapter illustrates very clearly how gender was central to the organisation of the ties between the women involved in the Hawthorne experiments, while at the same time emphasising that their construction of femininity was rooted in the wider setting of working-class familialism. O'Connor's chapter takes some of these issues further in examining how gender continues to be central even as the established orderings of modern society are becoming fragmented with the onset of late or post-modernity.

Allan's chapter is also concerned with the ways in which gender relations influence patterns of friendship. In contrast to these other chapters, he focuses mainly on male experience, and in particular on how different conditions of economic and domestic life alter the boundaries placed around male friendships. Aspects of class – the material conditions of employment, domesticity, and, indeed, leisure – are central to this analysis, just as they are in Oliker's, Marks's, Harrison's, and O'Connor's chapters. Like gender, class is a key influence on the patterning, content, and organisation of sociability. And, like gender, its influence is mediated by other circumstances in people's personal environment. Class, in other words, is not just a feature of people's employment or economic security; in friendship as elsewhere, its impact depends on its interplay with other aspects of people's contextual location. Marks's chapter illustrates this well. The women in his study developed their ties to one another as young factory workers, with their particular, and rather unusual, work situation playing a significant part in giving them their strong sense of group identity. But while their (and, importantly, their families') class location was of consequence in their friendships, so too it can be recognised that other factors such as their age, their marital status, and their ties to others in their households interacted with their class location in framing the ways their ties with their co-workers developed.

While less central to the analyses developed in this book than gender and class, other aspects of people's personal environments also help shape friendship patterns. Familial circumstances are clearly important, as many of the chapters illustrate. As noted, Harrison and Oliker emphasise how friendships articulate with the domestic relations of marriage. Marks is equally concerned with the impact of other familial and household relationships on friendship, including ties to parents and siblings, while Feld and Carter in their discussion of foci of activity indicate how divorce can radically alter people's opportunities for servicing existing ties and developing new ones. Age and life-stage, geographical location, religion, and migration histories are among the range of other factors that can influence friendship patterns, though these have not been considered explicitly in the papers in this volume. Most importantly, the impact of ethnicity on friendships and other informal ties is noticeably absent in the essays included. The existence of racism in all its forms is clearly of consequence in framing informal solidarities, just as, more positively, ethnic identity and commitment are also likely to influence the overall construction of friendships. Outside childhood ties, sociologists have in the main failed to analyse at all fully how ethnicity affects informal solidarities, or indeed how informal relations of friendship help sustain or counter wider divisions, be these between Protestant and Catholic in Northern Ireland, Afro- and Euro-Americans, or Asian and white British. Note also how Adams's discussion of technological change highlights the ways in which the salience of different factors in people's personal environments can alter as new means of communication develop.

Network

The discussion in the previous section has already indicated that friendship ties should not be considered alone. Each relationship is part of a wider complex or network of ties which may interactively all affect one another in diverse ways. Feld and Carter's chapter draws this out most explicitly. They show very clearly how the extent to which relationships are embedded in wider networks influences the forms of control that can be exercised and consequently the patterning of the ties. Their concern with foci of activity allows them to develop this in more subtle ways than some past studies have. In particular, because people are often involved in different foci of activity with non-overlapping memberships, their argument that overall network density may be less informative than the sectoral densities associated with each foci of activity is well made. They choose to examine how one social process – divorce – affects participation in different foci of activity, and they illustrate the ways in which network properties can alter as a result, but clearly their argument has a much broader applicability. At its heart is the contention that an element of the context in which friendships (and other ties of informal solidarity) emerge and are sustained is the constellation of other relations in which any tie is effectively embedded. The impact which such embedding has varies depending on the network's configuration, as well as the characteristics of its setting.

By its very nature the Internet would seem an ideal arena for examining this type of issue and seeing how incorporation in differently structured networks affects individual relationships. Unfortunately, though, as Adams points out in her chapter, researchers so far have paid surprisingly little attention to the possibilities of understanding electronic communication from a network perspective. Instead, the modes of analysis they have adopted focus almost exclusively on the dyad and the characteristics of the individuals involved. There are certainly difficulties inherent in using a network approach if data are confined to electronic communications *per se*. In particular, as Adams discusses, there are conceptual problems over determining when a 'link' should be considered to exist within these electronic networks, though such problems can arise with any analysis of open-ended networks. Certainly it would be surprising if future studies of electronic communication do not seek to situate their analyses more within a network perspective as the ease with which messages can flow through networks is part of the medium's radical properties.

Other papers in the volume do not address the network level of context so explicitly. None the less, the chapters by Harrison, Marks, and Allan all incorporate a concern with network implications into their analyses. In examining the issue of 'inclusive intimacy', for example, Marks investigates how the dense network of ties between the women in his study influenced the development of their individual relationships. He also examines how the network of domestic and familial relationships in which these women were embedded influenced the relationships which developed between them. Harrison, while not explicitly using the language of network, explores the interplay between marriage and friendship within her respondents' networks. In a different mode, Allan focuses on the extent to which some working-class male ties of sociability became less embedded in dense network structures as a result of changing notions of home, masculinity, and domesticity. It would certainly be useful to have more studies which explored in detail how the networks in which particular friendships, and particular sets of friendships, are embedded influence the character of the solidarities.

Community

One of the points we made in chapter 1 was that the four levels of context we identified do not operate in isolation from one another. Each links up with the others in ways that often make their empirical separation difficult. This is evident when we come to discuss the community level. The issues being addressed here inevitably overlap with some of the matters raised in the previous sections. None the less, in many of the papers, the impact of a community dimension is easy to recognise. Marks's chapter provides a good illustration. The women in his study were certainly involved in at least two 'communities', both of which influenced the solidarities they generated. The first of these was the Hawthorne factory or, from a narrower framework, the relationships of the RATR. This work arena provided the context for their (initial) involvement with one another, patterned the character of their interaction, and consequently played a crucial part in framing their mutual commitment. The conditions of the work-place – their relative isolation, their special status, their shared economic interests – shaped their relationships in a direct, though not deterministic, fashion. But, equally, the wider community to which these women belonged was also important. The formation of their relationships at a time of economic uncertainty, within a working-class and immigrant setting in which a particular form of familialism dominated, helped shape the pattern of reciprocal exchanges in which they became collectively involved.

While the community dimension is not highlighted in other chapters to the same degree, it is none the less evident. For example, in Oliker's analysis the backdrop against which middle-class women constructed their intimate friendships was one in which the divisions between home and work were becoming marked and in which geography was quite constraining. The women's lives were enmeshed in specific community contexts, albeit premised on their gender and class locations, which framed and restricted the opportunities they had for different forms of social participation. Feld and Carter's examination of foci of activity similarly highlights the importance of community-level context. In particular, the various foci of activity in which people can become involved depend in part on the specific forms of community association open to them, and this itself is a reflection of community structure and incorporation. So, too, Allan's discussion of changing male sociability is premised very much on post-war changes in the character of the working-class localities. His argument is that the patterns of employment, housing, domesticity, and migration found in established localities in the earlier part of this century encouraged a specific form of informal sociability. As these conditions alter – in other words, as community relationships change – so too dominant modes of informal solidarity will also be modified in line with the emerging community formations. As Adams points out in her chapter, the implications of new forms of communications for the development of community solidarities of different forms remain an open question.

Societal

The fourth level of context we identified in chapter 1 was the societal. The chapters in this book illustrate well how this level of context operates. All of them are concerned with the ways in which cultural, economic, and social transformations have had an impact on patterns of friendships. In their different ways, Oliker, Harrison, and Allan all focused on how broad-scale change affecting such areas as gender relations, domesticity, and employment influenced the nature of friendship solidarities. Without rehearsing the arguments they contain any further, it is evident from their analyses that friendship and similar ties of informal sociability do not lie outside the influence of macro-level structures, but instead are moulded by them in myriad ways, few of which are consciously recognised by those involved. Moreover, all the while patterns of friendship not only seem 'natural' and freely chosen, but more significantly ties of friendship continue to operate on the interstices of the structural elements which help shape them. That is, at an everyday level, friendships, like kinship, help individuals cope with the contingencies and demands made of them through their necessary involvement in the social and economic relationships of the wider society. At one and the same time, they are responsive to those relationships, and are partially constituted by them, yet all the while they appear as independent and individual constructions.

While the influence of different cultural, social, and economic orderings on friendships are apparent in all the chapters, those by O'Connor and Adams warrant particular mention here, as both are concerned with contemporary transformations. O'Connor's chapter addresses the question of how friendships, and more specifically women's friendships, will be influenced by the emergence of post-modernity within Western society. Irrespective of the terms used, it is evident that significant shifts are occurring within contemporary society. Old certainties are being questioned; new modes of relating are developing. People's positions within the social structure are less entrenched than they were, and their social identities more flexible. As O'Connor's chapter indicates, these macro-level changes, whose origins are far removed from issues of solidarity and sociability, influence the character of people's friendships. For women, new identities are becoming possible; dependence on particular men somewhat less central. Within this context, friends potentially play an increasingly significant role in self-validation, in sustaining identity, and in overcoming the problems and challenges of a predominantly patriarchal (and hostile) environment.

In her chapter, Adams illustrates how changes in the technologies associated with different historical periods have a direct bearing on the ways in which friendships and other such ties are organised. Moreover, in drawing on the integrative model of relationships she and Rosemary Blieszner developed previously (Adams and Blieszner, 1994), she shows how both the questions researchers pose and their understandings of what context comprises are bound up with the technologies of the era. At this stage, it is not easy to be precise about the ways in which the rapid development of electronic communication will impact on the patterning of friendships and other similar ties. However, what seems likely is that this 'revolution' in communication possibilities will, like others before it, lead to transformations in the forms of solidarity seen as culturally normal. Importantly, though, whatever transformations emerge will also be patterned by other elements within their societal context acting interactively with the developing technological ones.

Contextualising friendship: identity and social order

The papers in this volume have been concerned with the ways that friendships need to be situated contextually if an adequate understanding of their form is to develop. They have sought to demonstrate that friendships, like other seemingly personal ties, are not fashioned solely by those involved. On the one hand, they are relationships which are personally constructed through agency; they entail people making decisions about which specific others they are going to engage with, and about the contents of the informal solidarities which arise. On the other, it should be evident that these choices are not made in isolation. The diverse contexts in which they develop infuse them in ways which the friends do not normally prioritise in their cultural interpretations. That is, standard discourses of friendship emphasise agency above structure; they normally involve modes of construction and analysis which stress individuality and choice. Thus friendship is typically not defined as a tie which is grounded in circumstance but instead as one which emerges through the actions of each individual and the assessments they make of each other's personal qualities.

Yet, clearly friendships are social constructions as well as personal ones. Their contexts do influence the manner in which they are formed and the exchanges they come to involve. Through the diverse levels discussed above, friendships emerge with a content and pattern which reflect more than just individual volition. In this regard, precisely because friendships are so routinely interpreted culturally as individual action, they offer a particularly apt forum for sociological engagement. Like suicide, their apparent particularism camouflages the influences on them of 'external' relationships, be these economic, cultural, configurational, or whatever. Thus the challenge is to 'unpack' the articulations existing between friendships as they are experienced and the broader, 'given' characteristics of social and economic organisation which, in myriad ways, fashion them.

In the article cited earlier, Jerrome (1984, p. 715) suggested that friendships form 'the cement which binds together the bricks of social structure'. There are a number of ways in which this can be recognised. One is through the role that friendship, along with other informal ties, plays in enabling economic and social organisation to function. This is the perspective associated most famously with Eugene Litwak's (1960a, 1960b, 1985, 1989) pioneering work on the interplay between bureaucratic and personal forms of social organisation. His interpretation of the significance of the informal for the operation of the formal, and conversely of the ways in which the demands of formal agencies impinge on the informal sphere, questioned the then dominant understandings of the declining role of primary solidarities within modernity. However, Jerrome was focusing more on the role which friendships play in the construction of an individual's identity and sense of self. By way of conclusion, it is this aspect of the articulation between the personal and social realms of friendship which we will address here.

Many commentators have referred to the characteristic equality which imbues friendships. Essentially this refers to the respect each gives the other as a person and the acceptance that, despite potential difference, each attaches equivalent value to the other. If these are absent, it is unlikely the tie will be perceived as one of friendship. Equally if, within an existing friendship, this equality appears to be undermined, so too the relationship will be questioned. But as part of this construction of equality, friends usually – though not inevitably – share social and economic characteristics in common. This itself fosters a conception of social identity. Like the birds that flock together, the social location of our friends often serves to confirm our own self-identity. They help us authenticate our place in the world, our standing within the hierarchies and divisions of society.

Yet, more than this, our friends also provide us with a sense of individuality which at one level appears as a validation of our personal uniqueness. However, as mentioned earlier, our friends are typically able to do this without undermining the social roles we occupy. They distance us from these roles whilst confirming their significance for us. In friendship, as with other personal ties, we become more than the sum of our parts, yet these roles remain central to our ideas of self, to our notions of who we are, and, moreover, for many of the goals for which we strive. In being outside these roles, yet consonant with them, our friends, in numerous ways, challenge our pretensions and evaluate our claims, all the while confirming our personal and structural identity. Through such validation of the self, the significance of friendship in binding the 'bricks of social structure' together can be readily recognised.

So just as friendships take on characteristics of the cultural, economic, and social settings in which they arise, equally these ties are consequential in helping sustain the order there is within these settings. With changes in the dominant social formation, the patterns of friendship alter, and most significantly alter in ways which reflect the external changes occurring. But by and large these changes in friendship behaviour and orientation are not deliberate or self-conscious changes. Rather they are emergent changes occurring as a result of contextual shifts about which individuals have relatively little cognisance. Friendship behaviour, like other behaviours, is

adaptive and responsive, altering to mesh in with the developing constellation of cultural, social, and economic relationships. What individuals now
take to be appropriate, routine, and normal is the result of their location
within the modified social formation, and this is reflected in their patterns
of informal social solidarity. Thus gender divisions take on a different com-
plexion, employment practices change, or family commitment comes to be
seen differently. As such changes evolve, so they impact on the boundaries
of commitment and exchange within friendship in ways which can be properly understood only through attending to the broader contexts in which
they are based.

From such a perspective it is evident that modernity did not spell the end
of friendship. Most certainly community organisation changed; informal
ties were no longer as embedded in the locality as they once were for many.
Yet new patterns of informal solidarity and association emerged as the cultural, social, and economic conditions of modernity developed (Wellman,
et al., 1988). And as noted above, these new solidarities in turn helped
confirm the identities which were being newly constructed as the modern
replaced the established. Most importantly, these processes continue. To
the degree that we are now confronting an era of late or post-modernity, so
our patterns of friendships will reflect this, albeit differentially for individuals located less or more centrally within these developments. In particular,
they will resonate to the more flexible, fragmented, and uncertain tendencies inherent in this emergent formation, as both O'Connor and Adams
explicate in their chapters.

Particularly significant within this is the greater autonomy people have
over the construction of their personal lives. Changes in family commitment and dissolution, the wider acceptance of lifestyle diversity, and the
heightened prominence given to projects of the 'self' all point to an increasing openness in the individual's construction of his or her identity.
Convention is still of consequence, but its power is substantially reduced.
There is far more freedom, far greater flexibility to express the self in
different ways. If, under modernity, conformity was encouraged – though
even here less than in pre-modern formations – now it is diversity which is
celebrated. Identity construction is perceived as an exercise of choice; it
cannot so easily be read as an existing normative script. While it is most certainly possible to overemphasise the extent to which these types of change
are impinging on all sections of the population, there can be little doubt
that issues of lifestyle and identity are more prominent than in earlier eras.
The acceptance of diversity, the lessening of stigma, and an awareness of
choice have meant that self-identity now often appears to be rooted less in

structural location and more in individual volition. What matters is less the social positions any individual holds and more the commitment they have to a particular cultural grouping or ideology.

Even if such arguments about change are only partially accepted, there can be little doubt that identity is a more variable and fluid social property than it was. Within this context, friendship is likely to become of more rather than less salience. That is, if identity is no longer grounded as deeply in social position as it was, then association is likely to matter more. Who you are becomes even more marked by whom it is you spend time and socialise with. Thus, the value of friendship in supporting identity and providing a sense of self for many becomes greater: the flocking together of like minds in a world of greater diversity becomes a way in which boundaries are marked. And as, over time, different projections or images of self develop, informal solidarities like those of friendship will be a means of establishing and sustaining those new identities. As in Feld and Carter's discussion of marital separation and divorce, the friends through whom you achieve such modifications to identity will not necessarily be the same. There is routine change in friendship circles, and this will continue as identities become more changeable in conditions of late modernity.

In conclusion, this book has demonstrated the importance of seeing friendship contextually. Friendship does not exist as a 'disconnected' relationship even if some everyday portrayals treat it as such. Instead, it is a relationship embedded socially, economically, and culturally. Its forms and contents are responsive to those contexts, which, as the chapters in this book have indicated, operate at a number of related levels. As modern society continues to transform, so too dominant patterns of friendship will in turn be affected, changing to meet the new conditions of living. With increased diversity and significantly less stability in important aspects of personal life, informal solidarities like those of friendship are not rendered marginal. If anything they will become more important as signifiers of what and who we are. Even more will they cement the bricks of an increasingly fragmented social structure.

References

Adams, Rebecca G., and Blieszner, Rosemary (1994), 'An integrative conceptual framework for friendship research', *Journal of Social and Personal Relationships*, 11: 163–84.

Hess, Beth (1972), 'Friendship', in Martha W. Riley, Marilyn Johnson, and Anne Foner (eds.), *Aging and Society*, vol. III, *A Sociology of Age Stratification*, New York: Russell Sage Foundation.

Jerrome, Dorothy (1984), 'Good company: the sociological implications of friendship', *Sociological Review*, 32: 696–718.

Litwak, Eugene (1960a), 'Geographic mobility and extended family cohesion', *American Sociological Review*, 25: 385–94.

(1960b), 'Occupational mobility and extended family cohesion', *American Sociological Review*, 25: 9–21.

(1985), *Helping the Elderly: The Complementary Roles of Informal Networks and Formal Systems*, New York: Guilford.

(1989), 'Forms of friendship among older people in an industrial society', in Rebecca G. Adams and Rosemary Blieszner (eds.), *Older Adult Friendship: Structure and Process*, Newbury Park: Sage.

Oliker, Stacey J. (1989), *Best Friends and Marriage: Exchange Among Women*, Berkeley: University of California Press.

Wellman, Barry, Carrington, Peter J., and Hall, Alan (1988), 'Networks as personal communities', in Barry Wellman and S. D. Berkowitz (eds.), *Social Structures: A Network Approach*, Cambridge University Press.

Index

Structural Analysis in the Social Sciences